This Stubborn Soil

This Stubborn Soil

A Frontier Boyhood

WILLIAM A. OWENS

Nick Lyons Books

31 West 21 Street   New York, NY 10010

Library of Congress Cataloging-in-Publication Data

Owens, William A., 1905–
  This stubborn soil.

  Continued by: A season of weathering.
  Reprint. Originally published: New York : Scribner,
1966. With new introd. and an afterword.
  1. Owens, William A., 1905–   —Childhood and
youth. 2. Lamar County (Tex.)—Social life and customs.
3. Lamar County (Tex.)—Biography.   I. Title.
F392.L3609   1986   976.4′26306′0924 [B]   86–18535
ISBN 0-941130–19–3

For all my kinfolks,
especially Jessie Ann and David

Some said, John, print it; others said, Not so;
Some said, It might do good; others said, No.

—JOHN BUNYAN

INTRODUCTION

The knotty questions of heredity versus environment and free will versus determinism, as they relate to the shape of human lives, are not matters that often make me toss in my bed at night. With enough other worries already on hand, I tend to be grateful for this. But I do feel a recurrent perplexity, always mingled with pleasure, at the way in which an occasional bright youngster, bred up in circumstances that you'd think would suffocate him or at best squeeze him into being just like everyone else around, manages somehow to see himself as special, grabs hold of a dream, and follows it to places where he wants to be and can do things he wants to do. If you're teaching or otherwise working with the young, it only takes one kid like that every now and then to provide, if not grounds for optimism in times like these, at least a dose of equanimity in regard to the condition of our species.

On one level William Owens' *This Stubborn Soil* is a record of its author's own such youthful journey toward the light, a tale of progress from hard and narrow beginnings in rural East Texas during the early years of this century, toward escape to wider and more enlightened realms via the route of education. The book is loaded with a tenseness of remembered aspiration, inchoate in the boy's early years, increasingly conscious as he comes to see that books and knowledge can provide a way out of Pin Hook, Texas, and all of Pin Hook's limitations. If, indeed, there is to be a way out at all, for this is an honest work and it tells perhaps more about frustrations and missteps and setbacks than it does about success, even if success is what prevails in the end.

Someone once described Philip Carey, the protagonist of Somerset Maugham's *Of Human Bondage*, as the most reassuring hero in all of fiction, because after being bullied and oppressed in childhood and making every blunder he can possibly make as a young man, he emerges as a whole and functional and happy adult. There is much of that sort of reassurance in *This Stubborn Soil* also, and young Owens, though a vastly different person in vastly different surroundings, has the makings of that kind of hero. He is born into a dirt-poor, partly illiterate farming family, bereft of a father within days after his own birth, shut off from modern civilization's benefits by his region's isolation and the leached, unproductive, sandy land on which his people depend for their living, educated only sporadically because of the need to pitch in on field work (and even then in primitive schools with teachers who are sometimes ignorant or stupid or both), tormented and confused and often thwarted as to his own direction and hopes. Yet finally, at book's end, aged eighteen and with approximately an eighth-grade education to his credit, this improbable hero conquers the entrance examination at a small backwater college, thus starting a trek toward academic and literary distinction. And when he does pass that exam, by God you want to cheer.

The main reason you want to cheer is that by then you have come to like him and are very much on his side. And the reason for this is only in part that he is bright and ambitious and keeps on trying to be somebody. Mainly you like him because of the kind of warm and observant person the books shows him to be, both as a boy and the man who many years later is writing about that boy.

Astoundingly, there is hardly any resentment or anger in this recountal of events and pressures and restrictions that would embitter many, perhaps most sensitive youths for life. What there is instead is a contrapuntal blend of ambition and yearning with not merely acceptance, but full, affectionate, good-humored appreciation of family and neighbors and friends, of the few decent teachers and mentors that the boy finds, of the random books he manages to lay his hands on, of creeks and woods and field dirt and rain and ramshackle houses, of old hymns and ballads and jokes, of the taste of fried fish in the mouth—appreciation, in short, of the entire tough, religious, vital, deprived, backwoods world where Owens was born and shaped.

A portrait of that world is the other main dimension of *This Stubborn Soil* (which is aptly subtitled "a frontier boyhood"), and a fine dimension it is. The way of life and the outlook of the people among whom Owens grew up had more in common with those that Daniel Boone had known than with those of the twentieth century. The big wildnesses of bears and cougars and Indians and all that were gone, the land was depleted by long hard use, and Pin Hookers lived consciously within the shadow of modernity as manifested in such things as mail-order clothes and needed hardware, when there was cash to pay for them, and as seen in towns not far away with electricity, railroads, and other marvels. But some of them still lived in log houses, and most raised the bulk of their own food, made many of their own tools and utensils and implements, dipped their water from dug wells, cooked and heated with wood, worshipped an Old Testamental deity, and lived within the slow laborious rhythms imposed by farming with draft animals and human hands.

This way of life was not unique at the time, for it existed with variations across the whole American Southeast, in patches and belts of mountainous or rocky or thin-soiled terrain where bypassed rural Anglo-Celtic populations clung to the woodland, pioneer ways of their forebears, the only ways they knew. They kept on clinging in some places until World War II smashed the molds: growing up later than Owens, in a Texas city, I had glimpses of their world from time to time. But Owens saw it whole and from the inside, and remembers it in this book.

To those who love regional clichés, I suppose, this world will appear to have been an anomaly. It was intensely Southern without having anything to do with columned mansions and smiling black servitors, and it was quite Texan without having anything to do with cowboys and big ranches. But the facts are that tough independent yeomen were always the most basic element of the South's white population, and that Texas is, or was, a very Southern state, especially in its eastern forested sections. The clichés will not hold, as clichés seldom will. One of Owens' great-grandfathers, for instance, had had good land in Arkansas and even owned a few slaves, but he seems essentially to have been a yeoman pioneer, and when the Civil War came he enlisted not as a cavalier captain or colonel but as a private, a journey from which he did not return. And the circumstance that these descendants of his were reduced to scratching in sterile East Texas sand for subsistence is typical of what happened to multitudes of such folk in the aftermath of defeat.

At any rate they did scratch, and held their heads up, and Owens gets them down cleanly, with an impressive detachment that does not clash with the often humorous warmth of his presentation but somehow reinforces it. It is one of the marks of a good narrative for me—of good art, for that matter—that it does not tell but shows, and showing individuals and events and meanings sharply, without much analysis or moral comment, is something that Owens does with skill. If there is tension and unfairness mixed with low-keyed goodwill in the attitude of his people toward the few blacks in the neighborhood, it is not preached about but subtly demonstrated in three or four poignant scenes. If a revival meeting is highly comical you won't hear Owens say so, but you'll smile with him at the man who butts his head against a tree in frenzied regret for his sins. If a teacher is cruelly obtuse—but the list would go on and on, for this involved yet impartial viewpoint is basic to the structure of the book, giving it power and distinguishing it from most other recollections of childhood that I've seen.

We Texans have known since *This Stubborn Soil* first appeared that it is one of the best books ever written about our part of the world, but I think it is more than that. For anyone who cares about what Americans once were like and can feel the pull of such antique human traits as endurance and loyalty and persistence in the face of adversity, it is a fine, warm, often sad, often funny, and ultimately affirmative work, one that stays in your awareness for years after you've put it down. I'm delighted that it's being made available again in this new edition.

—JOHN GRAVES
May, 1986

PIN HOOK

If one was born in Paris or London or New York, or even in Dallas, to name a place closer to home, he has, when writing about himself, only to mention the city and the reader pictures place, buildings, people and he can go ahead to particulars about himself and his family. But since I was born at Pin Hook, Texas, a place whose character has not been made known to the world generally, I must begin by writing all I know or ever heard about it.

For as long as I can remember, Pin Hook has been a local force, like a strong character in a play, more so than any other community I have ever known—much more a byword than Woodland to the east or Novice to the west. As I see it now, the first settlers, the Witherspoons and McLemores, the Halls and Duvalls, who came up the Red River—the Rio Roxo of the Spaniards—from Arkansas and, leaving behind them the comparative safety of Pecan Point back on the river, settled along Little Pine Creek in spite of the danger of wild animals and wilder Indians, brought with them an attitude toward living that is still felt there—an attitude that makes the fiddle as useful as the plow and the Bible more to be treasured than all the libraries in the world.

English, Welsh, Scotch-Irish, a little French Huguenot, they were the trickle of a flow that for two hundred years had been moving slowly westward from the first settlements in Virginia, North Carolina, South Carolina. In their wagons and oxcarts, on horseback or, as they said, "footback and walking," these settlers came to a wilderness of oak and sweet gum made denser by huckleberry thickets on the uplands, by canebrakes in the creek bottoms. On grants from the Territory of Arkansas, sometimes with no grants at all, they staked out land for themselves which, when Texas became a Republic in 1836, they were able to claim, as deeds in the General Land Office in Austin show. In those days, in that place, land was easy to come by. Holding it was not so easy. With no better tools than a pollax and a crosscut saw they cut away some of the timber—enough for patches of corn and cotton and black-eyed peas. With the help of a few Negro slaves they built log cabins for themselves, the timbers hand-hewn with a broadaxe, the boards for the roof hand-split with a froe and a wooden maul. They cleared the land and worked it and found in a few years that, sand on the surface, red clay underneath, it was "too pore to sprout peas"—as worn out as the land they had left behind in Tennessee and Arkansas.

It was a lonely land they had come to. From time unknown, Indians had passed through it, leaving woodland trails, leaving camping sites where the white man's plow turned up arrowheads and bits of broken pottery. The first settlers had only these trails and the trail they had made themselves up from Pecan Point. Then there was the trail coming on a more direct route for the settlers who crossed the Red River at Fulton, Arkansas, and moved west over the land. In time, the trail up from Pecan Point extended southwest through what is now the county seat, Paris. With the establishment of a steamboat landing at Pine Bluff, where Big Pine Creek empties into the river, the settlers cut a road north to it and south toward new settlements on Blossom Prairie. Where these roads crossed, Pin Hook came into being, named by persons unknown, with a name given in derision or despair to countless other places by settlers who had found the reality less than the dream.

It was a land tortured by weather. There were wet springs when days of pouring rain put creeks out of banks and washed away cotton and corn. At times, before the water could drain off, dust storms blew down from the western plains, clouding the sky and making mouths gritty. Summers were long, hot, dry—worst in the dog days of August, when creeks ran low and scummy and the earth cracked in the sun. The people learned to be grateful for the first cool days of fall, and to bundle up in hard winters when blue northers swept down across Kansas and Oklahoma. They shivered in their shacks and said there was "nothing between them and the North Pole but a bobbed-wire fence."

During the thirty years between the coming of the Witherspoons to Pin Hook and the outbreak locally called the "war between the sections," only a few new settlers arrived, and those who had already claimed the land were struggling hard to set up plantations like those they had known in Mississippi and other states of "the Old Southwest." Such plantations had proved possible in the rich red earth of the Red River bottoms. At Pin Hook the land was against them. The log houses of the owners were larger but in other ways no better than the log huts of the slaves, and the fare for both showed up as a laugh in a song: "hog and hominy and poke for greens."

Wars came and went, each leaving its mark: the Texas Revolution, the Mexican War, the Civil War. Men and boys from Pin Hook must have gone off to at least one of these, but they left no record that could be carved on a tombstone. Nevertheless, the effects were there, especially after the Civil War, when the slaves took themselves and their freedom to the woods northwest of Pin Hook, where the Negroes still live. They were willing enough to come back and work by the day chopping or picking cotton but the white men, with little money for hired hands, worked themselves, their wives, their children.

After the Civil War a great number of settlers, displaced persons, came in from Tennessee, Arkansas, Missouri, and Mississippi. Needing land, they bought small farms from the people who had been granted the land but could no longer hold it. This was a second move toward poverty, the Civil War having been the first. Worn out, saddled with what they saw was not hope but despair, they cleared their twenty-five or fifty acres, built shacks of logs or boxing planks, and settled down to a cotton and corn and black-eyed peas existence, a living submarginal, exhausting to mind and body. The living was added to with what could be brought from the woods and creek—the game and fish—and the pigs and cows and chickens kept by barefoot wives and barefoot daughters. It was taken from, drained away, by malaria, hookworm, and a short-rations disease called by Pin Hookers "pellegrisy."

The will of at least some of the people was to have a living better than this. They did what they could for church and school. From the beginning, homes were opened for meetings any time a preacher passed through. They were also opened for a kind of subscription school that was better than no school at all.

It took them fifty years to get a school house—a one-room building on land that now belongs to the graveyard, like many of the homes built of logs and chinked and daubed with clay. This school, called Pin Hook and open three months each winter, was good enough for more than twenty years. Then a new one-room frame building was built between the crossroads and graveyard, on land deeded to Pin Hook by my father.

Pin Hook, a name good enough for the old school, was not

good enough for the new. In tribute to a man of some prominence in the county, the new school was named Faulkner. The tribute proved small. The name Faulkner appears in school and election records, but it is rarely used in other ways. The name never did fit the temperament or way of living of the people in Pin Hook. In time the school was absorbed by a county system. Faulkner seems likely to be forgotten, but never Pin Hook.

In winter it was school by day, debating club by night, where men met in all seriousness to debate such subjects as whether a Negro has a soul. In one of these debates the referee, to stop a fist fight, ruled that, in view of the strong arguments on both sides, a Negro could be judged to have half a soul. In summer, with the addition of a brush arbor under the oaks, it was a meeting house of church and singing school. It took them a hundred years to get a church building, and then it was secondhand, built from the lumber of the schoolhouse when, no longer needed, it was torn down.

Mostly Methodists and Baptists, Pin Hookers were religious in their own way—fervent in summer, cool in winter—and industrious when they had to be. Those who could, made music. Those who could not, listened. In meetings and Sunday night singings they sang hymns with a whang that gave a minor cast to every tune. At Saturday night parties they sang English and Scottish ballads, long and doleful tales of lords and ladies, of unrequited love, of murders as violent as anything on the frontier—and the people of the ballads were as real to Pin Hook as the singers of the songs. The language they sang or spoke, having existed some two hundred years with little benefit of writing or printing, was to anyone who had been outside "no end quare."

The Pin Hook I was born in was still a part of the frontier. The last Indian raid in Texas was only twenty years back and as fresh as yesterday in the minds of the people. Tales of the frontier were a part of daily life. So were the tales of the war between the sections and of that greatest of all heroes, Jesse James.

So I am from Pin Hook and Pin Hook is a part of me. All of my life has been a flight from it, but now, after many returnings, I see that it has overtaken me at last.

1

From the beginning, 1905 was a bad year for Pin Hook. It started out wet—so wet that farmers were late breaking land and planting. Through May and June the rain stunted corn and cotton, but not crabgrass and careless weeds. Water stood in the middles, or washed gullies across the fields. Little Pine Creek overflowed, leaving filled sloughs, muddy water that smelled of rot and swarmed with mosquitoes. Flies bred in the wetness. Seed ticks hatched on weed tops in clumps heavy enough to bend them over. Men going to work cattle in the bottoms tied strings wet in coal oil around their wrists and legs but still came home covered with ticks.

It was a year of sickness, of malaria, of swamp fever, of a run-down condition called "the dumb chills"—different from "the hard chills" of malaria. The blue quinine bottle was always on the table. There was almost always someone in bed. Men and women well enough to be up and around were called on to "set up" with the sick. Doctors were on the road day and night—one from Pin Hook, one from Woodland, two or three others from Blossom and Detroit.

It was a year of hard times. Corn planted did not come up. Corn saved for grinding at the mill had to be used for seed to plant over. Egg and chicken money went for doctors and medicine and the people had to make do or do without. They parched cornmeal and boiled it for coffee. In the spring they lived on hog jaw and poke "sallet," the greens of the poke weed. In summer they ate roasting ears and soft bread made from meal "gritted" on home-made graters. The man of the house made the grater by driving the side of a molasses bucket full of holes and nailing the edges to a board. He brought corn from the field when the kernels were hard enough to grit but not to grind. Children took turns at rubbing the ears up and down the gritter. It was the woman's job to turn the soft meal into bread.

Word came down the road from Blossom that cotton picking was going to be good on the prairie. A good hand could make up to a dollar a day and board if he was willing to drag a sack from daylight till dark, or, as they said in Pin Hook, "From can to can't." In the last days of August, the first days of September, men passed on the road, walking, carrying only what they had on, headed for Blossom Prairie, to that stretch of black waxy land that in good years made a bale of cotton to the acre.

Though it did not seem right for him to have to go, my father went with them. His people had been the first settlers in Pin Hook. He was kin to the Witherspoons, the Duvalls, the McLemores—the ones who first held the land. He owned fifty-five acres himself, as much as one man could farm, and a good three-room house built in an L, with a porch across the front and a brick chimney and fire-place. He had a barn, horses and wagon, some cows and hogs, and a few tools for farming. His cotton crop had failed and he had to have cash money for his family.

He was thirty at the time and had been married eleven years to Jessie Ann Chennault. When he was nineteen and she was fourteen he had brought a license from Paris and they had sat together on a trunk in her mother's front room for the ceremony. By 1905 they had four children: Monroe, eight, named for the President; Dewey, six, named for the Admiral; Charles Cleaver, three, named for my father and my mother's grandmother; and Linnie, two, named for my father's mother, Malinda Duvall, and my mother's mother, Alice Chennault. A fifth child was due in November.

So my father went to pick cotton on the prairie, leaving my mother to look after the children and place and to gather the nub-bins of corn and the scraps of cotton. Her mother, for many years a widow, came to stay with her.

He could not have gone far, or picked much cotton, for he was soon at home again, sick with something the women in the family had never seen before. Used to doctoring, they gave him quinine and calomel, and, when he was no better, doubled the dose. They also tried home remedies like snakeroot for purging and balmonia, the Pin Hook name for digitalis, for peartening up the spirits. Nothing seemed to do any good.

When there was nothing else to try, my mother sent for Dr.

Reeves, a Pin Hook man who, after giving up as farmer, fiddler, dancing master, and preacher, had sent off for medicine books and set himself up as a doctor. He lived on the north side of Pin Hook and kept his office and bottles and scales in a front room of his house.

By the time Dr. Reeves came, my father could not raise himself in bed for the pain.

"Rheumatism," Dr. Reeves said. "Looks like the beginning of sciatica."

He took his bottles and balances from his saddlebags and put them on a table. He weighed out bits of white powders and mixed them on a paper with the blade of his pocket knife. With the blade he divided them into doses and raked them into envelopes. He wrote the directions. Then he read them to my mother.

When he had strapped his saddlebags shut, he was ready to go. At the door he talked to my mother in a low voice.

"If these don't do any good, send me word. I've got some medicine at home that will."

My mother, worried that he might be making a mistake but too timid to ask him to start the better medicine at once, gave the powders and watched my father grow steadily worse.

The older women of the family came to help—all of them widowed, some of them more than once, with a shaking of heads and whisperings of what it is like for a woman to be left with a "passel of young'uns" to raise. Neighbors came, and soon the fireplace room, where he lay on the walnut bed, was crowded with children and with people who knew only that it was "neighborly to set up with the sick."

Dr. Reeves was called again. He had a new name for the sickness and a new medicine. He also had some advice for my mother: "Don't eat turnip greens. It ain't good for a woman in your shape to eat turnip greens." Any woman there could have told her the same thing. Turnip greens could bring on the scours, and the scours would start the baby.

The neighbors looked at our father and knew that he was a very sick man. Dr. Reeves had tried and failed. Now they wanted my mother to change doctors, or ask Dr. Reeves to change the medicine again.

"Can't hurt none to try," they said.

Dr. Reeves came again and my father was past knowing him.

"Meningitis," Dr. Reeves said to my mother. "That's what it is all right. I've been reading up on it."

Dr. Reeves put his bottles out on the table.

"I've got just the right thing for it," he said.

While they watched, he gave the first dose. By the time he left, my father was unconscious.

My mother, knowing that at any hour she might have to take to bed, sent the children across the fields to stay with Aunt Vick, my grandmother's sister.

It had been a year of trouble for Aunt Vick, after years of trouble. Her first husband had died of cancer, the second of a congestive chill. During the year her oldest son, Hedley, had run off from home. A deputy had come looking for him, but she never said why. She may never have known. Sometimes she got a letter saying, "Dear Madam: We hope our products have proved satisfactory." She had not ordered anything from the catalogue. The letters meant that Hedley was all right and that he was not in the hands of the law.

Hedley had left in crop time and Aunt Vick had to do the best she could with the help of her daughter, Maggie, and her son, Wade. It had not been a good crop year for them and they were down to nothing but baked sweet potatoes to eat when they had to take on the care of four children. They were near starving to death, Aunt Vick more than the others because she had to force herself to eat sweet potatoes. She had to keep the fire in the fireplace day and night and the dutch oven on the hearth always full. When a batch was done, the children peeled and ate their share, and begged for more. Aunt Vick had to eat the potatoes she put aside for herself to keep them from going down another gullet.

On November 1 my mother went to bed in the other room, worried about my father, afraid she would cry out in pain and disturb him. On November 2 I was born, with Dr. Reeves going from one room to the other to watch over both my father and my mother. The women were there to help him and to do what he might not have time to do. The women were the first to notice that I had been born with a caul. It was a sign of good luck, a sign that I would have powers beyond those of people born without it. Then they knew that I was a boy—a boy born with a caul. Any granny among them knew that I was different—that there was no end to the things I could do.

They told my mother but could not tell my father. He was not awake to hear the first cries of his newborn child.

When Dr. Reeves had gone, my mother sent for two other

doctors, one from Blossom, one from Detroit. They both came, looked at my father, and went away. It was too late for them to do anything for him.

Life and death came close together. Before my mother was able to get out of bed in one room my father was dead in the other, without coming to again, without knowing I had been born.

The women tending me talked of the wonder that had happened. I had been born with a caul. I was a son who would never see his father. For both, I would have special gifts—of luck, of foreknowledge, of healing. It was, they always said, making up for the loss of a father. They talked of it to my mother, helping her to take what comfort she could in this son who had been born under the signs.

Men came to help the women with the work that had to be done: laying out the corpse, bringing the coffin in a wagon from Blossom, digging the grave six feet down through layers of sand and clay. Women mixed the camphor water. The face had to be kept covered by a cloth wet in camphor water to keep it from turning dark.

The coffin was set in the fireplace room. Men came to stay with it through the night—men who had worked in the fields with him, who had been with him in many a square dance set, who between dances had listened to him singing old "ballets" and songs. The women sat with my mother in the next room, or around the stove in the kitchen.

The next day the children were brought home and held up for a long look inside the coffin. When it was time to go, the men carried the coffin by my mother's bed for the only glimpse she had of him after he was dead. Then, with the coffin in one wagon, some women and children in another, they set out for the graveyard, on the road to Pin Hook, in sight of the house. The ones going on foot cut across the field.

There was no preacher, no one to sing a song. The coffin rested beside the grave while a neighbor spoke a few words and made a prayer. Then, using plough lines for straps, the men lowered the coffin and covered it with dirt. There he would lie, head to the west, ready to rise when the Light would come from the east.

My father was buried, and the people who had stood around his grave had to move on, back to their homes, back to the jobs they had left off in the time of death.

My mother went in debt twenty-five dollars for a piece of

marble to set at his head. The stonecutter got the name wrong, making it "Charley Owen," but he added a verse which, when I was old enough to read, I could pretend was my father saying the only words he ever said to me: *'Tis not the whole of life to live nor all of death to die.*

My mother was then in a family of women who had lost most of their men: her grandmother, born Missouri Ann Cleaver, who lived on the Pin Hook road between the graveyard and the store; her mother, Alice Chennault, who had married off her two daughters and was "living around"; her mother's sister, Ellen Victoria, Aunt Vick; her mother's half-sister, Elizabeth Penelope Haigood, who lived across Little Pine Creek on the Novice road. All her life she had seen these women doing the work of men—plowing, cutting wood, feeding stock. In the beginning of winter she had to take up the work of a man and do what she could for the children.

The women of the family wanted to help. They wanted her to sell the land and give the children away. They wanted to take the children, in a kind of dividing up among them. When she told them that she wanted to hold the land and keep the children together, they begged her to give away the still unnamed baby. Again she refused, but for a long time they kept hoping she would change her mind. From the day I was born Aunt Vick called me her boy; Aunt Nellie, short for Penelope, often said, "He's still my pick of the bunch."

My grandmother took my mother's side, and came to live with her, to help with the children and to keep house while my mother went to the field. She had raised a family without a man. So could any woman who wanted badly enough to hold her children to-

gether. At the time she was a tall raw-boned woman of fifty and, as
the people said of her, "as stout as e'er a man." The strongest
daughter of the stronger Missouri Ann, she had survived the hard
times of the Civil War, the walk from Camden, Arkansas, to
Blossom Prairie, the hardships of making a living at Pin Hook. She
had buried a husband and a son. It was time for her to take a rest,
but rest had to be farther along the road.

The baby was to stay, and a name had to be decided on. My
great grandfather was William Duvall. My father had a young
cousin in Paris, William Hathaway, called "Willie" by the family.
He was a pretty town boy and my mother thought if I was named
for him I might grow up like him. So the first part of my name was
settled on. My grandmother, claiming her right to give the second
name, called me A. for her husband, my mother's father. It was short
for Aaron, but he was called A. and signed himself A. The name was
given but not used. People called me "Willie," "Billy," "W. A.,"
and "Bill," but almost never "William." They gave the name,
without knowing how hard it would be to live with.

In Pin Hook, November is often wet and gray but rarely
wintry. Monroe and Dewey could go to school, barefoot because
there was no money for shoes that year. In December and January
they would have to miss some days when blue northers swept down
and left ice on the ruts in the road, but they were pushed to get as
much learning as they could while they could. To give them the
chance, my mother cut and hauled wood to keep fires going in the
fireplace and cookstove. At night she helped them with their lessons
in front of the fire.

Three months of schooling and then they had to stop. By the
first warm days of February plowing had to start and Monroe had to
be a hand in the field. They hitched Old Maud, the bay mare, to a
kelly turning plow and began to flatbreak the land my father had
plowed the year before, taking it a square at a time, first for corn
and then for cotton. Hour after hour my mother went, holding the
plow in the ground, guiding the mare with rope lines looped over
her shoulders. When she was too tired to manage both, Monroe
held the lines. It was backbreaking, heartbreaking work, going as
they did from first light till first dark. Breaking the land was only
the beginning. Planting and cultivating still had to come.

While the days were chilly I was left in the house, propped in
an old rocking chair in front of the fireplace with a sugar-tit in my
mouth to keep me from crying.

By the middle of March the garden had to be started and the

hens set. New shoots of poke and dandelion and peppergrass were beginning to show along the rail fences and turnrows. My grandmother took on the jobs of garden and chickens, and picking "sallet" greens. The older children could trail after her. I had to be taken to the field, to lie on a quilt on the ground.

All that spring I spent my days in the field, sleeping, waking, crying when I was hungry or needed changing. When I was big enough to crawl, my mother tied me to a stake to keep me from going off into the woods where there were snakes and scorpions and long blue santafees with yellow stingered legs. Where the rows were long, she tied me in the middle of the field. When she was plowing and Monroe planting, she staked me between them, where one or the other could keep an eye on me.

My toys were the dirt, and a stick to dig the dirt. No one could live closer to the earth than I did. I dug the sand, I rolled in it, I covered myself with it. Before my first year had passed I had eaten the peck of dirt everyone, Pin Hook people said, is entitled to. I had learned the feel, the smell, the taste of earth.

That year and later I learned, hardly knowing I was learning it, how farm life is shaped by the land and the seasons—by what will grow and the days or weeks or months of growing time—of making the best of sun and rain and seed in the earth. In Pin Hook, corn had to be planted in late February or early March, the time of sandstorms out west. There were days when the sky was overcast with a cloud of red dust, and the sun shone through a muddy red. Corn planted then was in the ground on time. Corn planted later might twist and burn and never tassel in the drouth of late July and August. Cotton planting had to wait till the ground was warm. All in the month of May it had to be planted, plowed, chopped, to make it ready for fast growing in the hot moist days of June. Farming was going right for anybody who could say, "I found me a cotton bloom Fourth of July." In the heat of summer, crops had to be "laid by" with a last running of the Georgia stock down the middles. Once they were through laying by, Pin Hookers could rest a little before gathering time.

Gathering time came and my mother began to take heart. The crop was light, but she had made a crop. The land had not been lost; the children were still all together. My mother knew that she could go on. She could gather this year's crop. She could plant the next. She could see that the children got to school when they were not in the field.

Gathering corn came first, each trip down the field with the wagon taking a swath five rows wide. My mother took two rows on one side, Monroe took two on the other. The other children "carried the down row," the row of stalks knocked down by the wagon. I rode in the front of the wagon, with boards between me and the pile of pale yellow shucks.

Cotton picking came next. Grown-ups and older children dragged long canvas sacks down the middles, picking two rows at a time, their fingers working down the stalks, pulling out the white lint, leaving yellow burrs among the green leaves. The smaller children picked in flour sacks, and cried when the points of cotton burrs pricked their fingers. I rode on my mother's sack, or slept on a pile of cotton in the wagon.

Potato digging had to come before frost, while the sand was still warm and dry. The diggers had to work close to the earth. First the rows were turned up with a kelly turning plow. Then the diggers went on their hands and knees, grabbling in the earth with their fingers. It was a job for children. They could crawl and roll in the dirt as much as they liked. In moments of rest they could build sand houses and tunnels over their bare feet.

On the farm, sights and smells go with the seasons, and I learned them the first year, with each following year only a relearning: the green of young corn, the white of cotton blossoms slowly turning pink, the burnt brown of grass under an August sun; the sweetness of corn in silk and tassel, the dryness of dust in a cotton middle, the new-clothes smell of cotton lint when the face is pressed down into it.

The year passed. I was one year old, my father one year in the grave. Work had been hard, but there was enough to live on: milk and cornbread, sweet potatoes and black-eyed peas. Cotton money had to go for doctor bills and medicine. Times were bad, but they could be worse. Next year they would be better. At night they could be truly thankful when, after the Bible reading, they knelt beside hickory-bottomed chairs for the prayers they made themselves.

"If our health holds out," my mother and grandmother said.

3

Before the year was over, four generations were living in our house. Missouri Ann, my grandmother's mother, old and tired and dependent on her children and their children for a place to stay, came to live out the rest of her life with us.

She was born in Alabama about the time the stars fell, of a family who had come to Alabama from Missouri, to Missouri from Kentucky, and from what places before that she did not know. All she knew was that they had moved on and on, searching for better land, better chances. That, and her name Missouri for relatives who had stayed behind near Hannibal.

When she was fourteen her father took their belongings and slaves and moved to a new wilderness near Camden, Arkansas, on the Ouachita River.

When she was twenty-five, in 1860, she was still living on the Ouachita, married to Jesse H. James, and the mother of four children, the second my grandmother. They lived on their own land in Behistion Township and were well enough off to have a few slaves. Her life at the time was like that of many women in the South.

Then came the War between the States, and Arkansas sided with the Confederacy. When Jesse H. James felt that his duty to the South was greater than to his family, he went to Little Rock and enlisted as a private. Missouri Ann was left to take care of the farm, the children, and the slaves. It was a man's job and soon hers alone. Word came back that her husband had died of a fever a long way from home. From then on, even after she had married again, she signed her name M. A. like a man.

From the first it was a time of hardship. Confederate soldiers took the good horses and mules and left only the broken-down nags. Yankee soldiers came and took whatever was left. They took the corn from the barns and meat and molasses from the smokehouses. They ran over crops in the field and, when the slaves ran away, work came to a halt. Soon Missouri Ann was down to one slave, Mose, who stayed with her the rest of his life.

At one time Missouri Ann took her oldest children and crawled under the crib to pick up the grains of corn they could find, taking the rat-gnawed and weevilly with the rest. They crushed the little pieces into a coarse meal with which they made a round pone in a skillet. The rest they made into hominy, husking it by boiling it first in water mixed with ashes. Just when the hominy was boiled, the pone baked, a group of Yankee soldiers came to search the house. Missouri Ann knew what would happen to her bread and hominy if they found it. Before they could get inside the door she threw a quilt over the pot of hominy and sat down so that it was hidden under her skirts. Then she slipped the warm pone inside the bosom of her dress. Taking up a pair of carding combs, she carded cotton without stopping while the soldiers questioned her and searched the house. When they left, she and her children ate the bread and hominy.

Early in the war Yankee soldiers came to her house searching for Union deserters or Rebel soldiers home on leave. Disappointed at finding neither, put out because she would not talk to them, they cut open her feather beds and poured the feathers into a heap in a room. Then they brought a barrel of black molasses from the smoke house and poured it on the feathers. The mess made, they laughed at her and left her to clean it up.

Times were hard during the war. They were harder in the years after the war. Schools were closed. Children worked in the fields and woods, or were left to run wild along the Ouachita.

These were the years of the James boys—Jesse and Frank—who were claimed as cousins by Missouri Ann through her husband. At times she hid out two young men and later named them as the James boys. For the rest of her life she was bitter about the war. She thought the South needed more men like the James boys. When her son named his sons Jesse and Frank it seemed as right to her as it had to him.

After six years of Reconstruction, she had a passel of young' uns, and nothing else. The time had come for her to do what many around her were doing—pull up stakes and go to Texas, where they said a widow woman would have a better chance. Like women in her family before her, she loaded the few things she had left in a wagon and headed west, with the younger children in the wagon, the older children walking with her, driving their few head of cattle.

After thirty years in Texas, after thirty years of work, first as a farm hand on the black land, then farming her own place at Pin Hook, she had used up all her strength and everything she had made. There was nothing left for her but to sit in a rocking chair in front of the fire and nuss the baby, and tell stories that took her back to the war, to her hatred of the Yankees, her love for the James boys.

In February Linnie, the only girl in the family, took sick with a cold that turned into croup and then something else. Dr. Reeves came and tried his medicines but she got worse. He soon had to tell my mother what she already knew: He had done all he could and there was little chance that she would live. There was nothing left for him but to climb on his horse and ride out through the boggy lane.

It was too late to get help from outside. It had been a wet winter, and wagons could not get over the muddy roads. Fresh rain came, falling steadily till Little Pine Creek overflowed and cut off either road to town. The road to Blossom ended in a muddy lake. The road west from Pin Hook was worse. Only the bannisters of the creek bridge showed above the yellow water. A man on horseback could have got out, but they knew a doctor from town would turn back when he saw the overflow.

While my mother held her in her arms, Linnie died, quietly, at the age of two. The women in the family and neighbor women tried to tell my mother that it was a blessing: Linnie was better off; she would never have to go through the suffering they had all seen. They told her not to grieve too much. She did have four other children to think about, four other mouths to feed. It was God's will, and there would be a blessing in it.

There was no money for a coffin. No amount of money could have got men and wagon across the creek to bring a coffin from town. In a downpour of rain men brought boards and, sawing and nailing in the barn, put together a box and the women lined it with sheets. Other men dug a grave beside my father. The ground was soggy wet. Water seeped in and stood in a pool that had to be dipped dry for the burying.

The wagon carrying the coffin bogged through the mud to the graveyard. The mourners followed behind or cut across the fields. There was no preacher, no one to speak a prayer over the grave. My mother had to watch them lower the box and fill the hole with wet earth.

When it was over, she had to go back to the house with the living. Health had played out for one; it could play out for the others. It was the will of the Lord for her to work as hard as she could to keep the others well.

5

As soon as the rains slacked and the days turned warm, my mother was in the field again, flatbreaking land, getting ready for another planting. She could grieve for the dead from one end of the row to the other, but she could not stop for grief. A husband had been taken from her, and a daughter. "God's will be done." Words hard to say. Hard to go on working, knowing that no matter what she did death could change everything for her.

This spring she let Monroe stay in school as late as she could. To have any chance at all, he had to be able to read and write and do his numbers. Dewey stayed in school with him. She took Cleaver and me to the field with her. Again I was staked by a pallet, but instead of a sugar-tit I now had baked sweet potatoes. All they had to do to keep me from crying was to stuff my mouth with a baked sweet potato.

My mother was glad to have Missouri Ann with her. My grandmother could not read or write. With her there was no talk of books or reading. Missouri Ann was different. She had gone to school before the war. She had read books and wrote a good hand. As a little girl, my mother learned reading and writing from her, and with her help had written verses for Thanksgiving and Christmas. Missouri Ann was now too nearly blind to read, but she could call up things learned before the war: stories, songs, pieces memorized for reciting at school and Sunday School. She taught my mother and then my brothers a piece for Christmas:

> Will Christians remember
> This Eve of December
> When Christ the little Bethlehem Babe
> Was pillowed by a stranger
> In the humblest of manger?
> No fortune was there,
> Neither pride nor parade,
> And he was as poor as the barefoot
> Who wanders tonight.

She was now past seventy, and they could see how fast she was failing. Through the long hot days she sat in a rocking chair on the porch, sometimes dozing, sometimes waking to tell again the stories she had lived through in the war.

Then they knew it was time for her children to gather around her. Her oldest son had already left for Oklahoma, beginning the move to a new frontier. They wrote to him, but he was too far away to think of coming back. Her daughters were there—my grandmother in the house with her, Aunt Vick and Aunt Nellie close enough to come every day.

One day the next May, when they all knew the end was near, she called for my mother.

"Jessie," she said, "before I die I want to hear you sing and play the organ one more time."

My mother bent over her.

"What do you want me to sing?"

" 'There'll Be No Dark Valley.' "

My mother looked at the others and then at the organ, across the room from the bed, against the wall in a corner. She knew the song, the words. So did the others. She had sung it for Missouri Ann many times before:

> There'll be no dark valley when Jesus comes,
> To gather his loved ones home.

Words to sing over the dead, but over the dying? My mother looked at the three older women standing around the bed, all daughters of Missouri Ann, all a part of her, but none with her strength of mind and spirit. Still it was theirs to say.

Aunt Nellie shook her head and with her lips formed the word *no*. My mother did not sing, and the rest of her life was sorry that she had listened to the living, not the dying.

Missouri Ann died, and it was clear that a great deal had gone out of our lives. It was not only the link with the past, a link with men and women who stood up to the enemy, who fought the Yankees as long as they had any fight left in them. It was a link with books, with poetry, with a life a long way from Pin Hook.

They buried her at Red Oak, where she had lived once in her wanderings. They marked her grave with oak boards at her head and feet, and the grave was lost when the boards rotted away.

To her daughters she left her locket, her pin, her family Bible. To me she left a great deal more. Not two when she died, I could not remember her. I do remember her in an enlarged picture that hung on the wall. She was a woman of strong body, strong face. What did not show in the picture was that she was a maker of verse, a teller of stories, stories that from the time I could talk belonged to me.

6

Soon after, I crossed over from not remembering, though it took me a long time to separate things told me from the things I saw. Aunts and cousins liked to show off my memory. They would stand me on a chair and have me recite stories or count to a hundred without stopping.

"He's a heap o' company," they would say, "talking up peart like he does."

My mind was filling up with things to remember. I was four, going on five, and staying part of the time with Aunt Vick and her children still at home, Maggie Tippitt and Wade Grizzell. They said that Missouri Ann's looks had passed over Aunt Vick and settled on Maggie, the favor easiest to see in the strong, square chin. Wade had none of the favoring. His light hair and white skin made him more like his father's side of the family.

Aunt Vick's health was "jest tolluble," as she said day after day. If the days were chilly, she sat in a rocking chair in front of the fire, keeping live coals heaped on the dutch oven, baking bread or potatoes. On warm days she moved her chair to the hall between the two front rooms, where she could feel any breeze stirring. Wherever she sat, she needed someone to run for her. Wade was a half-grown boy and working in the fields or woods from sunup to sundown. Maggie worked like a man beside him.

When they came home at night, Wade sat by the lamp with the catalogue he had sent off for and looked at the things he would order if he had the money. Maggie pumped away at the organ, trying to learn the lessons and songs in the book my mother had studied. She had learned enough to play and sing:

There's not a friend like the lowly Jesus,
No not one, no not one.

During this time my mother let me stay with Aunt Vick to run
for her. It was better to have all the women in the family help raise
me than let me run in the fields and woods alone. I was too big to
be tied and not big enough to be sent to school. So all day long I
did the things Aunt Vick told me, and at night I sat on the floor by
the organ, listening to the rush of air in the bellows, and to Maggie
singing the only song she learned:

Jesus knows all about our troubles,
He will help till the day is done.

Looking at Aunt Vick, quiet in her rocking chair, I knew that
she was following the words with her lips. At times she talked about
her troubles. Hedley was still roaming somewhere, afraid to come
home. Ella, her other daughter, had married and moved off. After
trying to make a living farming, they had loaded their things on a
wagon and gone, first to Dallas, and then to Purcell, Oklahoma,
where we had kinfolks.

For the first time Dallas became a part of my memory. It was
more than a hundred miles away, and a big place. Aunt Vick said
she would be afraid to go to Dallas, it was so big. Maggie said she
could hardly wait to get on the road. She knew she could make a
better living in Dallas than she ever could farming. They laughed
at me when I said I wanted to go with her.

The running I did for Aunt Vick was little: to the bucket for a
dipperful of water, to the dresser for the comb, to the hens' nests for
the eggs, to the mantel piece to tell the time, till the clock stopped
and she had to tell the time by the sun. Sometimes she sent me to
the mailbox.

It was still hard for her to believe that she could send out to
the road and get the mail. All their years in Pin Hook they had had
to hook up a team to the wagon and drive the nine miles to Blossom for mail. Few letters went out. In bad weather or crop time letters might lie in the post office weeks on end. Then there was rural
free delivery, and Henry Ragsdale was the mail carrier. He was
good at coming every day, if the creeks were not out of banks, and
he kept good time. People without clocks marked time by him.
They would say, "Has Mr. Ragsdale passed yet?" Or, "It's nigh
about dinner time. I seen Mr. Ragsdale going by."

One day when I went the box was empty, the red flag down.

"It wasn't nothing in the box," I said, back at the house.

"Must a been a holiday," Aunt Vick said. "I wisht I had me a calendar so I could see if it was a holiday."

One day as I walked up the shady lane toward the mailbox I saw a long black snake in the road with his head high in the air. It was the kind they called a coachwhip. In Pin Hook they said coachwhips sometimes chased people. They had been known to wrap themselves around people and whip them to death with the long reddish-brown tails. Afraid to go forward, afraid to turn back, I stood in the sand of the road, trembling as if I had been taken down with a chill. While I watched, the snake lowered his head and crawled out of sight in the wild rose briers growing in the fence row. Afraid to pass where he had crossed, I waited long enough to have gone to the mailbox and went back to the house.

"No mail today," I told Aunt Vick. "Must a been a holiday."

The next day and the next I stopped short of where I had seen the snake and waited for the time to pass. When too many days passed without any mail, Aunt Vick sent Wade. They made a joke of it and laughed at me for being so lazy. I never told them about the snake. Aunt Vick stopped sending me to the mailbox.

Some time that year Eather Owens came to stay at our house. He was my father's double cousin—their fathers were brothers, their mothers sisters—close enough kin to be like one of our own family. He was seventeen or eighteen, and full of jokes and laughing. He had a good voice and liked to sing. With him there, music again became a part of our lives. Night after night, after supper, my mother played chords on the organ, "seconding" they called it in Pin Hook, while Eather sang old songs like "The Brown Girl."

My brothers usually stood beside Eather, taking turns holding the coal oil lamp. My place was in a corner between the end of the organ and the wall. I sang when I knew the songs. Most of the time I listened, trying to get the words by heart.

The ballads were long and sad, and the tunes were as sad as the words. I soon knew the words well enough to begin feeling sad before the sad part came, and to get the lesson of the song. My mother sang of Young Charlottie, the girl who froze to death because she wore silks to a dance instead of the warm clothes her mother asked her to wear. Or the killer of "The Oxford Girl" whose last words were:

> Oh, mother, they're going to hang me
> Between the earth and sky;
> Oh, mother, they're going to hang me,
> And I'm not prepared to die.

Not all the songs were sad.

"How about 'The Corn Dodger,' Eather?"

"You know I cain't second it," my mother would say.

She would sit on the organ stool with her hands in her lap while he sang a funny song with the refrain:

> She's a corn dodger,
> A didgy didgy dodger;
> He's a corn dodger, too.

We could laugh tears in our eyes at the words—knowing that a corn dodger was just a piece of corn bread fried in hot lard.

My mother also knew some funny songs. After some begging, she would turn around on the organ stool and sing "The Lazy Man." They started out saying it was Monroe's song, and then mine because I was even too lazy to go to the mailbox. The story was of a young man too lazy to hoe his corn:

> The careless weeds did grow so high
> They made this young man weep and cry.

By the beginning of the last verse they would all be looking at me, laughing, teasing:

> Now he's gone to court a widder—
> I'm in hopes that he won't git her—
> For a rake or a hoe or the handle of a plough
> Would suit him much better than a wife just now.

To make certain the lesson was not missed, my mother some-times told the story of the man so lazy that his neighbors put him in a coffin and started to the graveyard to bury him alive. On the way they met a man who, when he heard the story, said he would give the man in the coffin some corn to help him out. The lid of the coffin popped open and the man sat up.

"Is it shelled?" he asked.

"No."

The man lay back down.

"Drive on, boys," he said.

My grandmother, sitting through all of this, often without a word, would not let us go straight from laughing to the Bible read-ing and prayers. She would knock the ashes from her corn cob pipe and lay it on the mantel.

"Nigh about time for one o' my songs," she would say.

The laughing was over for that night, we all knew. My mother would turn back to the organ and open the songbook.

"Jessie, you reckon you could play 'Nearer My God to Thee?' "

She always asked for this song first, making *nearer* sound like *nea-raw*. My mother's answer was almost always the same.

"I reckon I can try."

She would pump till the bellows sounded like the hissing part of the Lord's Prayer. Then she would begin in her high clear voice the words my grandmother liked best:

> Though like a wanderer,
> The sun gone down,
> Dark clouds be over me,
> My rest a stone.

My grandmother would sit with her head bowed, her eyes closed, her hands folded in her lap. It was her song, a moment for thinking of death, of taking to heart the words, "Still in my dreams I'll be, Nearer my God to Thee." When the song had ended, while the sound still hung in the room, she would raise her head and move her black eyes from one to the other, making us all mark her words.

"When my time's come," she would say, "that's the song I want you to sing over me. I've said it before. I'll say it again. You hear me?"

I did not know what the others felt. I know that I felt awe, fear, dread that death would again shut off the singing and laugh-ing. My mother was the one who spoke.

"It's a long time off, but we'll remember."

After this, my grandmother often asked for her favorite passage of Scripture beginning, "In my Father's house are many mansions." That meant the singing had come to an end. Morning would come before daylight, and there was work to do: wood to be cut and hauled, brush to be burned.

My mother read the Bible out loud and prayed. When she prayed, the Bible and songs became part of her prayers.

Late spring, early summer, I was in the fields and woods alone. No one could take time from work to watch me. I could go and come as I pleased if I watched the sun and got back to the house before they came from the field for dinner or supper.

On soft, warm days I went along the branch that crossed our land and ran with clear water down to Little Pine Creek. In a way, Monroe had planted this place for me. When he was five or six he took sprouts of the honeysuckle growing over the porch and set them out along the branch. They spread and overran trees, making thick arbors green underneath and creamy white with blossoms where the sun struck. I found dark hiding places sweet with the smell of honeysuckle, with warm earth to lie on. Then I was afraid to hide there.

"I seen you in the honeysuckles," Monroe said. "You might step on a water moccasin down there if you don't look out."

Soon it was the same with the blackberry patches and plum thickets. It was all right to go to the edges, to the open ground around the edges, but not along the rabbit trails inside. Copperheads, the color of ground and dead leaves, liked to lie in the shade of the thickets. Anybody not watching might set a bare foot on a

copperhead. Better to stay out in the field, or on open paths in the
woods, where I could find all the sheep sorrel I wanted to eat.

"You look close along the rail fence you might find a quail's
nest," my grandmother told me. "Bring back the eggs. They beat
any kind, boiled done and salted."

I did find a quail's nest, the eggs pure white, thin-shelled, hard
to carry without breaking in the crown of a straw hat. Later I found
little quails, like tiny brown chickens, hiding in the leaves, scattering when I came close. One clear call "Bob White" would send me
to the fence rows.

One hot summer day I followed the others to the cotton patch,
where they were doing the last hoeing, the laying by. The sun hot
on my head, the sand burning my feet, I went to the fence row
looking for shade. It was a rail fence, higher than my head, zigzag-
ging along one side of the field. I tried sitting on the rails. Then I
tried walking the top rail. When the rail turned, I fell down
through weeds and grass and landed in a yellow jacket's nest. I felt
them before I saw them. Then they were swarming over me like
bees, stinging me on my face, hands, feet, and through my clothes. I
yelled and ran and, unable to get away from them, fell to the
ground, crying with the pain. My mother and Monroe came running into the thick of the yellow jackets, beating at them with
hands and hat and bonnet. Stung on their faces and hands, they
grabbed me up and ran to the open field, too far for the yellow
jackets to follow.

Soon my face was swollen, my eyes closed. The remedy was a
wet tobacco poultice, but there was no tobacco in the field. They
had to carry me to the house. My grandmother was the only one
who chewed, and she could not chew enough to cover the stings.
They stripped me naked and, all of them taking leaves from the
bundles of homegrown, chewed till I was covered with wet wads and
brown juice. They kept on chewing and laying on poultices till the
swelling went down—till they could hold my eyelids open and get
me to say that I could see a hand before my face.

The stings made me sick; the smell of tobacco juice made me
sicker.

9

Too young to work, to know what it was to rest after weeks and
months of plowing, planting, hoeing, day in, day out, morning till
night, I was old enough to know that a slack time came when crops
were laid by—a time when horses could be turned out to pasture,
when women could go visiting, when men knew it was all right to
go to the creek with a hook and line on a long cane pole. A time for
rest. Also a time for religion. Preachers knew that a man had more
feeling for a sermon at night if he had time for a nap in the middle
of the day.

Methodists and Baptists in Pin Hook agreed to have a union
revival meeting. It had been a long time, people said, since Pin
Hook had seen a real revival meeting. It was a good thing for
everybody to get together and make it a big meeting. No better time
than the hot days of August, the dog days. No better way to spend it
than listening to sermons from a preacher who knew how to preach.

I heard the talk. I watched the men build an oak pole frame
for an arbor on the school ground. I watched wagons come from
branch banks loaded with green willow brush to cover the frame.
Other wagons came with sawdust from the sawmill on the Pine
Bluff road. The men made a roof of willow brush, a floor of
sawdust deep enough for feet to sink in.

Word came from the preacher. The men were to hold prayer
meetings while they worked on the arbor. Women were to visit and
pray. Word came to my mother: She was to choose the songs and
play the organ. With the praying and singing we were in the revival
before the meetings started at the arbor.

On the first night we ate supper by daylight and, scrubbed and dressed in clean clothes, we walked out the lane and down the road in the greenish light of first dark. People were already coming in. Wagons and teams stood in the school yard. Men and women sat on benches made of rough boards laid across wood blocks. Kerosene torches hung from the arbor poles, making red smoky lights that drew moths and beetles in circling swarms.

The preacher, a tall bony man in a black suit, came in the wagon with one of the families and it was time for the meeting to start. My mother went to the organ and, the stool turned to the right height, sat down. In her long blue skirt and white lawn waist, with her black hair piled high on her head, she looked taller and prettier than she did at work in the field. She put a songbook on the rack and tested the pedals till there was a hiss of air from the bellows. Then she sat with her hands in her lap, waiting for word from the preacher.

My grandmother sat at the back of the arbor, away from the lights and bugs, with me on one side, Cleaver on the other. I sat with the feel of sawdust like rough sand on my feet, breathing the smell of drying willow, drying sawdust, and burning coal oil.

The singing started, led by the preacher, who walked back and forth across the front of the arbor, marking time with his right hand. The song was one we had practiced for the meeting, and I knew the words:

> I will arise and go to Jesus;
> He will embrace me in His arms.
> In the arms of my dear Savior,
> Oh, there are ten thousand charms.

The preacher went from song to song, getting the people ready for the praying and preaching, stirring them up to the revival feeling. It would not be a revival till the people danced and shouted all over the arbor, or fell in trances in the sawdust.

I stayed awake through the singing and praying. I watched and listened as men and women stood up from their benches and testified what God had done for them. The preaching was long and I went to sleep, my head on my grandmother's lap.

When I woke up, singing had started again and the preacher was calling sinners to the mourner's bench. This bench was at the front of the arbor, at the preacher's knees, under his hands. While my mother played the organ, while the people sang, the preacher gave the call. The words of the song became a part of the call:

Earnestly, tenderly, Jesus is calling,
Calling for you and for me.
See at the portals He's waiting and watching,
Watching for you and for me.

In the chorus the people sang "Come home," the preacher shouted "Come home." When they sang "Ye who are weary come home," he talked to them about the weariness of life, the rest in heaven for the ones who would come forward and confess their sins.

Men and women, some of them singing as they went, left their benches and crossed the arbor to someone unconverted, or to a known backslider, to plead with them to go to the mourner's bench and confess their sins. Some went, and the song changed to "Almost persuaded now to believe."

There was some shouting, and the people knew it was going to be a good meeting. They talked about it on the way home that night and sent the word up and down the road the next morning.

The second night more people came and there was more shouting. The third night on the way home my mother said,

"Did you hear me? Five people shouting all around me and I went right on playing. Never missed a note."

The glow that touched her also touched my grandmother.

"I do wish Nellie'd come to the meetings," she said. "Her girls is old enough to go to the mourner's bench."

She was talking about Aunt Nellie Haigood, her sister, Missouri Ann's youngest daughter. From their talk I knew that Aunt Nellie had joined the church when she was a girl, but did not take to religion the way the others did. She had lost her husband and had three daughters to bring up. She went to the fields or woods and worked like a man. She was raising them to work like men. If work needed doing on Sunday, they worked on Sunday. She had put her letter in the Baptist Church at Novice, but months went by when she did not set foot inside the door.

My grandmother talked to my mother and Aunt Vick and they sent word to Aunt Nellie to come to the meeting.

Before the meeting was half over they were glad they had. One of our near neighbors, a man said to be hard of head and heart, went to the mourner's bench and got religion. It was more than anyone had expected, and shouting broke out all over the arbor. He danced around the mourner's bench and then ran in and out among the people shouting and praying. He circled outside and stopped beside a big oak at a corner of the arbor. Falling to his knees, he began butting his head against the tree and begging forgiveness for his sins.

The preacher, seeing him in his glory, jumped up on the benches and danced from one to the other, shouting for the people to look upon the work of God, begging them to open their hearts and raise their voices. The organ stopped; the singing stopped. My mother and grandmother knelt with the people struggling at the mourner's bench.

Aunt Nellie came at the end of the meeting, in the wagon with her girls. We knew she was coming. She had sent word that she wanted my grandmother and me to go home with her for a visit. We could come home next time someone was passing.

The meeting was good that night, but the shouting was quiet, and no one fell down in the sawdust. Aunt Nellie listened to the singing and praying and preaching.

"It was a good sermon," she said to my grandmother, but she had nothing to say when the call came for mourners. She could have spoken to her daughters, but she did not. When the call was over, not one of them had stepped forward.

After a last prayer, a last song, the revival was over and we went to Aunt Nellie's wagon. They sat in cane-bottom chairs. I lay on a quilt by the endgate.

It was a long trip, north to Pin Hook and then west across Little Pine Creek and more than half the way to Novice. I could hear my grandmother and Aunt Nellie talking, not about the meeting but about the hard times and the way they had to live. I lay still, looking up into the dark trees overhead, waiting for the sound of horses and wagon on the bridge across Little Pine Creek.

We crossed the creek and the girls started singing, their voices high and thin and echoing in the woods. First they sang songs from the meeting, and then a song my mother sometimes sang at work in the field:

> No never alone,
> No never alone,
> He promised never to leave me,
> Never to leave me alone.

Someone was crying, but the singing went on:

> I heard the voice of my Savior,
> Telling me still to fight on—

The wagon stopped with a jolt and Aunt Nellie jumped flat-footed to the ground. Up the road she went, shouting at every jump, giving way to all the sorrow and grief and gladness stirred up in her. Up the road, and down again, past the wagon she went, shouting, crying, crooning, begging God to have mercy on her and help her. As if she had to, she trod the dusty road, up and down, till she was worn out and her voice barely made a sound. We waited, with nothing to do but wait.

Quiet again, she came out of the darkness and climbed up to her seat in the wagon.

"I had me a good shout," she said.

Then she took up the lines and drove home.

Crops were not as good as they should have been. Corn grew big stalks, little ears. Cotton went to leaf. Boll weevils hid under thick leaves and bored into the squares so that they fell off before they bloomed. There would be enough corn to get by on for meal and feed and seed, but none to sell. By the end of August my mother knew there would be a little cotton, a little money, but not enough to go on through the winter—not enough even to buy shoes and clothes to start the winter. It was all right for me to go without shoes. I had never had a pair and, still too young for school, I could stay indoors when the weather was cold. Monroe and Dewey would have to have shoes. They were too big to go to school barefooted.

There was talk of going to the prairie to pick cotton, and my mother began to think she should try it. As she said, she could leave us with my grandmother for the month of good picking and come back with enough money to carry us all through the winter. My grandmother did not think so. She thought a woman out by herself would have a hard time getting a job picking cotton. She thought my mother was too slow at picking to make more than her room and board. My mother argued that any money she made was better than none.

When my grandmother would not let her start out alone, my mother went to Aunt Vick's to get Maggie to go with her. It took no begging. Maggie was ready to go picking cotton on the blackland, or anywhere else that would get her away from Pin Hook.

She was a tall, gaunt girl with big square teeth and lips too short to cover them. In all her life she had had only one beau, and, at twenty-five, was looked on as an old maid. Her one chance for marriage had come that summer, and now it was off. The man was an old widower with several children, some of them older than Maggie. On Sundays he came and sat with her in the front room, taking up the one rocking chair, leaving her to sit on the organ stool. Warm days I sat with Aunt Vick in the hall.

"Miss Maggie," we could hear him say, "I would take it kindly if you would sing and play something on the organ."

She still had not learned anything but "No Not One." Her hands were awkward on the keys, her feet heavy on the pedals. Her voice had a whang when she talked; it was whangier when she sang. She knew she could not do well, but, willing to do her best, she put her voice, hands, and feet to work on a song that may have pleased him once, or twice, but not forever.

My grandmother said she "No Not One'd" him to death. Whatever happened, he stopped coming to see her. After a time they said he had married a widow who could not play or sing but who owned a good farm with some cattle.

When my mother talked to her about going to the prairie, Maggie had given up the organ, and any hope of finding a life for herself in Pin Hook. She listened to my mother and then wanted her fortune told. She had thought of going to Dallas. The fortune might help her decide between Dallas and the prairie.

That night she came to stay at our house, for my mother to tell their fortunes. After supper she boiled two eggs—one for herself, one for Maggie. When they were hard as rocks she cut them in half, took out the yolks, and filled the halves with salt. Then each ate two halves, salt and all, and they went to bed without a drink of water. If the fortune worked right, they would dream of the men to come into their lives and see their faces close enough to know them when they met.

Next morning the talk was not of fortunes but of going to the prairie. My grandmother had given in. So had Aunt Vick. All they had to do was put their sidesaddles on their ponies and start out. My mother talked about the money she would make. She also talked of leaving Pin Hook for good. Not yet thirty, with four years of hard work behind her, she could not see much hope.

My grandmother did not keep them from going, but she went around the house with a frown on her face, a grumbling in her voice. It was not right for two women to go off by themselves. No telling what might happen to them out on the road like that. She was crying when my mother led the pony up to the doorstep and climbed on.

With me holding on to her, my grandmother went with them as far as the front gate.

"I'll be worried till I hear from you," she said.

Still crying, she watched them ride up the lane at a trot. They came to the road and, waving white handkerchiefs, turned toward Blossom.

"Ain't no telling," my grandmother said. "Just ain't no telling."

There were days of waiting for us at home, when we went every morning to the mailbox to meet Mr. Ragsdale, looking for a letter, hoping for some word of where they had gone, what they were doing. Some days, after the mail carrier had passed, my grandmother would take us across the pasture and fields to Aunt Vick's. They would sit on the back porch, talking in voices too low for us to hear, keeping us quiet not with words but with the look of worry on their faces. In the late afternoon we would go back home, with my grandmother walking ahead, talking half to herself, half to us.

"Two weeks is a long time not to hear. I've got a good mind to leave you with Vick and start out walking looking for them."

Then a letter came from my mother. They had gone past Blossom and all the way to Deport before they found a farm where cotton pickers were needed. It was a big farm and they had a good place to stay. They had turned their ponies out in the farmer's pasture and were working from daylight till dark, picking in the best fields they had ever seen. There was enough picking to keep them going till frost, and they did not want to come hcme till they had made every penny they could.

Again we went to Aunt Vick's, and found her in the kitchen crying. Monroe was not with us to read the letter, but my grandmother remembered everything in it. Aunt Vick listened but did not stop crying. With me standing between them, she told my grandmother what had happened.

Wade had gone to the mailbox and brought back a letter that she thought was from Hedley, though the name on it was not his and the men's suits on the enclosed sheet of paper were too fine for him or Pin Hook. This time there was a return address, in a town in West Texas, and an order form for size and color.

"He wants to hear from me," Aunt Vick said, "and he's going to."

My grandmother set her lips tight.

"It's risky."

"Not if I don't say more'n he asks me to. Wade wrote in the blanks and put in Victoria Grizzell. When he sees my name he'll know I'm all right. What else can I do? Turn my back on him in trouble?"

"No, not if you want to take the chance."

An envelope with a printed address had come with the letter, but it was not stamped.

"You got a stamp, Alice?" Aunt Vick asked. "I tore the place upside down but couldn't find anything that looked like a stamp."

"No. I hunted but couldn't find one to send Jessie."

Aunt Vick held the envelope in her hand.

"You got two coppers, Alice? I've got to get a stamp."

"No, and no way to get none till Jessie sends some."

Aunt Vick went through the hall and back to the kitchen.

"I don't know what to do. The letter's got to go by return mail."

My mother's letter lay on the kitchen table, the stamp good as new but marked with wavy lines of black ink. Aunt Vick looked at the stamp carefully.

"I've a good mind to use it again," she said.

"You cain't." My grandmother looked worried. "You'd get caught and be sent to the pen—"

"Not if I wash out the marks. If I wash them out and paste it on right nobody'll ever see it."

My grandmother shook her head.

"If I'd ever a thought a sister of mine—"

Aunt Vick began walking the floor and crying.

"Now, Vick." My grandmother was crying with her.

Then my grandmother gave in. They would send the letter and risk getting caught with the marked stamp. Working together, they soaked the stamp off in cold water. Careful not to tear it, they laid it on the table and with wet fingers rubbed the black streaks. The red faded to a deep pink, and the marks looked like rubbed-out pencil lines. When they dried it in the sun, the marks were so dim they had to look twice to see them. The gum had all been washed off. Aunt Vick made a thin paste of flour and water. On the envelope, the stamp looked old, but not marked.

Afraid to leave it in the mailbox, afraid Mr. Ragsdale might take a look at the stamp and turn them in for what they had done, my grandmother let me stay at Aunt Vick's that night so I could meet the mail carrier the next day. He would take the letter from my hand and put it in his bag. Once it was in among all the other letters, no one would notice the difference.

I did, and felt it that night, the next morning, and on the way to the mailbox—started out early by Aunt Vick, who wanted to make sure I would not miss the mail carrier. I was afraid that Aunt Vick would be caught and turned in—that she would go to the pen and I would never see her again.

I put the flag up on the mailbox and walked back and forth on the hard clay road. When a long time had passed, I saw the mail carrier come around the bend by the schoolhouse, sitting high in his buggy, letting his horse plod along with loose reins.

When he was nearer, I could see the smile on his thin, sun-browned face. Almost to the box, he reached down into a bag and brought out a letter.

"Got a letter for you this time. Looks like Maggie's writing."

Afraid to say anything, I reached up and took the letter, and forgot to give him the one I had to mail. He saw it and laughed.

"You want to mail that one?"

I handed it up to him, still unable to get a word out. He laughed again.

"Looks like you about forgot to."

He took the letter, glanced at it without really looking at it, and dropped it into a canvas bag. With a cluck to his horse he went on down the road, and I ran as hard as I could to the house.

Aunt Vick and Wade were waiting for me on the front porch.

"He say anything?" she asked.

"He never even looked at it."

Some of the worry went out of her face.

"'You got a letter from Maggie," I said.

She took it from me and with shaking fingers tore it open at the end away from the stamp. Then she handed it to Wade.

"Read it out loud."

It was a short letter and full of good news, from the "I take my pen in hand to drop you a few lines" to the "We are both well and hope you the same." They were picking cotton for a man named John Rhodes, who was working a place on the shares out a ways from Deport. Picking was still good, but it would not last much longer. They had been to a party on Saturday night, and had been asked to another one. No word of when they might be home, but it would be when the picking was done.

Aunt Vick listened and then looked at Wade.

"I'll go tell Alice," she said.

With me following behind her, with her skirts lifted above her ankles, she struck out at a fast walk across the pasture.

One day without letting us know my mother came back just as she had left, riding her pony, sidesaddle, with a bundle tied on behind. She had on new clothes and shoes, and a fine white wool shawl around her shoulders. She was laughing and talking and kissing us all at the same time. She untied the bundle and brought out sacks of candy and packages of wax—the word we used for chewing gum. Picking had been good and she had brought money for shoes and clothes for us.

My grandmother felt the shawl.

"How much did you pay for it?" she asked.

My mother had to tell her that it was a present from Mr. Rhodes, and that she had told him he could come to see her. My grandmother was bound to find out more about him. We heard some of the questions, some of the answers. He was a widower with five children, the oldest, Monroe's age, the youngest, mine. The youngest were twins, a boy and a girl. He was a renter, but the land he rented was the best black waxy, good for a bale an acre nearly any year.

"Better let him stay there."

My grandmother said her mind then, and she never changed it. The more she found out, the more she grumbled. Over and over she said, "You better let well enough alone."

There were letters from my mother to "Mr. John Rhodes, Deport, Texas," and letters to "Mrs. Jessie Ann Owens, R.F.D. 3, Blossom, Texas." It was make two trips to the mailbox or wait for the mail carrier every day.

One day Mr. Rhodes came driving down the lane in a shiny

new buggy with a team of fine horses. A finer rig had never been seen in Pin Hook. He tied up to the fence in front of our yard gate, and came toward the house. He was a tall tanned man with dark brown moustache and brown eyes, and his suit and hat were brand new.

My mother saw him coming and ran to hide. In Pin Hook, she would have been called fast or feisty if she had gone out to meet him.

I waited in the door till he toled me out on the porch with a handful of candy teddy bears, pink and brown. He pushed at me on one shoulder and then the other, and scuffled with me till I doubled up my fists. Laughing at me, he swung me up and gave me the sack of teddy bears.

My grandmother came and, with a word to me to go out and play, took him inside. I went to the west end of the house and squatted in the chimney corner, where I was warmed on one side by the sun, on the other by the dark red bricks. One by one I ate the teddy bears till they were all gone.

After a while I heard them in the front and went around the house. Mr. Rhodes was on the porch, ready to go down the steps. This time my mother was with him, dressed in a white waist and a blue worsted skirt. She had wrapped the white shawl over her dark hair and around her shoulders. She gave me a quick hug and let him help her up the buggy. He got in beside her and turned the horses up the lane.

"Jessie," my grandmother called, her voice sharp, whiny, "look out for that shawl. You'll get it caught in the wheel."

My mother pulled the shawl tighter around her shoulders, leaving the ends to fly out behind her.

"Out of the frying pan into the fire," my grandmother complained.

When the buggy was out of sight on the road to Pin Hook she told us that they had gone to find a preacher to marry them. Inside the house, she told us that things would never be the same again. We would be taken to Deport to live; she would be left behind to live with some of the other kinfolks.

"I nussed the last one of you," she said, "and she's taking you off with her. She says it's to keep you together. If it was just that, she'd keep you right here on the land you own. Mark my words. In a year's time you'll be scattered, and no place of your own to go to."

We listened, but we did not believe her. We were going to live

with Mr. Rhodes at Deport. We were going to live on the blackland. Blackland people called people from the sandy land sand-
lappers. Times would be better with Mr. Rhodes. He had brought
me a sack full of teddy bears. We had seen his fine horses and
buggy. We did not know he had rented them from a livery stable in
Paris.

Before sundown my grandmother took me across the pasture to
Aunt Vick's and they made down a pallet for me by the fireplace.
After supper I could see them coming and going, getting the room
across the hall ready for my mother and Mr. Rhodes. I could hear
them, talking in low voices, voices that came down to me over the
rustle of long skirts, talking on the wedding night that the marriage
would not work out, that two sets of children would be worse off for
it. Either one could have said what I heard: "It looks to me like she
drove her ducks to a bad market." I went to sleep listening to their
talk.

Late in the night, when all was quiet, a shotgun went off under
the part of the house where I was sleeping. By the time I was up on
all fours the house and yard were full of sounds of men running
and yelling and banging on sweeps. Around the house they went,
with guns blasting, cowbells ringing. Aunt Vick took me in her
arms and tried to stop me from crying.

"It's a shivaree," she said. "They're shivareeing your mammy
and Mr. Rhodes."

I cried harder.

"They gonna hurt them?"

"Not if they get up and pass out a treat. They're just having
fun. They might ride him on a rail a piece, but they won't hurt
nobody."

I stopped crying and Aunt Vick took me to the porch to watch.
I could see dim shapes circling and circling the house, all the men
of Pin Hook together at once, making all the noise they could make.
Men put their shotgun barrels under the porch and blazed away. I
could see the fire and smell burning powder. I thought I could
hear the rattle of shot.

A hen squawked and I thought of the chickens. On hot days
they rested in the dust under the house. A few of them roosted there
all night.

"Stop," I yelled at the men. "Stop shooting. You'll kill all the
chickens."

The men nearest me stopped and came to where I stood shivering in my long drawers.

"Look at him," they yelled. "He thinks we want to shoot the chickens."

They laughed and slapped their legs and got the others to come and see me trying to stop the shivaree. Wade was with them, carrying a sweep and hammer.

The noise stopped, my mother and Mr. Rhodes came out, with the lamp lit, and with sacks of candy and tea cakes from the store. It was the treat they all expected. The shivaree was over. The men laid their guns and sweeps and bells on the edge of the porch and went up to shake hands and take a treat.

Aunt Vick let me stay long enough to see that everything was all right. Then she took me back to my pallet.

On the way to Deport, we were like any of the other families that had left Pin Hook to find a better living somewhere else. The horses were hitched to the wagon, the wagon piled up with stove and beds and chairs, the younger children on top on a feather bed, the two cows tied behind the wagon with ropes. My mother sat on the springseat, driving. Monroe sat beside her, his light curly hair almost white in the sun, his thin face tanned brown, his blue eyes watching ahead to every bend in the road. There was no crying for the things left behind. The place was rented. The things we lived with were in the wagon with us.

We had talked ourselves out about Deport, but some of the things had to be said again in the wagon. Making a living would be easier on the blackland. There was a saying at Pin Hook:

"You can make a better living by accident on the blackland than you can by trying on sandy land."

It was time of year for school. Monroe and Dewey would be going to school. My mother would not have to go to the field to plow. They would not have to stay home from school to help her.

The trip was no more than twenty miles but it took the rest of the day and late enough at night for me to go to sleep on the feather bed. I was carried into my new home without waking and bedded down with my new brothers and sisters.

When I woke in the morning, I was on a pallet on the floor, sleeping with Ollie and Collie, the twins, who asked me my name and told me they would soon be six years old. I found my mother in the kitchen, cooking breakfast. Mr. Rhodes was at the barn feeding.

That first morning we all crowded around a table too small for us—a table so small, a family so large that there would have to be a first and second table every meal. At four biscuits apiece, the number Mr. Rhodes said we could have, my mother had to bake fifty at a time to have any left over. She laughed. Cooking for her family was like cooking for the hands at chopping and picking time.

After sunup, three Rhodes children—Oscar, Elmer, and Mamie—and three Owens children—Monroe, Dewey, and Cleaver —went down the road to the one-room schoolhouse. I was left at home with the twins. I wanted to see their toys. They watched the things unpacked from our wagon. We had brought as many things from our house as they had in theirs, but I had more new sights and sounds to learn:

The land was black and flat and treeless. The house we lived in sat close to a black dirt road that in dry weather packed down hard and smooth like concrete—in wet, got churned and worked to a sticky wax that people said would bog a duck. Cotton rows came up close to the house and barn. Leafless brown stalks stretched away as far as I could see. The house was no better than our house in Pin Hook, and smaller till a new room was added for a sleeping place for the older boys.

In that first morning I learned what it was like to run through cotton stalks higher than my head. After school, I watched the older boys scrapping cotton on land so rich they had to reach up to get the bolls left by the last picking. The rows were long, the fields not broken by fences or trees. There were only a few houses in sight, and slender telephone poles along the road.

Telephones were new to me. We did not have one in the house, but there were poles on either side, strung with wires soft green against the blue sky. I could not listen in on a telephone, but I could put my ear against a pole and listen to the sound of wires in the wind. It was a low humming sound that seemed to be part of something a long way off. I tried to believe that it was made up of the voices of many people, and that I would see them if I followed the wires far enough. It worked when I was by myself. When the others were around they said, "The wires don't go no place past Deport." I had not been to Deport, so I had to believe them.

The older boys sang words that made a joke of a song we had sung at Pin Hook:

> Jesus lover of my soul
> Help me up a telephone pole;
> When the pole begins to bend,
> Help me to the other end.

The words stayed in my mind, and I heard them every time I listened to the humming.

One morning my mother called us in and told us that a neighbor down the road had died in the night, and that Mr. Rhodes would take us to the funeral, to let us see the dead man in his coffin. I had been too young to know anything when my father died. Ollie and Collie could not remember their mother.

The day was wet and cold, and the mud of the road like black wax. It balled on our shoes and made a gray-black coating on our long black stockings. The wagon waiting to take the coffin to the graveyard stood half hub deep in watery ruts. People going in had tracked mud on the steps and porch, so that we walked in mud to the front door.

In the front room, the people were waiting for the preacher to begin. I saw the people first, and then the long black coffin, set in the light from a window. Mr. Rhodes picked me up and held me over the coffin so that I could look down on the white face, the white hair, the wrinkled hands folded over black coat, white shirt.

There was time for each of us to look, and then the service began, with the preacher leading some men and women in singing "Jesus Lover of My Soul." Mr. Rhodes stepped back with us, so far that I could not see the coffin, only the dark-britches legs of men standing in front of us. I knew it was there, and what I had seen inside was death.

When it was over I backed out the door and went home by myself. My mother met me at the door.

"You see him?" she asked.

I nodded.

"Did he look natural?"

I did not know. I did know one of the songs.

"Sing it."

I sang the words as I thought I had heard them.

> Jesus lover of my soul
> Help me up a telephone pole—

"They never sung no such a thing," she said.

I wanted to sing the rest to show her, but she would not let me. It was a bad song. She would whip me if she ever heard me singing a bad song.

I did not know a bad song from any other kind, but I soon learned. In the barn one day I heard the older boys singing some words and giggling over them. It took no time at all for me to learn the words and tune:

> I thought I heard my grandmother say
> Funky butt, funky butt,
> Take it away.

I went to the house, straight to the kitchen, and, when the others were at the table, sang it to them.

Without a word my mother took me by the arm and pushed me out to the backyard. With her right hand she broke a limb from a bush. With her left she switched my legs till I promised never to sing it again.

"Just don't let me catch you," she said. "You do and I'll double the dose."

There were times when we missed Pin Hook. I missed my grandmother and the visits to Aunt Vick. I missed going to the woods by myself. At Deport there were no woods in sight.

My mother missed being part of a place. At Pin Hook she had sent the "Pin Hook Notes" to the Blossom *Bee* for a long time. She had to keep up with the news. In Pin Hook people brought her their news so they could see their names in the paper the next week. Now we lived on a road where people passed by, but we did not know them and there was not a Deport paper.

14

When we were first at Deport there were many jokes between my mother and Mr. Rhodes over how "my children" and "your children" were becoming "our children" at school and at home. But there was some trouble almost from the beginning, partly because there were too many of us living in a house much too small. My mother was good at mothering; she tried hard at stepmothering. In the fights among us, she could not help taking sides with her own. At any sign of favoring, or anything they thought was favoring, the other children ran to their father to tell. Before long, any fight among the children ended in rough talk from him, tears from my mother.

Some of the fights started with me. I was the youngest, and used to being the baby. I fought, cried, tattled to keep my place and when they called me crybaby or sugar-tit I scratched and clawed anybody in my way.

Mr. Rhodes tried to even things out. On Saturdays he went to Deport in the wagon and brought back sacks of flour and red beans, buckets of molasses and lard, and a big piece of side meat which we called middling. For the older children grub was treat enough. For the younger he brought candy teddy bears, which he counted out one by one to make sure we had an even number.

The others always ate theirs at once. I saved a few of mine and hid them in dark places in the house or barn, the places I had learned to hide in when I wanted to be by myself. With a teddy bear in my mouth I could keep myself busy an hour. We did have more to eat and wear at Deport than we had at Pin Hook, but there was less than I had thought there would be. The fine team and buggy went back to the livery stable, and we never saw them again. When we went anywhere, and that was only once or twice to visit new kinfolks, we went in the wagon, or walked. But with a teddy bear in my mouth I could think that Mr. Rhodes would bring us more things the next time he went to town.

The others hunted for my teddy bears, and finding them was easy. I could not keep away from the hiding places. To them, it was finders, keepers, and the safest keeping place was down the gullet. They ate the teddy bears and I fought them till one or more of us got a thrashing. I got my way in the house but not behind the barn. Behind the barn they fought me for tattling, and my only chance to get even was to tattle again. The fight seesawed back and forth, and at times it was the children of one family against the children of the other.

One day my mother told us that she was looking for a new baby and that she would find it before long. At Pin Hook they had told me that cows found their calves in hollow stumps. Now I remembered what I had heard:

"Old Reddy found the prettiest surly calf."

"Where?"

"In a hollow stump."

"How'd she know it was there?"

"Go ask her."

My brothers told me to ask the bull, and my mother said she would wash my mouth out with soap if she heard me use that word again.

I went out and looked at the treeless land. Not a stump in sight. To me, that was the answer: No stump, no baby.

Behind the barn, where we were playing house, I learned more about babies. Collie told me how babies got started, using words bad enough for a mouth washing if my mother heard him. Ollie did not use bad words, but she did pull down her drawers and showed me where babies come from.

"It'll be a baby," they said. "Just wait and see."

This time I did not tattle on them. Back at the house, I asked my mother if she was still looking for a baby. When she said *yes* I went behind the barn again to ask more questions.

One morning I went to the kitchen by myself and found my mother washing dishes and crying. Monroe had left home. He had put his clothes in a flour sack and gone to Pin Hook to get a job. Going on fourteen, he was off on his own to bind himself to some farmer for room and board and enough money for clothes.

I could not keep from crying. Monroe was the one I looked up to. He was the one who took my side in fights. At the times when I was afraid of Mr. Rhodes, I could always go to Monroe.

"When's he coming back?" I asked.

"He says he won't. He's going to stay at Pin Hook."

He did not come back, and he did not write. Without him, I knew that things had changed.

He had not been gone long when I woke up one morning knowing that I was in a strange bed in a strange house. Ollie and Collie were on the pallet with me. I started crying and woke them up. We soon knew we were at a neighbor's house, down the road from ours. The woman gave us mush and milk but I would not stop crying.

In the middle of the morning, leaving the others at her house, she took me by the hand and led me up the hot, hard-packed road. They let me stay in the room with my mother a few minutes. Her eyes were red, her face swollen, but she sat up in bed and tried to laugh me out of being a crybaby. I stopped, but started again as soon as we were out on the road.

The next morning, while the dew was still on the ground, the three of us were taken up the road, home. Mr. Rhodes met us at the door. He had on clean work clothes, and was smiling.

"Come see our new baby boy," he said.

My mother was sitting up in bed, with a red-faced baby on the pillow beside her. He still had no name, and did not seem to belong to us. It took time to get used to him and to the hippens drying on the line, longer for me than for the others. I was no longer the youngest. Someone liked the name LeRoy, and it soon became his— the *Roy* of it.

In the hottest days of August my grandmother came from Pin Hook, riding sidesaddle on her bay pony. She had come to see how we were living at Deport, and to let my mother know that things were not going well at Pin Hook.

She did not like what the renter was doing with our place. He had let most of the land "lay out," land rented to him on the shares, and the house was beginning to look run down. Another year and it would not be fit to live in.

When Mr. Rhodes was in the field she talked about Monroe. Still without a job, he was going from pillar to post, out of health and looking thin as a rail. She had met him on the Blossom road, walking toward Pin Hook, pushing an old bicycle through sand too deep to ride in. He was going to Aunt Vick's, but she could not help him long. Maggie had a job in Dallas and was sending money home, but not enough to feed another hungry mouth.

Aunt Nellie had packed up and moved to Oklahoma, to a farm close to Purcell. Monroe was talking of going out there, too, if he did not find a job at Pin Hook.

They talked together and cried. The trouble was that my mother was not keeping her children together. Then I was sent out to play with the other children.

One morning my grandmother left, on the Deport road, with the sun hot and bright on her black bonnet and dress. My mother watched her go. Then, her right hand shaking at her side and tears on her face, she went back to the house.

15

In the middle of cotton picking, Monroe came to Deport again, not to stay but to help us move back to Pin Hook. He came in the night and I saw him in the morning, standing in the kitchen door, tall and thin, his curly hair grown long and roached back from his high forehead. My mother, with a set look on her face, was taking hot biscuits from the stove. Never one to talk much, she was quiet in a way that made me know something was wrong.

Between then and field time all of us knew that everything had been settled, and that my mother was taking her children, including the new baby brother, back to Pin Hook to live. As the cotton had not been sold, there was no money for her for a new start, but she was to have one of the new-ginned bales in the yard and all the things she had brought with her. Anything she could not take in the first load would be kept till she could send for it.

Even with all of us in it, the kitchen was quiet, with the quiet of sadness. Time for words and crying had passed. It was time for leaving, and we all knew there were reasons to go, reasons to stay. We had never had the feeling of kin, but we had lived long enough together to be more than friends. Good-byes were quick, almost wordless.

Mr. Rhodes took his cotton sack and swung it over his shoulder. He went out the door and to the field, followed by his children. I watched them till they were bent over the rows picking, almost out of sight.

My mother began loading the wagon with the things she wanted to take with her—beds and chairs, feather beds and quilts, as many things as she could pile between the springseat and the bale of cotton. On top they made a hole for me and the baby among the featherbeds and quilts.

Once the loading was done, they lifted us up to the hole. I could not look down at the house or road. There was only the hot blue of the sky and the smell of fresh-ginned cotton seeping in through the quilts.

I heard the sound of trace chains when they brought the horses out and hooked them to the wagon. I heard my mother saying "Saw now" and knew they were tying the cow to the back axle. Then I could hear them climbing up. When my mother was on the springseat I could see her white bonnet and shoulders, and her arms moving as she pulled the reins to right or left.

To sell the cotton, she had to take the long way around by Detroit, to the cotton yard, where buyers cut into the bagging with sharp knives and tested the lint by pulling at it with their fingers. They were wasteful of other people's cotton. They pulled out bigger wads than they needed and then threw what was left over to the ground. Negro men with tow sacks went around the yard picking up the lint. It was theirs to pick and sell.

A price by the pound was bid, the price taken, and the bale was unloaded from the wagon. My mother had in her hand all the money she would have to start over again, and there was still the long trip to Pin Hook.

She bought cheese and crackers at a store and, with Monroe driving and more room for all of us without the cotton, we went out the Red Oak road. While we ate, she nussed the baby. Then she chewed crackers till they were soft and then with her finger put them in his mouth. We passed the Red Oak graveyard, where Missouri Ann was buried, and took a road that branched off to Pin Hook.

Sitting together in the wagon, listening to the sound of steel tires cutting into the sand of the road, we talked of what it would be like to live in Pin Hook again. My mother said as much as she ever said about why she left Deport. She wanted to be in our own house, on our own land, where no one could drive us out and we could keep what we made for ourselves. She wanted to be close to church. Not once had she gone to church at Deport, and she missed playing the organ and singing. She wanted to get back to Sunday School and school for us. She wanted her children to have a chance to go to school.

I was under age, but at Pin Hook they would let me go to school. She wanted me to start as early as I could and stay in as long as I could. It would not be easy, but easier than on the blackland.

The day was hot, the road deep with sand. Sweat turned the horses dark in patches around the collar and where trace chains rubbed their sides. The cow walked with her head lowered and her tongue hanging out. When we were past Red Oak, on a woods road wide enough for a wagon, we knew we had to stop and rest and miss getting to Pin Hook by sundown.

At a wide sand bed Monroe stopped and let the horses stand with slack reins, slack traces. He went down over the front wheel and started to the back of the wagon.

"Don't let the cow get down," my mother told him. "We'll have a time getting her up again."

Before he got to her she was down, lying in the sand with her legs stretched out, her mouth open, her eyes rolled back so that only the whites showed. She looked like a possum sulled, playing dead. Monroe pushed her with the toe of his shoe but she did not move.

"Sulled all right," he said.

He pulled at her and lashed her with a rope.

"Better let her lay," my mother said. "She'll get up again when she gets rested. We'll have to take our time."

While we were resting we heard the sound of an engine on the road from Red Oak. As it got closer it was louder than a cotton gin or a thrashing machine.

"It's an automobile," Monroe said. "Coming this way."

He climbed up the wagon wheel and took the reins. Tired as they were, the horses began rearing their heads and stomping in the sand, skittish enough to run away.

"Want some help?" my mother asked Monroe.

"I can hold them all right. They can't run with this load."

We were all leaning forward, watching and holding to the sides of the wagon, when a red automobile came out of the woods and pulled through the sand toward us. We stared at it and at the two men on the seat.

The road was not wide enough for them to pass. The driver slowed down and blew his horn. The horses jumped to the side of the road. Monroe let them go, but the cow was dead weight in the sand. The car stopped and they stood still.

"Cow dead?" one of the men asked.

Monroe looked back at her.

"Sulled."

The men laughed. My mother looked away from them, her face red under her bonnet.

"We tried to make her stand up," she said, "but she won't."

The men stopped laughing.

"You better pull her to one side so we can get by."

Afraid to drag her, afraid of breaking her neck, my mother took the lines and Monroe and Dewey went to make her get up. They tried kicking and beating her but she only rolled her head and bellowed.

"Try twisting her tail," one of the men said.

Monroe took a good grip on her tail and twisted till she got to her knees and then to her feet. With him twisting and Dewey beating they got her past the automobile. With a roar and a cloud of dust it went on and was soon out of sight. The cow, with her head lowered, kept on walking.

Afraid to let her stop, my mother went on driving, her bonnet pushed back, her lips tight.

"I reckon they thought we were a sight," she said.

She was glad it would be dark when we got to Pin Hook. Nobody would see how we looked, coming back. I did not care how we looked. I had seen an automobile. I could tell people in Pin Hook I had seen an automobile.

16

With no house to move to, no more crop to gather, nothing for the winter but the money from one bale of cotton, my mother left us at Aunt Vick's and went from place to place looking for work. She had left the blackland when cotton picking was at its best, and would not go back. Better to own a little piece of sandy land than rent a hundred acres of blackland. Better to hold us together till we could get back into our own house. She would have taken us to the field at Pin Hook, but the crop was light and people wanted to save money picking their own.

Then she heard from Samantha Green that it was a good cotton year in the Red River bottoms and that anybody could get all the picking he wanted. Manth, as everybody called her, and my mother went horseback down to the Rucker farm at Slate Shoals, between Big Pine Creek and the River. They found plenty of picking, but no place to stay. The best the farmer could do for them was set up a pair of tents, side-by-side at the edge of the cotton fields. They told him to set them up and came back to get their families.

Manth had only her mother, who was old and blind, and a daughter, Lily, who was about my age. She had once had a husband, but he had left her at crop planting time, with no money and no way to make a living. She had moved to a log house on my mother's farm for the winter, but she had to make money or starve.

My grandmother could have stayed with Aunt Vick, or with Uncle Charlie and Aunt Niece Kitchens. Aunt Niece was my mother's sister and they lived at Novice. She wanted to go with us.

She was afraid for my mother to go off by herself, and she could help with the children and cooking while my mother picked cotton. They sent word to Aunt Niece to tell her where we were going and loaded the wagon.

They had to leave the organ and the heavy bedsteads at Aunt Vick's. They would need the bedclothes and cooking things on the River. My grandmother could not help seeing that we had so much less than we had before we went to Deport.

"Three moves equals a fire," she said, with an edge in her voice.

Then we were in the wagons, ours in front, Manth's following, and on the road north from Pin Hook. My mother and grand-mother sat on the springseat, my mother driving, my grandmother holding her black parasol. We crossed Little Pine Creek. At Big Pine Creek we left the sandy land and drove on the hard-packed red waxy of the bottomland. Then we were on the Rucker farm, not near the big house and barns but in the field, with the shacks of the Negro day hands between us and the big house.

The tents, white canvas stained along the bottoms by red mud, had been hung from the center poles, but the pegs had to be reset, the guy ropes tightened. Every minute lost now was time lost from picking. Working like men, the women drove pegs and tied ropes. The older boys went for wood and water. Beds would take up the space inside the tents. Cooking had to be done outside, over an open fire, out under the trees.

Our tent had two beds: one for my mother, grandmother, Roy, and me; the other for Monroe, Dewey, and Cleaver. The other tent also had two beds, but they set up only one at first. Easier to sleep three in a bed, Manth said.

Lily and I, too little to work, ran up and down the road and far enough out in the fields to see the pickers, mostly Negroes, moving slowly up and down the rows. We ate from our hands, under the trees, and played on the dirt floor of the tents.

The next morning we were in the field before sunup, wakened by Negroes on the road, out early, to be ready to start picking at daylight. My grandmother, who had said the night before that we all had to go to the field, walked ahead of us, tall and straight in a gray work dress, her face hid by a slat bonnet.

"Make haste," she called to us. It sounded like *mekeest*. "What we don't get, the niggers will."

The Negroes, men and women, down to children big enough to walk, were ahead of us, down the rows a ways working without a sound, picking the stalks clean. We took rows next to theirs and went to work. I had my floursack, but I also had to watch the baby, who was left on a pallet at the end of the row. I could pick the stalks around the pallet.

The weather was good, the picking better than anything we had ever seen, even on the blackland. Cotton bolls hung open and white among the thick green leaves, and the lint weighed heavy. By the first weighing, when the sacks were dragged to scales hung from a wagon tongue, we knew we could count on more than five hundred pounds a day, at fifty cents a hundred.

We were making money, and saving most of what we made. The tent was furnished free. So was the water from the well. We could pick up sticks for the fire in the strip of brushy woods along a creek. Day after day our food was bread and beans, flour gravy and black molasses. Twice a day the fire had to be built up for cooking. In the middle of the day we ate on our sacks and drank from the water keg at the weighing wagon. Every night at the last weighing the man counted up what he owed us and paid in cash.

The weighing wagon did not come to the field on Sunday and there was no picking. There was work to do: washing clothes in a tin washtub, patching cotton sacks, getting up wood and water. That done, there might be rest for the next day's picking.

On a bright Sunday morning we saw a wagon come around a bend in the road and knew it was Uncle Charlie and Aunt Niece Kitchens. They were on the springseat, their children in the wagon bed behind them, sitting on a quilt, dangling their feet out over the road. Aunt Niece had on a small black hat, "fine enough to wear anywhere" my grandmother said; Uncle Charlie had on a wide gray stetson.

In the kissing and crying and laughing, we soon found out why they had come. Aunt Niece was worried about us, living off in a tent like that. They wanted to hunt pecans in the woods if we would go with them. More than anything, they wanted to see Red River. They had never seen that much water at one time. Neither had we, but from where we were picking we could see the river bluff and the tall cottonwoods on the Oklahoma side.

Picking pecans came first, in a stretch of tall trees between Big Pine Creek and the River. With buckets and sacks we went on all fours through the brush, pushing aside red-brown leaves so we could see the gray-brown nuts or green-brown hulls. It was like picking cotton, only more fun. Pecans dropped under leaves and sticks and slid out of sight. A dry pecan could be cracked open with the teeth and the goody picked out.

In the late afternoon, when the sun was beginning to turn red in a purplish sky, Uncle Charlie started toward the river, and we followed him. He was a tall man, wide in the shoulders and stout as a mule. He was a good swimmer. Monroe had watched him tread water, keeping himself under, with one finger out to show how steady he was.

We came to the edge of a bluff and I was looking up Red River—at red water and red sand, fiery red where the sun struck, purplish red where bluffs and trees left shadows. The riverbed curved unevenly, up and down, and the water made its own curves in the sand. Up the river we could see the bluish sandbars of Slate Shoals. Across, the land was Oklahoma. I was looking at Oklahoma, and wishing we could cross over.

Uncle Charlie started down the bank.

"You going down to the water?" Aunt Niece asked.

"I want to get me a taste. I never tasted river water before."

He went down slowly, testing each step ahead of him for quicksand, and stopped on a sandbar where the River cut in. We watched him dip with his hat brim, drink, and wipe his moustache with the back of his hand. We went closer to him, but not all the way to the water. We stopped at the dry end of the sandbar and waited for him to bring water on the brim of his hat. It tasted of wool and sand and muddy bottoms, but it was Red River water, and we had crossed over from before to after drinking it.

After the wagon had gone, the older boys went back down to the sandbar to wash themselves. When it was sundown we started back to the tent, on a shortcut across a big hay meadow. Rough stubble cut my feet. Sandburrs stuck and stung like bees. I sat down and cried till Monroe took me on his shoulders and carried me.

I had seen Red River, and the taste of it was in my mouth.

17

While there was still cotton in the fields the rains became heavy, falling from gray skies that did not change from morning till night. All day and all night the water came down, keeping us inside the tent, with cold bread and meat to eat when we could not keep a fire going long enough to cook.

I could start a leak by holding my finger against the tent top till the water dripped through. This was fun for me, but my mother stopped me and they moved the bed I was standing on to a dry spot. Then the canvas was soaked through and water dripped down in so many places that there was not a dry spot the size of a bed. Water stood on the ground outside and ran in enough to wet the dirt floor. Sticky red mud balled on our shoes inside the tent.

My mother worried about the baby. He had been moved from one part of a bed to another till he was fretting and crying. He had to be kept dry or get pneumonia. When there was nothing else to do, my mother got out my grandmother's black parasol and started to open it. My grandmother stopped her.

"It's bad luck."

Anybody in Pin Hook knew it was bad luck to open a parasol in the house. So did my mother, but she came to the bed where I was sitting under a quilt with the baby. It was night and a lantern was burning on the tent pole.

"A tent's not a house," she said. "It won't be like opening it up in the house."

She opened the parasol and held it over us. Water dripped on it from the tent and ran off the sides. With other things to do, she gave me the handle to hold.

"I'll bound it brings bad luck," my grandmother said.

"It might," my mother said, "but I don't know what else to do."

"Me neither. It just shows that pore folks has pore ways."

She had seen hard times often enough before, and she talked about them. She had camped out in the Red River bottoms before when she was a girl, when they were moving from Arkansas to Texas. They had no tent and had to sleep under the sky.

All night long my mother and grandmother took turns holding the parasol over us. By daylight they knew that cotton picking was over for them that fall. It was time to go back to Pin Hook and find some kind of place to live till we would move back to our house.

The rain had stopped but the sky was dead gray and there was a chill in the air. My mother had her final settling up for the picking and pinned the money inside her waist. Monroe brought the wagon and they loaded wet beds and quilts without waiting for them to dry.

While it was still morning we were ready to go. As we drove out to the road, Mrs. Green, Manth, and Lily stood outside the flap of their tent. Mrs. Green was crying in her old blind eyes. Manth and Lily looked pale and sick. They had no place to go, no place to live but a leaky tent in a muddy field. They would not have that when the last of the cotton had been picked.

Late in the day we drove back through Pin Hook, with no one to see us pass but Old Man Latimer, standing in the door of his store. No time to stop and buy from him. We had to get to Aunt Vick's and get unloaded before dark.

When we went down the lane we saw her wagon at the front gate, with the hoops up and a new wagon sheet tied over them. We knew what that meant. Aunt Vick had made up her mind to pack up and follow Maggie to Dallas. My grandmother began to cry. Aunt Vick was the last of her brothers and sisters to leave Pin Hook.

In by the fireplace there was kissing and crying, and talking about what all of us would do. Aunt Vick said something to my mother that made her sit down in front of the fire and cry as if she had given up. We soon knew what the trouble was. The man renting our house had not moved out. He would not get out till he got good and ready.

"He said you could try and put him out," Aunt Vick said, "but it won't get you nowheres."

So we were back in Pin Hook, owning a house but with no place to live. Aunt Vick had rented her place and the people were waiting to move in. When she left, we would have no place to go.

Three widow women sat by the fire talking of how men take advantage of women who have no way to help themselves. They also talked about the man causing the trouble. They had seen him get a dose of religion and dance all over the brush arbor, but it had worn off. My mother had not managed well, and he was not willing to move out to help her.

My mother heard of a house on the Blossom road across Little Pine Creek that would be empty till after Christmas. It was a log house, with square-hewed logs laid one on top of the other, and with post-oak clay chinking and daubing in between. It was small but dry, and the fireplace threw enough heat to warm it through. By night we were in it, and our clothes and quilts were hung up to dry.

With a place to stay, with her children around her, my mother began to take heart. We were back in Pin Hook, where there was both school and Sunday School. We had been out of both too long. We had the organ, and it was like old times to have the Bible and prayers and songs at night.

My mother went to Blossom and bought new shoes and Sunday School clothes out of the cotton picking money. For me there was a blue suit with knee pants, black shoes with long black stockings, and a blue felt hat with a red feather. The hat was not loose and easy like my old straw hat. The tight leather sweatband made a red mark across my forehead. It was the finest hat I had ever owned, and I was so proud of it I wanted to take it to bed with me.

Sunday morning we were up early. My grandmother would stay with the baby. My mother would walk with the rest of us the two miles to the schoolhouse for Sunday School. I had to be told several times how to behave myself while my mother was playing the organ and when we went to classes. Whatever happened, I was to keep quiet, and do whatever I was told.

Once we were on the road, my mother walked so fast that I had to trot to keep up.

When we were in sight of the schoolhouse I thought of my hat.

"What do I do with my hat?" I asked.

My brothers wanted to tease me, and my mother was too far ahead to hear them.

"Give it a sail," they said. "When you get to the door, take it off and give it a sail."

There were wagons in the school yard. People had gathered outside the door in the sunshine. I could see my mother going ahead, bowing and nodding to neighbors.

When I came to the door, I looked at the people and then at the school yard covered with brown oak leaves. Doing what I had been told to do, I took off my hat and gave it a sail. It curved up and out and fell on the leaves, the feather bright red against the blue and brown. My brothers began giggling, and men and women laughed till tears were in their eyes. My mother heard me bawling and came back for me.

Monroe went for my hat. My mother took my hand and jerked me along the aisle to a bench at the front.

Knowing that people were laughing at me, I had to sit there through the singing and praying and long talks. Then I got a Sunday School card with a colored picture and a verse to memorize.

After a long time it was over and we began the long walk home. My brothers teased and I fought. I got nothing else out of Sunday School that day.

The next morning I was on my way to Pin Hook school, with my tin dinner bucket in one hand, a United States history in the other. The school was not graded, and books were scarce. Pupils were expected to buy books or bring the books they had at home. Monroe had the arithmetic that my father had studied. The others had books bought when we were at Deport. There was nothing left for me but the United States history. I could not read it, but I could pick out the big and little letters, and look at the pictures.

I was just under six, and short for my age. I had to go at a trot
to keep up, down the steep hill to the creek, across the creek, and
through a shortcut on a path through fields and woods.

The school was a one-room wood building without a well or
outhouses. Water had to be carried in a big bucket from Aunt
Vick's. The girls had to take one side of the woods behind the
schoolhouse, the boys the other. The teacher was Miss Mollie
Hefner, who had got her certificate for teaching by studying on her
own and taking examinations at the county courthouse.

When we came on the school ground, Miss Mollie was standing
in the door with her school bell in her hand. She was my mother's
age, but a little taller, a little heavier. Her hair was sandy red and
her pink skin was covered with red-brown freckles. She laughed in a
good-hearted way when she spoke to us. Then she swung the bell
down with a quick jerk of her wrist.

It was second bell, bell for books, for lining up and marching in, the smallest in front and stairsteps to the tallest boys in the
back. She took me by the shoulders and placed me at the bottom of
the steps. There were about twenty-five of us. The older girls were
big enough for long skirts; the older boys had on overalls and work
shirts and brogan shoes.

Miss Mollie tapped the bell for attention.

"March in."

She stood aside and we marched past her and down an aisle
between rows of old-fashioned benches. The pews for Sunday
School were now the benches for school. The boys went to one
side, the girls to the other, with the two front benches saved for the
little ones. Miss Mollie took me by the hand and led me to a front
bench. Between me and the wall blackboard there were only two
things: her desk and the recitation bench where the pupils sat while
she heard their lessons. She kept us standing for saying the Twenty-
third Psalm and the Lord's Prayer. I knew both by heart, but my
grandmother called it "psa'm."

In her school there was no time for quiet periods. While some
of the boys and girls read aloud to her, the others got ready for
recitation by reading over and over in lip-moving whispers. As no
two children had the same readers, she had to take them one by one.
Briefly they stood before her, on one foot and then the other, the
girls mumbling, the boys hawking out words like phlegm from the
throat. I had nothing to do but listen, always to parts of stories,
never to a whole story. Days and days could pass between the beginning and the ending.

I soon knew the sounds of the schoolroom, and the smells: chalk dust on the blackboard, the rags kept wet to wipe off slates, shavings from cedar pencils sharpened with pocket knives, biscuits and side meat sweating in tin buckets with holes punched in the lids.

Before I knew enough to raise my hand for a drink, the water bucket was empty, and would not be filled again till morning recess, when two of the older boys would go down the road to Aunt Vick's well. When they brought it back, dripping down the sides, the older ones passed the tin dipper from one to the other, above my head. When the bell rang for books, the bucket was dry, and I had not been able to get a drink.

Arithmetic for the older boys and girls came after recess. One after another they stood in front of Miss Mollie and said multiplication tables, all the way from one times one to twelve times twelve, sometimes with long gaps in between, while with their hands behind their backs they counted on their fingers.

My time came late in the morning, after two boys had been sent to the well for water.

"Can you count?" Miss Mollie asked.

My mouth dry from thirst and chalk dust, I nodded.

"How far can you count?"

"A hundred."

"Without making a mistake?"

Again I nodded.

She smiled and told me to face the schoolroom so they could all hear me. At home it was easy, but not with the older boys and girls looking at me ready to laugh. My throat was dry, my face hot.

Miss Mollie formed the word "one" with her lips and I started counting and giggling, unable to stop either. Miss Mollie smiled. The others began to laugh out loud. They were laughing at me, but I could not stop. My giggling turned to laughing, and I could feel tears in my eyes.

The distance from one to a hundred had never been so long. I knew I had to go all the way, and they did not stop me, even when I swallowed words wet down my throat.

I said "one hundred" and went back to my bench. The others were still laughing. Miss Mollie smiled at me and rang the bell for dinner time.

She kept me in to ask how I had learned to count so young. Some of her scholars took a year to learn as much. When she let me go, the water bucket was empty, and I had to eat cold biscuits dry, sitting alone by the brush arbor, watching the older boys in a game of two-eyed cat.

That was my one recitation that day. The rest of the time I sat on my bench listening to the others, or looking at words and pictures in the history book.

At home that night the talk was of school and the need to get an education. Miss Mollie had started out with no more schooling than my mother had and was now a teacher. John and George Haley, who had been in school with my mother, had left Pin Hook and worked their way through school. What they had done we could do if we would work hard enough.

The next day at school I stood before the whole room and said the ABC's through without stopping or giggling. The others watched and listened, but did not laugh. They did crowd me away from the water bucket, and it was empty every time I got the dipper in my hand.

The third day there was nothing for me to recite. I had done more than was expected of me. Miss Mollie thought I would have to get a different kind of book. She could not set lessons for me in a United States history.

Recess came and dinner time, and I did not get a drink of water. Monroe had been told to help me, but he was playing two-eyed cat and forgot. When books took up after dinner, I did not listen to the others reading their lessons. I sat with my back to Miss Mollie, looking through the open door at the road, wishing school was out, and over.

I heard a wagon coming up the road from Pin Hook. Then I saw it was Aunt Vick's wagon, with the wagon sheet up, with Aunt Vick and Wade on the springseat under the canvas. I knew what it meant. They were on their way to Dallas, and I would never see them again; they were gone, and I had not said good-bye. I set up such a crying that lessons had to stop. Miss Mollie sat on the bench beside me and tried to quiet me, but I kept on, even when the wagon was out of sight.

When the bell rang to let us out of school, I knew I was never going back. It was not what I had expected, or wanted. Three days of going without water and no regular lessons, and too little to keep up with anything. I would be better off at home.

On the way home I told my brothers, and they did not seem to mind. They would not have to watch out for me. When I found a good Barlow knife in the road, they let me keep it. It was the most I got out of my first time at school.

Before we got to the house we saw Aunt Vick's wagon in front of the gate and her horses in the lot. They were going to stay all night with us and get an early start in the morning. We came up behind the wagon and saw that they were taking everything they owned with them. They had tied cane-bottomed chairs on behind, and hung the water bucket from the coupling pole.

That night, bedded down on a pallet by the fireplace, I knew why Aunt Vick had stayed another night. She was still begging my mother to give me to her. She talked of how lonesome she would be away from home and relations. She talked of what it would mean for me to be raised in Dallas, but they were not going to live in Dallas. Maggie had found a place for them in Vickery, close enough for her to ride the interurban to work and far enough out for Wade to keep his wagon and team and for Aunt Vick to raise chickens. With no education, no trade, Wade would have to earn his living driving his team. With all helping, it might be a slim living, but there would be enough for me and I could go to school and get to be somebody.

They did not know that I was awake, hearing them talk about me. I wanted to go, but I also wanted to stay. I had heard enough about Dallas to know that it was a fine place to live. People might be better off to go there than to Oklahoma.

My mother was no more ready than she had been to give me away. She had left Deport to keep us together. Things were not working out well, but she still wanted to hold on. Late in the night she talked to Aunt Vick of what she had in mind. She had heard that Blossom had a good school. She was looking for a place close to Blossom, close enough for us to walk to school and work in the field when we got home. I went to sleep knowing that I was not going with Aunt Vick.

When daylight came, the horses were hitched to the wagon and Aunt Vick and Wade hugged and kissed everybody and climbed up on the springseat. I could not bear to see them go. While the others were crying together outside, I went behind the door and hid myself in the coats and dresses.

The wagon was going. I could hear the wheels rocking in the ruts. I could hear Aunt Vick saying what she said before she went out of the house: "You'll come to Dallas some day. I'll send for you and you'll come." When the wagon was out of sight the others came in and warmed themselves by the fire.

Schooltime came, and my brothers went without me. No one tried to make me go.

"No need'n starting him too soon," my grandmother said. "He'll pick it up in no time when he gets ready."

When the others had gone to school, I lay on the floor in front of the fire with the United States history, looking at the pictures and spelling out words to my mother.

There was a sadness in her face, and in my grandmother's, like the sadness I had seen when the wagons left for Purcell, only with more worry. They were now the last of Missouri Ann's family at Pin Hook, and they would go when they found a place.

In the bleak days of January we moved again, this time to a twenty-five-acre farm a mile and a half northeast of Blossom. The land was deep sand, not very good for corn and cotton, but good for fruit and vegetables and sweet potatoes—crops that could be planted when school was out and gathered before it took up again.

The house had one big room with a fireplace, a shed room for the kitchen, and a front porch. On the back side of the field, away from the road, it faced into woods of red oak and huckleberry—a good windbreak against the blue northers that swept down in February and March but a dark gray wall for anyone who tried to look out the front door. My grandmother, staring into the woods, said it was a lonesome place that would take a long time to get used to. It was made lonesomer at night by the faraway whistle of a freight train.

My mother had agreed to pay six hundred dollars for the house and land. As she was afraid to part with the homeplace at Pin Hook, she paid a hundred dollars down and signed a mortgage for the rest. That mortgage was at once a worry: payments would have to be met or we would lose the place and all we had put into it. We worked and saved; we made do or went without. My grandmother stopped our grumbling by telling stories of farms and homes that had been taken to satisfy mortgages. It did not matter that we were a family of widows and orphans, she said. Banks had no hearts for widows and orphans. Lying on my pallet at night, I listened to their talk and wondered where we would go if we lost the place.

"We can always go back to Pin Hook," my mother said.

Not all was worry. The move had been made to get us close to a good school, and Blossom had a good brick school with two stories. My older brothers started the first Monday after we were in the new place, the three of them taking shortcuts across the field, with dinner buckets in their hands and money for books and tablets and pencils in their pockets.

I was left behind, too young to go to school that year, or the next, for the law said that a pupil had to be seven by September 1 of the year he started. I could go only by paying extra, and anything extra had to be saved for the mortgage.

So I stayed at home and read and studied in front of the fireplace. My mother taught me what she could, while she carded cotton or quilted. On bad days she was in the house all day and could help me with words and the meaning of anything I was reading. Other days, I read by myself and sounded out words the way they looked: *col-o-nel* for *colonel, mizzled* for *misled,* and *Anty-tam* for *Antietam.* When words were too hard, I skipped over them.

I was learning. My grandmother, listening to me read words she could not tell one from the other, watching me print capitals of letters she had never learned to make, told me that I was going to be good in books. I was going to be a good scholar in school.

"I wisht I'd a had the chance you'll have," she said.

She meant it. For the first time in her life she was living away from friends and relatives. Before, when she had anything to say, she could put her sidesaddle on a pony and ride over, or cut across fields and pastures on foot. Not one of her brothers and sisters could write, and Dallas and Purcell were too far off for visiting. Letters between them had to be set down by somebody else and read out loud by somebody else. Letters were few and far between, and she worried about not hearing.

At night I learned as I listened to my brothers at their lessons. The school at Blossom was graded and they were in different rooms with different teachers and different sets of books. At night they all had to read and spell out loud. They talked of teachers and recess and, something new to me, chapel.

One night Monroe told us that he was going to sing a song by himself in chapel—not a song out of a book but one of the songs the teacher had heard him singing. It was "The Brown Duck," one of my father's songs, and he was going to stand by himself on the stage and sing it to the whole school. My mother was proud of him, and glad that at Blossom he had the chance.

He had to practice. Every night he stood in front of the fireplace, tall and straight, and began: "The fox jumped up one moonlight night And called to the moon to give him light." We listened, and laughed at "Old Mother Flip Flop jumped out of bed."

The weather turned warm enough to work in the field, but they stayed in school. My mother went to work, cutting and burning sassafras sprouts, getting ready for the first plowing. I followed around after her, feeling the soft sand on my bare feet, smelling sassafras sap cut and burning.

Several weeks before school let out for the summer Monroe gave up books and went to the field to help with plowing and planting. I was in the field with him all day long every day, sometimes walking in the furrow behind him, watching for things the plow turned up—field mice dens lined with cotton lint and straw, once a long black snake not yet awake from his winter sleep. He hit it once with a stick, and let me beat the head to a pulp in the sand. After I knew it was dead, I watched for the tail to wiggle, for snakes never really die till sundown. This snake had not been awake enough to wiggle. I turned him on his belly to keep it from raining and left him in the furrow.

There were jobs for me to do, like setting out sweet potatoes. While it was still winter my mother had dug up a patch of ground and laid seed potatoes in it close together, side by side. Then she heaped it over with earth, making it into a bed. With warm days the sprouts showed through. Monroe pulled up the sprouts and dropped them by hand in the furrows he had made. My job was to cover the root end with sand and wet it down with water from the well. The sand chapped my hands and knees, and my back ached from stooping and carrying. At night the plants lay wet and limp; in the morning they were crisp and growing.

Eyes had to be cut from seed Irish potatoes—another job I could do. I sat on the back doorstep with a tow sack of reddish-pink potatoes at my side and two buckets in front of me. With a pocket knife I cut off the eyes, cutting only as deep as I had to, leaving the center of the potato for eating. Irish potato planting time was a good time. All winter we had been doing without potatoes. Now there was enough of the leavings for fried potatoes and potato soup. Before I was half through with the cutting, I could smell potatoes cooking in the kitchen, some of them flavored with wild onions pulled from a place on the branch.

There was more work than all of us could do, and we went from daylight till dark six days a week. On the seventh we rested, but we did not go to church or Sunday School. There were no country churches nearer than Red Oak or Post Oak, and my mother thought we would be looked down on if we went to church in Blossom. What we had, or clean shirts and duckings, were good enough for the country, but they would be laughed at in town.

"Better stay home than be made fun of," she said.

I would not have minded. I had been to town once, and wanted to go back. It was late in the day and my mother had to get something at the Womack store. Afraid to come home by herself in the dark, she took me along, trailing behind her, trying to keep up with her quick, short steps. We passed town houses and came close enough to the cotton oil mill to get the frying smell of cooking oil. We crossed the railroad tracks and came to a wooden store big enough to hold clothes and groceries, farming tools and coffins.

Left to wait on the store porch, I stared across the railroad track, past the wooden station, at another line of buildings—more stores, a brick bank building, a newspaper office with THE BLOSSOM BEE printed on the window. I heard a train whistling, coming from the east, the short whistle of a passenger train, not the long wailing of a freight, and knew that at last I would see a train.

It came in a rush of white steam and boiling black smoke, and stopped at the station, close enough for me to see the engineer and fireman, the wide open door of the baggage car, and passengers leaning out of windows to get a look at the town. A black cloud of smoke rolled across the road and I felt it in my eyes and tasted it deep in my breath. My brothers had tried to tell me about the smell of coal smoke. Now I knew, and liked it. It was a part of town.

With another rush of steam the wheels started a slow turning and the train moved on. It was soon gone, but I remembered the sound, the sight, the smell.

My mother came out of the store and we crossed the tracks in the greenish light of first dark. As we went we watched lights go on in stores and houses—not the orange-red light of coal oil lamps but the white light of clear electric bulbs. My mother walked straight ahead, across the tracks and dirt road, and turned to the right on the concrete walk in front of the stores. I lagged behind, looking in at doors and windows, at the lights, at people with faces sickly pale under the lights.

We came to the end of the row of stores and turned north, walking on a dirt path that was separated from front yards by white paling fences. Lights were on in the houses and I could see women setting tables in big rooms used only for eating. Everything they used looked good enough for Sunday.

On the dark country road my mother stopped to catch her breath.

"How'd you like town?" she asked.

"More'n anything I ever seen. I wisht I could go back."

"You will, all you want to, when you start to school."

I did not believe her. I did not believe my brothers who said: "I wouldn't live in town for anything. You couldn't pay me enough to live in town."

My mother went ahead and I tried to keep up but my mind was not on the road or walking. I was thinking about town. We came to our field and started across it. Ahead of us, against the darker shadow of the woods, we could see a light burning in our house. From there, town might have been a hundred miles away.

In early summer, when field work was caught up, Monroe and Dewey made extra money cutting firewood in the heavy timber to the north of us. Monroe was fourteen, Dewey twelve, and both of

them light for the work of sawing down big oaks. My mother sent
me with them. I could carry water, or run for help if they needed it.
In the morning we would have a breakfast of biscuits or corn bread
and flour gravy made of cooking oil and gravy. Sometimes we had
middling meat, sometimes not. When the sky was beginning to
show through the treetops we walked through the woods. They
carried the crosscut saw and axe, a glass jug of water and a tin
dinner bucket. I trotted to keep them in sight through huckleberry
thickets and over dim wagon roads made by woodcutters before
us.

I knew the woods closer to the house. My morning job in the
early spring was to follow the old turkey hen and find her nest.
From daylight, when she came down from her roost in an oak tree
near the house, I had to keep her in sight. I tried hard, but morning
after morning she gave me the slip. She would sidle along through
the brush, keeping watch out for me and for bugs and worms, at
times staying a long time in one place, at times darting ahead faster
than I could run. The color of sticks and leaves, she would hide and
I could not find her. Afraid to go back to the house too early, I
played along the branch and hunted sheep sorrel in sunny patches.

One day I did find her, sitting on her nest in a brush pile, not
from following her but from fooling around till I could go to the
house and not be in trouble. The nest found, I still had to watch
her till the eggs hatched. Baby turkeys had to be brought to the
house for raising. They would die if they got wet with dew.

While Monroe and Dewey cut wood, I went farther and farther
away, bound to them only by the sounds of saw and axe and falling
timber. Only when they cut stovewood could I help them. Then
they set up stakes measuring the height and length of a rick, and I
stacked in sticks as they split them. At times they called me for
dinner, and we rested in the shade.

With so much time in the woods, I learned the shape of leaf
and tree, the color of bud and flower, the smell of old leaves, and of
green leaves cut down and drying in the summer heat.

All week my brothers worked like men. Sundays they were part
man, part boy. When the sun was high overhead we went to the
woods again, not to cut wood but to blaze trees for felling—red oaks
and post oaks, tall and straight, the limbs high up, the trunks, clear
of knots and warts, good for splitting.

At times in a patch of second growth, where the trees stood
small and close together, Monroe would shinny up a sapling, starting a game of follow the leader. Running on the ground under him,

I watched him climb to the top of a slender sapling and bend it over to the next one. Climbing, swinging, climbing again, he could travel across a thicket without touching ground. Dewey and Cleaver could follow him. I tried, but the sapling I climbed was too big, my weight not enough to bend it. I had to come down again, with my arms and legs scratched and my hands shaking.

"You got to learn how to swing and drop," Monroe told me.

I tried, not in the woods where they could see me but on the walnut tree down by the well, after feeding time, when I thought they were all at the house. The first limb was high, twelve feet or more, and I was out of breath when I swung myself over it. Without waiting, I swung from it and started for the end, climbing hand over hand. The limb did not bend. When I had gone as far as I could go, I was higher than when I started, and too tired to go back. I had to drop. I yelled once for help, and let go, with no sense of how to hold my legs to get a spring in them.

I fell in a heap, with the breath knocked out of me, too hurt to cry. I heard the sound of running feet and then Monroe was picking me up.

"That's not the way to do it," he told me when he knew what I had done. "Walnut limbs'll break before they bend. You'll get yourself all stove up falling stiff-legged."

I stood up, and then sat down again, too shaken in my bones and joints to hold myself up. Monroe washed my face at the horse trough and waited till I felt better to take me to the house.

On another day Monroe showed me how to draw water from the horse trough. With his pocket knife he cut a forked jimsonweed stalk from a bunch growing by the lot fence. He sat on the ground beside me and cut the prongs of the fork, making one longer than the other. The stalks were hollow, with holes as big as a pencil. He stopped the butt end up with mud and hung the short prong over the edge of the trough into the water. The long prong almost touched the ground. He sucked on the long prong with his mouth and a stream of water flowed out. He lifted the stalk to break the flow.

"Try it," he said.

I sucked on the stalk till I felt warm water in my mouth. Then I turned it down and watched the water run on the ground. It was fun, but the jimsonweed left a strong taste in my mouth and I did not try it again.

On a Sunday I went to the woods to watch Monroe make a steam engine with a whistle. He had found a five-gallon coal oil can on the road. He had tried to make the iron teakettle on the stove whistle. The oil can was bigger and better.

He took us to a place where a sandy-bottomed branch wound in and out among tall oak trees. While Dewey and Cleaver built a fire, he put water in the can and plugged the spout with a whistle whittled from a hickory limb. After long waiting, steam rose and boiled out, but there was no whistle—only the sound like a boiling teakettle.

Monroe whittled a whistle with a smaller opening and plugged the spout. This time there was a whistle, but it was watery when it should have been clear and sharp.

Again Monroe whittled and plugged. By now the fire had burned down to a bed of red hot coals. The can hissed and sizzled when he put it on. Steam began to build up. There was a rumbling, and the can lifted, first on one side and then on the other. We watched the whistle and waited. This time the sound had to be good.

"It's leaking."

Not steam but a fine spray of water was coming through the whistle, and the can was beginning to bounce.

"Get away," Monroe yelled.

We watched a side of the can cave in like bent paper. Then we ran and hid behind trees.

I was close enough to see the can, bouncing and turning, with all sides drawn in, and steam coming out in a fine thin whistle. Then the whistle was lost in a rumbling and the can rose up, straight into the branches high overhead, and burst with a crack and a spray of boiling water.

We were out of reach, but close enough to see what might have happened to us.

21

Christmas that year, not one to look forward to, was one we could always look back on.

On the day before Christmas Eve, my mother said at breakfast: "How'd you like to go to your Aunt Niece's for Christmas?"

We had not seen them since fall, and it was our time to visit them. She had not asked us for Christmas, but, in the way of Pin Hook, we knew she would have if she had thought of it, or had taken time to write. There was no way to let her know we were coming. Anyway, it would be fun to surprise her driving up in the wagon.

Christmas Eve morning we were up before daylight, shouting "Christmas Eve Gift" to each other, laughing, hurrying to get the wagon loaded and on the road. It was ten miles to Novice. The trip over muddy roads could take all day or more, and there might be no passing at all on the lane from the main road to Aunt Niece's house.

We hurried, but the sun was high before we were in the wagon, with my mother driving, my grandmother on the springseat beside her, and the rest of us in the back among the quilts and pillows, the jars of canned plums and peaches, the boxes with pies and cakes.

The road was rough, the horses slow enough for us to hop out and stretch ourselves with walking. The sun was already to the west when we passed the Walnut Ridge schoolhouse. It was no more than a hand high when we came to the lane where we would turn off. The mouth of the lane was at the top of a long hill that began at Nolan Creek. Another wagon was coming up the hill, close enough for us to see a man and woman on the springseat, and children behind them on kitchen chairs.

There were two houses close together on the lane, both made of boxing planks, both unpainted but weathered a soft gray. We passed the first, the old Kitchens home place, where Aunt Sis, Uncle Charlie's sister, a strange, silent woman, lived alone, shut up in the house most of the day, summer and winter. Uncle Charlie and Aunt Niece lived in the next—a house with one big room, a shed room for the kitchen, and an open front porch.

We stopped at the front gate and Monroe got out to open it. It was a wide, heavy gate made of oak timbers fourteen feet long and an inch thick. We had passed through the gate and closed it behind us when the front door opened and Aunt Niece came out to the yard gate to meet us.

"Christmas Eve Gift," she called, her soft voice raised as much as she ever raised it.

My grandmother, first out of the wagon, ran toward her.

"Well, give it here."

They were laughing and crying, hugging and kissing. By the time we were out of the wagon, Austin and Ruthie came around the house.

"I told you somebody was coming," Aunt Niece said to them. "That old rooster's been crowing all morning."

While they were getting hugged and kissed, the other wagon stopped at the gate. Aunt Niece saw them and started toward them.

"It's Sallie and her folks, come to spend Christmas."

Sallie Holmes was Uncle Charlie's sister, and she was there at the front gate with her husband and seven children. I saw the look on my mother's face and knew we might turn right around and go home again. There were five in the Kitchens family and their hired hand, Othal Johnson, seven of us, nine of the Holmeses.

"You don't have room," she said to Aunt Niece. "You cain't sleep this many."

Aunt Niece laughed.

"We'll make out. We'll just have to bunk a little closer together. I been wishing all day somebody'd come for Christmas."

The Holmeses stopped their wagon beside ours and the hugging and kissing began all over again, and somebody asked about Uncle Charlie.

"He went to Paris to get Christmas," Aunt Niece said. "Him and Othal. They took a bale o' cotton to sell."

We knew by the way she said it that we could expect a good Christmas.

"You young'uns go watch for him," my grandmother said. "You ought to see him coming up the hill afore long."

We did see him, before dark, a man in a broad-brimmed hat, another man with him, and wagon and mules against a winter sky. He was a tall man and strong, with broad shoulders and straight back. By the time they started up the hill we could tell which was Uncle Charlie, which Othal. When we opened the gate for them, he had pushed his hat to the back of his head, showing his heavy suit of dark brown hair, and was smiling under his wide moustache. At other times I had been afraid of him, but not now, not when he leaned out at us and said, "Christmas Eve Gift."

The wagon had to be unloaded, the boxes and sacks and buckets taken to the kitchen or smokehouse, the ones he would let us carry. The others got slid under beds, out of sight. Uncle Charlie opened a big package of firecrackers and lined the little packages up on the mantel piece. To us, Christmas was the time for firecrackers, and I had never seen so many outside of a store. He stacked boxes of roman candles beside the firecrackers. He handed Monroe a sack with a pound of loose black powder, and brought in six boxes of shotgun shells.

"I'm aiming to get me some squirrel hunting this Christmas," he said.

He had something else that I saw first in the kitchen—a gallon jug of whiskey which he had set on a shelf with the sugar bowl and some glasses. The men would pour whiskey in a glass, pile in the sugar, and add hot water from the teakettle on the stove.

"Christmas ain't Christmas without a hot toddy," they said to each other.

Aunt Niece, working at the kitchen stove, shook her head. She knew that Uncle Charlie and Othal had sampled the jug on the way home. She did not know how much more sampling they would do before she could set tables for so many.

Neither did my grandmother.

"You gonna make some music after supper?" she asked Uncle Charlie. "Seeing the fiddle box under the bed made me recollect. It's been a whet since I heard any fiddling."

"I might get out the fiddle after supper," Uncle Charlie said.

But he did not. After the first table the men and bigger boys built up a big fire in the pasture between the house and front gate. Then, while the women stood on the front porch to watch, Uncle

Charlie gave the little children firecrackers and showed how to shoot them. He put a paper fuse against a live coal. When it had lighted it he threw it away from the fire into the dark.

"Don't ever let one go off in your hand," he said. "And don't throw it close to nobody. Somebody might get hurt."

While we went through the firecrackers he had given us, the men made a trip back to the kitchen. This time they brought the jug with them and set it in the back end of a wagon. They brought out more fireworks, and Monroe had the sack of powder in his coat pocket.

"Time for a roman candle," Uncle Charlie said.

He took a long red roman candle and went to the fire.

"You all watch now," he said. "I'm gonna hold it like I was aiming to shoot the gate."

Outside the rim of firelight the night was of a soft, heavy blackness. He lighted the fuse and ran out of sight. We heard a fuzzy pop and a white ball of fire rose and, like a single star, floated through the night, followed by other pops and other stars—red, green, white, red, green, white, enough to take the breath of anyone who had never seen a roman candle. At first he lighted them one at a time, making them last as long as they would. Then he gave one to Othal.

"Let's me and you light up and make out like we're having a battle."

They did, away from the fire, in night so black we could not see them, but we could see the balls of fire, flying straight, stopping when they hit, and dropping to burn out on the ground. The match was even, and they came back to the fire laughing.

Othal stopped close to the blaze to see how to start raveling the string that held together a package of firecrackers. When he did, Uncle Charlie tied a full package to his coattail and set fire to a fuse. At the first pop, Othal whirled toward us. Then he saw what had happened and began running and threshing his hands behind him, but he could not stop the popping. Down through the pasture he went, out of sight, but we knew where he was going by the popping.

Uncle Charlie doubled over, laughing.

"He lit a shuck all right."

Uncle Charlie straightened up and started running, with firecrackers tied to his coattail and popping. Then all the men and bigger boys were running through the night, with firecrackers popping off their backs, in their pockets, in their hands. The smaller children took up the running, without firecrackers—just running, around and around the house, and through the house, but not in the pasture.

The firecrackers gone, they went back to roman candles, chasing each other, firing at such close range that the smell of powder mingled with the smell of burning cloth. Dewey got a hole in the front of his shirt. There was a smell of singed hair. They kept on running. Into the yard they went, and around the house. Children my size went under the house, behind the blocks of the foundation.

On the porch the women were having their say.

"Look out for the door."

"Look out for the bed."

"That'n hit the bed."

"They'll burn the house down shore."

With hands and feet they put out the balls of fire that came in the house and on the porch.

Then the roman candles were all gone and the men, out of breath, stopped running. It was quiet, and we came out as far as the yard gate.

Uncle Charlie was not ready for the fun to be over. He went up the steps and across the front porch. Aunt Niece was standing in the door, with the lamplight behind her. He lifted her chin with his finger and went on past her, to the chimney corner where he kept his double-barreled shotgun. Then he came out with the gun under his arm and a box of shells in his hand.

Near the fire, he loaded both barrels and set the stock against his shoulder.

"You aiming at the gate?" Othal asked.

"You got to aim at something."

He fired, and after the blast we heard shot rattle against the gate.

"Got it first shot," Othal said, and ran for his own gun.

In no time at all, five guns were blazing away at the gate, and the little children were running for hiding places under the house. I shivered at the sound, but felt safe, for their backs were to us and they were aiming at the gate.

Then Othal came running around the house, loading and firing as he ran, and some of the others took after him. The women had run inside, but I could hear them telling the men to stop. Too scared to stay under the house, I crawled out and started for the door. In the darkness I ran straight into Othal's knees, and he let a double-barreled blast go off right over my head, leaving a burning flash in my eyes and a ringing in my ears.

"You gonna kill somebody."

The women were saying it first, and then some of the men.

After another round the shooting stopped, the shells all gone.

I got inside to my mother and she held me in her arms till beds for the children had been made down on the floor. Then she put me down and pulled a quilt up over my head.

The next morning the children were up by daylight and out in the yard and pasture, picking up the firecrackers that did not shoot and empty shotgun shells still smelling of burnt powder. We went to look at the gate, and found it half hanging from the posts, with the timbers drilled and splintered by shot.

When we went to the house again the men were at the barn and Aunt Niece was in the kitchen, fixing herself up. She had combed her black hair up all around and piled it in a big knot on top of her head. Her lips and cheeks were pink from pinching. She was smoothing powder on her face with a puff made from real moleskin.

Uncle Charlie came in with a backstick for the fireplace. My grandmother was waiting for him.

"You ruint the gate," she said.

"I reckon we did."

He laughed, and the light in his blue eyes showed he was not sorry. She frowned and went out to the front porch.

Aunt Niece came in, with a peeled orange in her hand.

"Christmas Gift," he said to her.

She went up to him and stuck a slice of orange between his teeth. They were both laughing without making a sound, and once he leaned over and kissed her.

"I had me some Christmas," he said.

22

It was spring, and I was alone in the house, with nothing to do but go over books I knew by heart, or watch a wren building her nest in an opening above the front door. Breakfast had been before daylight, and by the time the sun was two hours high I was hungry. The pots and pans on the stove were empty. There was nothing left to eat in the safe. In the smokehouse I found a partly cut ham hanging from a rafter. I cut off a slice and ate it raw. The salt, set deep, was strong enough to sting my mouth and make me crave something green to go with the ham. There was a brown stone pickle jar at the back of the smokehouse. The summer before I had watched my mother filling the jar, with a layer of cucumbers, a layer of salt. With my sleeve rolled up, I fished around in the mushy brine. The pickles were all gone, and I wanted a pickle more than I had ever wanted anything.

Outside, at the edge of the woods, I saw pokeberry stalks pushing up through the leaves. The year before my mother had made good pickles from pokeberry. I looked at the sun. Plenty of time for me to make pickles before anybody came back. I punched up the fire in the cookstove and set the kettle on. Poke had to be parboiled to take out the poison. Then, with a bucket and knife, I went through the woods and along fencerows looking for poke.

In the woods I found a patch of May flowers, each with a bud or bloom hung at the fork of the stem. In May, the apples would be yellow and ripe and acid to the taste. Now there were only the white flowers, thick petaled, with a heavy bittersweet smell. I picked a flower and carried it in my hand, at times holding it to my nose till I had to take it away to breathe.

Down the fencerow and back, and I had nearly a bucketful of poke sallet stalks and leaves. The stalks had to be boiled and the skins peeled off. Then they had to be soaked in vinegar till they were pickled. I was hungry, and that took too much time. I held a stalk in boiling water and in no time at all I could strip the skin off with my fingers. I dipped it in a jar of vinegar and held it there long enough for the pale green to change to lemon yellow. Then I ate it. I could taste the stalk raw in the middle, but the vinegar outside was a stronger taste and I wanted more. I kept on, boiling, dipping, eating, till I had finished half the stalks in the bucket.

Then, with a sourish taste in my mouth, I lay down on the bed with the May apple flower on the pillow close to my face. I tried to read newspapers pasted on the wall, but my head began swimming and I knew I was sick—poisoned on pokeweed pickles. Scared, I called for help, but nobody came. The pain in my stomach stopped me from calling. When I thought I was bound to die, the writhing turned to retching. I leaned my head over the side of the bed and covered the floor with a mess of half-chewed pokeberry stalks. When that was over, I was too weak to sit up, and my eyes felt funny.

When my mother came in, she found me in bed, and knew that something was wrong. She grabbed me and shook me and I was glad she was there.

"What made you so sick?" she asked.

"I et the pokeweed."

"Raw?"

I said yes without lifting my head.

"I thought it smelt like raw pokeweed. It's a good thing you throwed it up. You'd a died if you hadn't a throwed it up. You couldn't a stood the poison."

She put cool wet cloths on my face and cleaned up the mess on the floor. Then she found the May apple flower and laid it on my pillow. I began retching again, and she had to take it away.

The next morning I was able to sit in the rocking chair and watch the wrens come and go. My mother was in and out of the house, and then in the kitchen cooking poke stalk pickles. The smell was enough to make me sick, and when they were done I could not eat a bite.

23

In the middle of summer, when the crops were laid by, we rested through the long hot afternoons, and again at night, between supper and bedtime, sitting on the front porch, looking into the dark woods, listening to the sound of katydids and of bullbats flying. On these nights there was little talk, and most of it was lonesome talk of other times, other places, of Camden, Pin Hook, Red Oak.

"I been laying off," my grandmother said one night. "I been laying off a long time to go see your Uncle Jack and Aunt Julie."

Uncle Jack Chennault was her husband's brother, Aunt Julie his wife. They lived at Red Oak, a good part of a day's walk away.

"I've been so lonesome to see them. It's been on my mind till I cain't hardly think of anything else."

She went the next morning, taking me with her, walking a road we had never traveled before. I had gone with her to Uncle Jack's another time, up from Pin Hook and back in a wagon—too long ago for me to remember the road or the looks of places and people. I remembered clearest sitting in the back end of the wagon on the way home, holding a ripe peach in my hand, wanting to give it to both my mother and Aunt Vick.

My grandmother, in gray chambray skirt, waist, and sunbonnet, kept to the middle of the road and did not look back. The sun was hot, and sweat made circles under her arms and dark spots on the back of her waistband. I felt the sweat on my face and the sand burning my feet. I ran from shady place to shady place, and in the time of waiting tried to think what it would be like when we got there. I knew about Uncle Jack. His family and Missouri Ann's had lived close to each other on the Ouachita. My grandmother had often talked about him and my grandfather when she talked about the move from Camden to Texas.

Though I could not remember her, I knew that Aunt Julie was different—my grandmother called her "quare." She was half Cherokee and, though she had lived with white people all her life and had been married to two white men, she would not give up the ways of her Indian mother.

"Julie ain't much for talking," my grandmother said when we had stopped to rest. "It's nothing aginst her, no more'n her Indian pigeon toes, or going around the place barefoot in the dead o' night."

"How come she does that?"

"The Indian in her, I reckon. With her it don't do to ask questions."

She started on the road again, and I saw that her feet pointed straight ahead.

At Red Oak, my grandmother turned off the road and into the graveyard. Talking to herself, she went among the wooden markers till she came to some graves with boards at the head and foot but with no names on them. She stood a long time staring at a mound of earth that had been packed down and rutted by rain. Sage grass browned by the heat almost hid the boards.

"That's Ma's grave all right," she said aloud. "Pore Ma, that she should have to be brought here."

She knelt and brushed the sand from the headmark. Then she cleared away the brush and weeds. She pulled the grass from another long grave, and then a short one. A space had been left between.

"That's A.'s grave," she said of the first, and then, "That's Charlie's. He died before he was as old as you are but I still get lonesome for him."

She pronounced the *are* as *air*, with a shortness of breath but a tenderness in her voice. It did not sound like her, and I saw that she was crying. She reached out and put an arm around me, for the first time that I could remember. For me, I knew, and also for the little boy she had lost a long time ago.

With the toe of her shoe she drew a line across the open space.

"I want to be buried right here," she said. "When I lay this old body down I want it put right here, with them."

The sun was low when we left the graveyard. It had set when we went through the last stretch of red oak woods into the open in sight of Uncle Jack's house. It was of unpainted boxing planks, two stories in front, one story in the L at the back. There was a red brick chimney at either end of the two-story part, and a flue on the roof of the L for the cookstove. Smoke was coming from one chimney and the flue.

"Lizer sees us," my grandmother said.

She came out the kitchen door, a tall, thin woman with a sweaty face and sweat spots on her dress. She and her husband and children had come home to live, and I had been told to call her "Cousin Lizer."

"Law me alive," she said to us. Then she called back through the kitchen door, "You all come on out. We got company."

Uncle Jack came first, his long hair and beard white in the orange-gray light. Then we saw Cousin Dud and the three children: Mary, Elmer, and Mattie Lou.

We all met at the side gate and I stayed back behind my grandmother, but I still had to go through the kissing. Uncle Jack's kiss was no more than a brushing of his white beard across my face. Lizer's was with lips on which drops of sweat had gathered. It was wet, and she smelled of things cooking on the stove. When I could, I wiped my face on my sleeve.

"You'uns don't look at the kitchen," she said. "We got caught making cider and soap at the same time."

We went inside the hot kitchen and saw the oilcloth-covered table set with white plates and bone-handled knives and forks and spoons.

"I'll just put on more plates," Lizer said. "We'uns was about ready to set down."

"Where's Julie?" my grandmother asked.

"Inside, with the hoecake."

We found Aunt Julie in the room in front of the kitchen, stooping over the fire on the hearth, turning a flat piece of corn bread on a flat cooking iron. She was a little, dried-up woman with dark skin and black hair pulled straight back from her wrinkled forehead. She stared at us with round black eyes.

"It's me—Alice," my grandmother said.

Aunt Julie looked us over again and straightened up.

"Come in, Alice," she said.

They came together, or my grandmother came against her, but it was not like the kissing of kinfolks. I could see that she had too much Indian blood to be like kinfolks, or talk like kinfolks.

When the hoecake was done, we all sat at the kitchen table,

with Uncle Jack and Aunt Julie side by side, the hoecake in front of them. It was for them and no one else. They helped themselves to beans and greens, but let the biscuits and corn bread pass by.

"You always eat hoecake?" I asked.

"Three times a day," Uncle Jack said. He smiled at me. "You want a taste?"

I tasted it, and it was as flat as meal and water.

"You chew it enough, it'll turn sweet," he said.

That night I slept with the other children upstairs, for the first time knowing that I slept in a two-story house, and that the ground was farther down than I could drop.

The next morning I was in the kitchen before daylight, watching Cousin Lizer making hoecake. It was cornmeal, salt, and water, and nothing else. This time she baked it hard and flat in the oven.

Aunt Julie never ate any other kind of bread. It went back to her Indian people, to the hard times when they were moving from place to place and could not get anything else to make bread. Aunt Julie was used to it, and Uncle Jack ate it to humor her.

Soap made the way Aunt Julie liked it took a long time, but it had to be made that way. She would not waste money on soap bought at the store, and soap made from bought lye left her skin raw and burning.

At the L of the house, where the kitchen joined on to the other part, they had an ash hopper big enough to hold the ashes from a year's fires in the cookstove and fireplaces. All the ashes went into the hopper, and a trough was set so that with every rain some water trickled down on the ashes and was caught in a wooden keg at the bottom. This was the lye water for making soap, and for husking hominy.

Cousin Lizer had a pot of soap in the second day of boiling, in an iron washpot with the three legs set on three bricks. It was our job to keep the fire going under the pot, hot enough to keep it boiling but not enough to make it boil over. It had started out as a layer of hog grease on lye water. In the second day the lye had worked, and there was one liquid, needing only to be boiled down to the thickness of soap.

In the middle of the day Aunt Julie came by and saw that the soap was made. She pulled away the fire to let it cool and covered it with boards. Our job done, we could play, told so by Cousin Lizer, not by Aunt Julie, whose stern eyes and tight mouth kept us from asking.

The game was a new one to me. It was a game of running,

counting with sticks or gravel, and chanting over and over the
rhyme:

Chickamy, chickamy, cranie, crow,
Went to the well to wash my toe,
When I got back
One of my old black chickens was dead.

With it, and with resting under the blue-green cedars at the
front, cedars planted by Aunt Julie after everybody told her they
would bring bad luck so close to the house, we passed the day. Then
the soap was cool enough to be dipped up in buckets and carried to
the barrel in the smokehouse. It was thicker and darker than sorghum molasses, and smelled of wet ashes.

When it was all in the barrel, Aunt Julie took the gourd
hanging on the side and dipped some into a pan of hot water. The
water turned milky white and she stirred some foam to the top.
Then she rubbed the tips of her fingers together in the water.

"Turned out good," she said, and set one gourdful by the
dishpan, another on the wash shelf on the back porch.

That night, when we went to wash our feet for bed, we sat on
the back steps and covered them over with soft soap, up above our
ankles. Aunt Julie was right. When it was washed off, it left the skin
feeling clean but not burning.

At first we were kept out of the garden, where Uncle Jack was
digging pits and Aunt Julie was setting up the cider press.

"You'uns dassen't get in the way," Cousin Lizer said. "You'uns
go to the orchard and help pick up the apples."

Cousin Dud climbed the trees and shook down the apples.
When he had come down again, we picked them up and put them
in thick tow sacks. Then he put the sacks, one at a time, on a
wooden slide and, pulling with ropes tied around his waist, took
them to the garden.

When we had all that could be pressed in a day, he sent us to
the kitchen to carry out the jars and bottles Cousin Lizer was washing.

In the garden, the press was set up, the storage pits dug. Aunt
Julie was washing apples in a washtub. Uncle Jack was chopping
them up with a butcher knife and piling them in the hopper. At
one side they had beeswax heating in an iron kettle over a low fire.
The whole garden was sweet with the smells of apples and boiling
honey.

When the hopper was full, Cousin Dud stood beside the press

and turned the screw slowly. Aunt Julie held a gourd dipper under the spout. When it was full, she tasted and nodded, without smiling. Then the gourd went around, from lip to lip. When it was empty, Aunt Julie patted me on the head and held the gourd under the spout.

"Drink it all up," she said.

I did, and it was sweeter than the apples in the orchard.

There was no time to waste. Apples and juice could not stay out in the sun long. Uncle Jack chopped, Cousin Dud turned the screw, Cousin Lizer held jugs and jars under the spout and filled them. Aunt Julie pushed in stoppers, screwed on lids, and sealed each one with hot beeswax. Then she buried them in the deep holes Uncle Jack had dug. She would put in a layer, cover it with tow sacks, and pile on a foot of dirt.

"How come you bury it?" I asked when she started a new layer.

Cousin Lizer answered.

"If light gets to it, it will turn to hard cider and vinegar. It's the Indian way. You'uns come back when it's Christmas, it'll be sweet and good as it is now."

Cider making kept us children busy for a while, but not for long. Mary and Elmer had something to tell me that had to be told in their hiding place under the house, where no one could hear.

We left the bright sunlight of the garden and crawled into the twilight of their hiding place. It was a shallow hole, hollowed out by dogs in the sandy earth. When we sat up in it, our heads were close to the sleepers, and dust from the floor above hung around us. I could see them, but not clearly.

"You hear about the calf?" Mary asked in a whisper.

"What calf?"

It sounded like a riddle she was asking me.

"The calf with a human head."

She and Elmer said it together. It was not a riddle. They leaned toward me and I could feel the heat from their faces.

"A cow had a calf over at Red Oak," Mary whispered. "They say its head favors the man that was its father."

I was scared by the thought, but I had to hear more.

"What'd it look like?"

Mary put her lips close to my ear.

"They say it's all over hair, but the eyes is blue and the mouth turns up like a human mouth."

They could not tell me any more. We sat close together and

whispered the things they had told me till the twilight changed to dark.

I knew they had not seen it, but I had to ask them.

"You seen it?"

"No."

"How come you know about it?"

"*She* told us."

By the way they said it, I knew they meant Aunt Julie.

"She told us, but she ain't told nobody else."

When it was dark outside, Cousin Lizer called us to supper and I sat where I could see Aunt Julie's face. The look that had been in her eyes at the cider press had gone. No need asking her anything.

The next day when we were on the road home and passing through Red Oak I had to say something. I walked beside my grandmother and looked up so I could see her face.

"You hear about the calf?" I asked.

"What calf?"

"The calf with a human head."

She turned on me with her mouth tight and her hand up.

"Shut your mouth or I'll slap your jaws."

She meant what she said. I said nothing else and, after a hard look at me, she started along the road.

When we were out of Red Oak, she spoke to me over her shoulder, or said it so I could hear her.

"I told Julie there's ways o' letting young'uns know things without scaring them to death."

She said nothing more about Aunt Julie's Indian ways.

24

In November, after I had passed my eighth birthday, after the last of the crops had been gathered, I went to school, wearing blue knee pants, long black stockings held up with white rag strings that had to be kept rolled out of sight, and rough, high-topped shoes. I carried my dinner in a tin molasses bucket, and a tablet and speller under my arm. In the gray light before sunup we set out across fields of dying cotton and dead cornstalks, with Dewey ahead, Cleaver behind him, and me still farther behind, so afraid of school that I kept going over things I had memorized.

My mother was certain the law was wrong that kept me out of school till I was eight years old, By rights, I should have been through the primer and first grade. The way to make up lost time, she decided, was to put me in the second grade with Cleaver, who had been in school three years, or parts of three years. She was sure the teacher would keep me once she heard me count and multiply and read.

"Tell her you're as good as in the second grade," she told me.

We came out of the field on a sandy road, where there were scattered houses and other boys, all older, wrestling and cutting up on the way to school. We caught up with them and walked with them, out of the country into the town, through the roads and shacks of nigger town, past the nigger church, the nigger school. The school was of unpainted wood, and children were playing in the yard, waiting for books to take up.

We went through a part of white town, past the stores, and across the tracks to a red brick school set in a big treeless yard. The bell had rung, and the children were lining up by classes. Cleaver

had been in the second grade the year before and knew where to go.
We came up at the end of the line and were marching in before
I had time to look around.

The teacher, Miss Monty Hutchens, was a young woman with
pale sandy hair and brownish eyes without the sign of a smile. The
line was long; she had more pupils than desks in her room. She
knew Cleaver from the year before, but she did not know me, we
looked so little like brothers. He had black hair, brown eyes, and
skin speckled as a guinea egg. My hair was light, my eyes blue, my
skin fair. She watched me follow him to the room and crowd in a
seat beside him.

"He's my brother," Cleaver said to her.

"You visiting today?" she asked me.

"No'm. I'm starting to school."

"Are you in the second grade?"

"Yes, ma'am."

"May I have your report card?"

"I don't have airn."

"You must have if you were promoted to the second grade."

Cleaver told her that I knew enough to be in the second grade.
I had studied at home and could read and write.

She shook her head, but she added my name to the class roll
and gave me a seat away from Cleaver, with two boys on one side of
the aisle from me, and twin girls on the other. Cleaver was to help
her with the younger pupils.

At last I was in school, in a room airy and light, breathing in
the smells of chalk dust and cedar pencils and ruled tablet paper.
There were copybooks on desks, words on the blackboard waiting to
be copied. It was not like Pin Hook. The boys and girls were all
close to the same age. They read from the same books, and recited
together. They were ahead of me, I saw when they recited, but I
wanted to stay with them.

A bell rang and the teacher went to stand by the door.

"Line up for chapel," she said.

We lined up and marched to the seats for the second grade at
the front of the auditorium. I had heard so much about chapel that
I felt at home. I wished Monroe had come, but he was at home,
getting the land ready for winter plowing.

The principal, a man in a dark blue suit, came and stood in
the center of the stage. A teacher came in behind him and seated
herself on a stool at the piano. I had never seen a piano before, or
heard one. My eyes were on it and on her while the principal led us

in the Lord's Prayer. I said the words, but I was thinking of the piano.

"Now we will all join in singing 'Day Is Dying in the West.'"

Her hands had been resting on the notes. Now they moved up and down like lightning, and my ears were full of sound—bright, happy, singing sound. I was half out of my seat at the shock of it. It stopped, and everybody looked at the principal.

"The chord, please," he said.

His voice was far away and rough, but she brought her hands down in a loud, deep chord.

"Now, all together."

I had never heard the song before, and there were not enough books to go around. I did not care. I could hear the words they sang, but I wanted most to hear the piano.

At first, when the words were "Day is dying in the west, Earth is sinking into rest," there were only chords—soft chords full of the sadness when dark is coming on. Then they were louder, rising above the sound of singing. At "Holy, holy, holy," there were no chords, only a rippling sound that went from low to high, from high to low, played by fingers faster than the eye.

The song was over and the woman left the piano. After some words from the principal, we had to go back to our rooms, to reciting lessons. Chapel would not come again for another week. I liked school, and chapel was the best part.

My first lesson was spelling, and Miss Monty soon found out that I had not studied spelling the way it was done in school. She sent us to the blackboard and told us to write the words she gave us. I had never written on a blackboard, and I did not like standing with my back to the room. I would not know if anybody laughed at me.

"Black."

She said the word loud and clear, and said it again. I knew the word in reading, but I could not spell it. The room was full of the sound of chalk pushed over slate. I turned to her, hoping she would spell it for me with her lips the way Miss Mollie had done. She looked straight at me and I could see nothing friendly in her face.

"Sit down."

She meant me, and I went to my desk, rubbing my eyes with my fists, to wait while she worked with the others on spelling and arithmetic.

At recess she kept Cleaver and me in, but she talked only to him. He was to tell my mother that I was not ready for second grade and would have to be put back, maybe to the primer.

Through the rest of the day I sat in class, listening to the others read, afraid to tell the teacher that I could read as well as any of them. She had said that Blossom was a graded school. Everybody had to pass first grade to go to second grade. I could sit in second grade one day and no more.

At home, my mother was put out at what Cleaver had to tell her. The teacher was to blame, she said. She had not tried me on reading. No pupil should be put back for missing the first word the teacher gave him.

"You're going back, and you're going to spell," she told me.

That night, in front of the fire, we studied spelling—all of us except my grandmother and little brother. The spelling book had page after page of rows of words, all to be learned by heart. It was not enough to learn the lesson for the next day. I had to memorize lessons ahead, and spell the words out loud without a stutter. At Pin Hook, they said a good speller had a good education. That night I was started on the way to becoming a good speller.

At school the next day, after Cleaver talked to her, Miss Monty let me try one more time. When I went to the blackboard for spelling, I listened carefully and wrote slowly. When my work was graded, all the words were spelled right.

After recess, at reading time, Miss Monty gave me a book and told me to read it to the class. The story was about Henny-Penny and Chicken-Licken, and easier reading than the Bible or my United States history.

At the end of the day she told me that I could stay in second grade, but that I would have to study hard to keep up.

25

One night the older boys who walked to school with us came to our house for a game of hide-and-seek, or as we called it, hiding-seek. It was a warm, moist night, light enough for us to use a porch post for home base and hide in the edge of the woods, light enough for us to see each other like running shadows.

The "it" had to stand at home base with eyes covered and count to a hundred by fives while the others hid themselves behind fences or trees or the well box. He had to count loud, and the sound of "Five, ten, fifteen, twenty" echoed through the night.

The counting over, he still had to give them a chance. He could open his eyes, but before he could leave home base he had to chant:

> Bushel o' wheat,
> Bushel o' rye,
> All ain't hid
> Holler *I*.

This had to be followed with another chant:

> Bushel o' wheat,
> Bushel o' clover,
> All ain't hid
> Cain't hide over.

After this, he moved away from the base, searching shadows and hiding places as he went. To catch anyone, he had to find him, call him by name, outrun him to the base, and count "One, two, three" before he got there. The first one caught was "it" for the next game. The ones he could not find came in "free" when he gave up and chanted:

> Bushel o' rye,
> Bushel o' ree,
> All ain't caught
> Come in free.

I was the smallest one playing, and "it" so often that I was run ragged. Once when Monroe was counting for me, I went farther into the woods than I had gone before and crawled inside a brush pile. It was dark around me and, far away, I could hear Monroe calling, "All ain't hid cain't hide over." I made myself small and quiet, knowing this time I would go in free.

I heard the sound of running, of counting "One, two, three." Then all was quiet and I lay trembling, waiting for the call, "Come in free."

What I heard was the blast of a shotgun on the road south of us, a mile away, but sharp and clear on the night air. It left a roaring in the woods, and above that I heard a man screaming, "Oh, my life! Oh, my life!"

I came out of the brush pile and ran to the yard as fast as I could. The game was broken up. The others were in the yard with my mother and grandmother. We could hear the sound of a wagon on the road and the man screaming over and over, "Oh, my life."

"He needs help," Monroe said. "I'm going—"

My mother tried to stop him.

"I've got to go," he said. "I'll be careful."

He and some of the other boys went running across the field in the direction of the sound. We stood in the yard close together, listening and wondering what had happened. The man's voice grew weaker and stopped, or we thought it stopped. It had been in our ears so long we could not tell. Then the wagon stopped and there was nothing for us to do but go inside and wait by the fire for Monroe to come back.

When he came, his face was white in the lamplight, and his voice shook when he told us what he had seen. A chicken peddler on his way home after selling his chickens in Blossom had been held up. He would have given up his money, but the robber got scared and shot him in the stomach. Monroe had helped put him to bed at a house on the road, and then run back to tell us.

"They know who did it?" my mother asked.

"He didn't know, but it sounded like a nigger. They sent for the sheriff and bloodhounds to trail him, and a doctor."

"No telling what'll happen next," my grandmother said.

What she meant was that the killer might come our way, and that we had better not go to sleep, not till daylight had come. They built up the fire and we sat close to it, waiting, and listening.

Late in the night we heard a bloodhound bark and begin the high wailing that told us he was on the trail. We stood in the front yard and followed the sound of hounds, first as they went in circles in the woods, and then along the railroad track toward Blossom.

"I'll bound he's hiding in Blossom," Monroe said. He wanted to go and see, but my mother would not let him.

Next morning we heard what had happened. The robber, a Negro man thirty years old, had gone straight home and crawled into bed in all his clothes, tired and wet from running. The bloodhounds went right to the door and bed. The sheriff had jerked the covers off and found him trying to hide his head. He was taken at once to the calaboose in Blossom and had owned up to the crime.

"They say they'll lynch him," Monroe said.

My grandmother nodded her head.

"It wouldn't surprise me none."

When we went to school that morning we went close enough to the calaboose to see that a crowd of men were standing around, talking. We could not hear what they were saying, but we knew from their grim faces that they were waiting for a chance to lynch the "nigger."

At school, all the talk was of the nigger. The children did not play; the teachers stood around with worried faces. The calaboose was in plain sight, a building they could break into without much trouble. The crowd was bigger, and more men were coming, horseback and walking, enough to break doors and bars and take the nigger.

At recess, the older boys began going quietly across the tracks, and the teachers did not try to stop them. The younger boys followed, and I went with them, to stand around with the men, staring at the walls and door.

"He in there?" a man asked.

"He's in there," another man said. "Nobody but him. Take a look in. You'll see him. I reckon you might know him."

The windows were too high for me to see in, but I knew he was in there and they were going to take him out. There were enough to do it. I could not see what they were waiting for.

We saw the other children lining up to march in and some of us went back. The older boys stayed, and saved the life of the

nigger. The men were afraid they would tell. They could trust each
other, but not the boys. It was broad daylight and the boys knew all
of them. It would not do in court to have the boys naming names.

While they were trying to send the boys back to school, the
sheriff came from Paris with enough deputies to take the man out
and take him to the county jail, where he would be safe from
lynching till his trial.

At dinner time, the calaboose was standing open and the men
no longer stood around it. They were still in town, bunched around
stoves in the stores, talking about how to punish the niggers for
what the man had done, and how to put them down if they should
start an uprising.

On the way home from school we went through town and
nigger town. We passed the nigger church and nigger school. No-
where did we see a nigger. All their places were shut and silent,
while they waited for the storm to pass.

"They know when to take to tall timber," the older boys
said.

The peddler died, and the boys were blamed bitterly for getting in the way of the lynching. The killer was tried and given a
sentence less than death. The bitterness grew. So did the talk.

"How you ever gonna keep them in their place?" people asked
each other. "If I'd a had my say, he'd a swung on a rope from a
hickory limb."

26

That winter my grandmother decided to learn to read and
write. Her brothers and sisters, nieces and nephews, were spread all
over Texas and Oklahoma, and only by letters could she keep in

touch with them and find out what was happening to them. My mother was too busy to write, and had to be begged for every letter that went out. It was the same with a letter that came in. My grandmother had to sit with it in her hand waiting for someone to find time to read it to her, not the first time but every time after that till she knew the words by heart. At times she wished they were all back at Pin Hook, close enough to run in on each other any time there was something to say.

She wanted me to be her teacher. She never said so, but when I was studying in front of the fire, making letters in my copybook, she would sit in her rocking chair and study the letters with me till she knew their shapes. Then she would copy them with a pencil. I was eight; she was fifty-eight, and her fingers were stiff from hard work and tetter. My letters were reasonably like those in the book. She shaped hers to her own way of thinking. At first she and I were the only ones to know for sure what they were. After weeks of practice, she could make them good enough to be read by anyone.

She wanted to write a letter to Monroe, who had gone out on his own, to make his own way. He was in Dallas, staying at Aunt Vick's. A letter to him would be a letter to all of them—Aunt Vick, Maggie, Wade.

Before she could settle on what to say and how to say it, he was back home again, telling us what he had seen and done in Dallas. I had seen the town of Blossom, but nothing bigger. Wanting to believe, but not quite believing, I listened to him talk of tall buildings, of streets at night bright as day, of streetcars and interurbans. He had not been able to find work, but he was glad he had gone. Anybody ought to see Dallas.

I wanted to go. So did my grandmother. She figured out a way and a time to go. The first letter she ever wrote was to Aunt Vick and Maggie, telling them when to meet her at the station.

That letter took a whole Sunday, with me lying by the fire spelling out the words as she wrote them down, a letter at a time: "I seat myself with pen in hand." This much she remembered from Missouri Ann's letters. But not pen in hand for her. There was not a pen in the house, and she had not learned to make letters with one. Pencil would have to do. The ending she also knew: "This leaves us all tolerably well and hope it finds you the same. Alice."

In between, in unjoined letters that wavered above, below, across the lines, she managed to tell them when to expect her on the Santa Fe. She also promised to bring them a bundle of Jerusalem oak to kill the mites on the chickens. It was hard work for her. At the end she said, "I wouldn't a been tireder cutting cordwood all day."

She tried to learn to read in books, but gave up after a little while. There were too many words, and what they told her she already knew, or had no interest in knowing. It was different for me, she told me. If I expected to be anybody, I would have to be able to read as well as the next one.

We saw signs nailed to telephone poles on the Blossom road: CIRCUS. FREE STREET PARADE. COME ONE. COME ALL. FREE TOYS FOR THE CHILDREN. We had never seen a circus or a clown, but the laughing faces of the clowns on the signs made us want to go. All the way home we talked about it: not about seeing the circus itself—there would never be enough money for the circus—but going to the street parade and getting free toys.

On the road home, it was easy to talk about going to the street parade. At home, we began to see that we might not be allowed to go. It was not the money but the work. My mother was not sure we could be spared from a full day of work.

"We'll have to wait and see," she said.

The longer we waited, the more I built up in my own mind what it would be like, and the toy I would get. Some days it was a horse on wheels, others a tin railroad car. I saw all these things, but I did not tell anyone what I saw.

When the day came, we were up before daylight. By breakfast time we had fed and watered the horses and slopped the hogs. The sun came up in a fair sky. The day would be hot but clear.

"We going?" we asked, still at the table.

My mother looked at us, her mouth firm, unsmiling.

"You think you can behave yourselves?"

We were sure we could, even after she told us that she was going to stay at home with my little brother and let us go with my grandmother. We promised to mind everything she said.

The sun was high and hot by the time we started out. Monroe and Dewey went ahead on the path through the field, and were soon out of sight. My grandmother walked with Cleaver, looking strange in her black bonnet and black dress so long it touched the ground at every step. I kept close behind her, my bare feet burning in the hot sand.

As we went, she told us what minding her meant. She would find us a place on the plank sidewalk and we would stay close to her. We could stand or sit, but not run or play. She did not want to have to raise her voice to us. When the street parade came, we were to hold her hand. That way we wouldn't be run over.

I was afraid of missing my free toy.

"If anybody gets a play pretty, you will," she told me.

She stopped and made us listen to her.

"You take what they give you," she said, "and say 'Much obliged,' no matter what it is. If it ain't nothing but a piece of hockey on a stick, you take it and say 'Much obliged.' You don't, you'll get a skinning when you get home."

The road between the stores and railroad track was already crowded with wagons and buggies and people on foot—the biggest crowd I had ever seen. My grandmother took us by the hand and led us to the sidewalk in front of the dry goods store.

"We c'n see as good here as anywhere," she said.

The people were looking down the road past the oil mill, where the parade would start.

"Time they was coming," they said.

When it was away past time, we heard a steam piano, loud and shrill above the low hum of talking.

"Here they come."

The first thing I saw was a clown in a red and white suit carrying a big straw basket. He was dancing from one side of the road to the other, laughing, talking, and dipping his hand into the basket every time he saw a child.

"You'll get something all right," my grandmother said. "It's him that's handing them out."

She took me by the shoulders and pushed me to the front of the crowd. He saw me and opened his mouth in a wide grin. I started backing away, but he grabbed my hand and made a joke of shaking it. When the people around us had laughed, he gave me a penny lead whistle in the shape of a bird. I looked at him and then at my grandmother. I had got better toys than this from a Cracker Jack box.

"Try it," she said, and I knew she meant it.

I blew on it and got the shrill cheep of a bird—so little when I had wanted so much. It was hard to say it, but I had to.

"Much obliged."

He had already turned his back, and could not have seen me wiping my face on my sleeve. I went back and stood with my grandmother.

"I told him much obliged," I said.

The street parade passed, led by wagons painted red, white, and blue and pulled by horses too pretty for workhorses. Other clowns leaped and danced, but they had no gifts. I looked for elephants and lions, but there were none. There were monkeys in high cages on the backs of wagons—too high up for me to get a good look. The steam piano came last, played by a clown who kept yelling for the crowd to follow him.

People walked behind the steam piano and we went with them to the open lot that had been made into circus grounds. In the center there was a big brown tent with green and red flags drooping in the still air. The door was open, and the clowns were doing what they could to get the people to go in. We could not go in, but we could watch the clowns and imagine the things they told us.

Not all the people went inside, even when the clowns told them it was the last chance.

"We c'n watch the flying jenny," my grandmother said when the tent flap had been closed.

We went to the far side of the circus ground, where a merry-go-round had been set up inside a fence. It was my first time to see one, and I stood as close as my grandmother would let me, staring at the painted wooden horses going up and down in a slow gallop. There were children on the horses, some of them boys and girls from my class at school. There was a bench between two big green geese for the smaller children.

It would have been fun to ride, but my grandmother did not give in. As she said, it was better to be there looking than not to be there at all.

When she was tired of looking, she got us all together and we walked through the crowds and out on the road home.

The road was hot and dusty and I was tired. Purple paint from my whistle had come off on my hands.

"It ain't much of a whistle," I said.

My brothers laughed at me.

"What'd you expect?" they asked. "They only give you something to get you to come. They didn't think nothing about you."

I began to cry. I had never thought about it that way at all.

28

Monroe went in the wagon to meet them at the train in Blossom. Aunt Nellie Haigood, my grandmother's sister, was moving back to Texas. She had made a good living in Oklahoma, but a good living was not everything. She had lost her daughter Bessie, who had been killed by a runaway horse. She had almost lost the other two when they got typhoid fever. Now, she was coming back, bringing Willie and Myrtle with her, hoping that a change of climate would be good for their health.

It was a good thing for us. We had outgrown our farm and had to find a bigger place with more land to work. Our place was the right size for Aunt Nellie and she wanted to rent it. It was close to the end of gathering time, a good time for moving.

My mother and grandmother talked about moving back to our place at Pin Hook, but did not. My grandmother wanted to be close to Aunt Nellie. My mother wanted to be close to better schools. Renting on the shares—one-fourth of the cotton, one-half of the corn—was something to worry about; they would have to plant more, gather more to come out even. Before Aunt Nellie came, they had rented the Womack place, about two miles north of us, and were ready to move in.

This new place had a bigger house, with two front rooms, two shed rooms, and a long front porch. The outside was of rough, unpainted pine boards; the inside had been papered with newspapers now too old and yellowed for reading. The house mattered, but not as much as the land. The land was deep sand, good for peas and potatoes, and just as good for corn and cotton. We would raise a fine crop, and our share would bring more than we had ever had before.

We saw the wagon coming down the lane and went to the gate to meet them. My mother and grandmother got to the wagon first. I stayed back, dreading the kissing and crying that would take place. Aunt Nellie climbed down over the wheel. Then she and Monroe lifted the girls down.

Aunt Nellie was then in her forties, a powerful woman with a voice rough and deep like a man's. For fifteen years she had done the work of a man, and she had the muscles and grip of a man. She had given up worrying about her looks; her skirt and waist had been cut like sacks, and hung on her like sacks. When her hair hung down in her eyes, she took the scissors and whacked it off. She met us with a toothbrush of snuff in her mouth. For years she had been afflicted with "pellegrisy," and it had left blotches of albino white on her sun-browned face and hands.

"You don't look good, Nellie," my grandmother said, after the kissing.

"I don't feel good. I'm plumb wore out. Gentlemen, if I ain't had a time, two sick on my hands at once. Look at them now. They look a heap better'n they did."

They stood holding on to each other, trembling, their faces thin, their eyes staring out of the whiteness like brown doorknobs. Their hair had fallen out from the fever till bald patches of scalp showed through. Willie was nineteen, Myrtle fourteen, but they looked old, and they were so feeble they had to be helped inside the house and to chairs with pillows on them.

"Bring me my can," Aunt Nellie said to Monroe when they were settled.

He brought her spit can from the wagon and set it on the hearth beside her. She rubbed her wet toothbrush in a can of snuff and put it in her mouth.

"I been needing me a new toothbrush," she said to me. "You reckon you could get one and chew it for me? If you could find a slippery ellum root, that makes the best kind."

While my brothers unloaded the things Aunt Nellie had

brought with her, I went down to the branch, looking for a slippery
bark elm. It was getting dark, but I found one and dug out a root
the size of a toothbrush. I slipped off the bark and chewed one
end, working it back and forth between my teeth till I had made a
good brush.

After supper, we sat around the fire. Aunt Nellie dipped with
the new toothbrush and told us what it was like to go through a
spell of typhoid fever. She told of fever so high that they were out
of their heads days at a time—of the spasms they had when they
threw up till there was nothing more in the stomach to be thrown
up.

"It's a sight to see what they went through," she said.

"They'll pearten up," my grandmother told her. "You get your
things here and get settled, they'll pearten."

Aunt Nellie had chartered a freight car to bring her furniture
and tools, horses and wagon.

"It might take till spring," Aunt Nellie said, "and I cain't wait
that long to start plowing."

While they talked, the fire burned down and the room got
chilly, but no one was ready to go to bed. We sat close to the fire
and listened to Aunt Nellie talk. She was not sorry she had gone to
Purcell. There had been years better than any she had ever known
at Pin Hook. If it had not been for typhoid fever, she would have
stayed there. As it was, she had come back, and she was not sorry.

"I just hate it that I couldn't bring Bessie with me," she said,
and began to cry.

"I never did see how it could a happened," my grandmother
said.

Aunt Nellie stopped crying and told us. Bessie had married a
boy named Goatch and they had set up housekeeping not far from
Purcell. They had been married only a little while when one day
they started to town in a buggy. The horse shied at something on
the road and ran away. Bessie jumped from the buggy and died
before Goatch could stop the horse and get back to her. They would
never know what killed her. She did not have a bruise on her
body.

She did not blame Goatch. She did blame herself that they
had never had a picture taken of Bessie. Not till she was dressed
and in her coffin did they remember they did not have a picture.

"I couldn't stand it not having something to remember her
by," Aunt Nellie said, "so I got some made."

A man had come out from Purcell to make pictures of Bessie.

Aunt Nellie went to a valise and got out some large pictures. She held one up by the lamp.

"That's me and Goatch with her," she said. "We had to sort of stand the coffin up to make it."

The coffin was at an angle, so that the girl in it seemed half standing up. Her round white face was only a shade darker than the white coffin lining. Her dark eyebrows and lashes seemed dead black against the whiteness. Aunt Nellie was on one side of the coffin, her face and eyes caught in the depth of grief. Goatch was on the other side, stiff and staring, and the shock of death had not gone out of his eyes.

Aunt Nellie passed that picture around. Then she held another close to the lamp.

"The picture maker said he could open her eyes in one picture for a dollar extra, so I let him go ahead and do it. I told him her eyes were brown, but he did not get them right."

This was a picture of Bessie alone, half-standing in her coffin, with her eyes open and staring.

"It ain't like her in the eyes," Aunt Nellie said, "but I'd druther have it than nothing a-tall. It sets me remembering."

The picture was passed around and cried over. Then it was set on the mantel for the night.

29

By the time we moved to the Womack place there was talk that we had made a mistake in moving. The house was bigger, but not better; too much of the land ran to post-oak flat. There was more land than we owned in the places at Blossom and Pin Hook, but we would have to make more crops to pay the rent and come out ahead, or even. With luck and hard work, we might come out ahead, and there was enough land to keep everybody working at home. Monroe and Dewey would not have to hire out part time.

We moved long after school had started, and then more time passed while my mother and grandmother talked about the school we should go to. Only three of us would go. Monroe had to work the land we had rented. Roy was too little.

I wanted to walk the four miles back to Blossom, but we had moved out of the Blossom district to the Walnut Ridge district. No transfer had been made, and Blossom would not take us back, without payment as outsiders. We could go to Walnut Ridge, three miles away, or to Linden, also three miles away, if they would take us without transfers. Both were in what was called "walking distance," as set by the law of the time. The shortest way to Walnut Ridge was on paths through fields and woods, and across creeks that overflowed with heavy rains. The road to Linden was open and public.

Then my mother heard that George Haley and his wife were teaching the Linden school. He had married Miss Mollie Hefner, and they were teaching together. Better for us to go to teachers we knew than to strangers. They knew us and would not ask for transfers.

With no more than that to go on, we set out one morning in late November for the Linden school. We had quit school too early in the spring to get report cards. We might have been promoted, but we had no way of knowing. We were told by my mother and grandmother that we would have been if we had stayed in school, and we could tell that to the teachers.

The school was a two-room white frame building set in a grove of oaks. It was on a sandy road, and there was a bare sandy playground in front of the door. We were late, and books had taken up. We had to look at the building from the outside and tell which was the "big" room, which the "little." Dewey would go to the "big" room, Cleaver and I to the "little."

We came to the door and would have turned back, but we were afraid to go home. Better to face strangers than a hickory switch at home. Pushing against each other, Cleaver and I went through the door and found ourselves looking straight into Miss Mollie's face. She looked at us a moment, trying to place us, and then smiled.

"Don't I know you?" she asked.

"Yes'm," Cleaver said.

"At Pin Hook?"

"Yes'm."

She put her hands on our shoulders and turned us around to face the room.

"Look, boys and girls," she said, and there was a kind of laughter under her voice, "we have two new boys from Pin Hook. Let's try and make them feel at home."

She gave us a desk together and never asked about grades or report cards or whether we had transferred from the Walnut Ridge school. She did tell us that we were to call her "Mrs. Haley," not "Miss Mollie," and her name was written with chalk on the blackboard, "Mrs. Mary Belle Haley."

Linden was not as good a school as Blossom, but better than Pin Hook. It had two teachers and two parts, primary and elementary. Mrs. Haley did not keep the boys and girls separated by grades, but she did use graded books in arithmetic, reading, and spelling.

We soon knew that she had passed county examinations and raised her certificate to a permanent, but she had not changed as a person, or as a teacher. In spelling, when we were standing in a row in front of her, she still shaped letters with her lips to help a boy or girl who could not remember. No one wanted her to change. She was a good teacher as she was.

At recess, we saw Mr. Haley, a tall, thin, red-necked man who looked as if he had just come in from the cotton patch and put on a white shirt and black coat. The older boys were in a game of "Anthony, Over," and he was standing at one end of the schoolhouse, watching both sides to see that they played fair. Dewey was playing with them.

A boy stood on one side with a twine ball in his hand, his team ready to run.

"Ant'ny," he called.

"Over," the boys on the other side answered.

The boy threw the ball and started around the house. A boy on the other side caught it and hit the boy who threw it. Mr. Haley had to call "fair catch, fair hit," and the boy was lost to his side. The game went on. Once he had to pick me up and brush me off when a boy knocked me down trying to get away.

I liked Mr. Haley. My grandmother had said, "I knowed him when he was nothing but a shirttail boy." Before recess was over I was glad we had gone to Linden.

In chapel, Mr. Haley led the prayers and singing with hardly a change in his face, or his voice. With nothing to pitch the tune to, he would start off in a key low enough for his raspy voice and too low for the rest of us. He believed in singing songs with lessons in them, like "Just before the Battle, Mother," with its words of farewell and then the sad refrain: "But, oh, you'll not forget me, mother, If I'm numbered with the slain." Chapel was better at Blossom. They had a piano at Blossom.

After supper that night there was talk of school, of Miss Mollie, of George Haley, but mostly of George Haley.

"He's sure raised hisself," my mother said. "You've got to give him that, and he's done it without help from anybody."

What he had done, anyone might do, she told us. He had studied all he could at Pin Hook, and then gone on his own, studying when he could, taking county examinations as fast as he could get ready for them. Now he had a permanent certificate. Teaching was easy work and he was looked up to.

"No need'n staying behind a plow all your life unless'n you want to," she said.

30

The organ was one of the last things moved to the new place. While it was on the front porch waiting to be taken inside, I saw that dauber wasps had crawled inside and built their mud nests. Some of the notes had been stuck down so that they played all the time when the pedals were pumped. Some reed slots had been covered over and made no sound at all. When I told what I had found, my mother shrugged her shoulders. No one had time to play the organ anyway.

One day when I was home from school and the others were in

the field, I looked at the organ, closed up and silent in a corner, and knew I should clean out the dirt dauber nests. I moved it away from the wall and took out the screws that held on the paneled back. Nests clung to it and to the wooden flap that opened when the knee swells were pushed out. Under this flap were the key slots, some of them hidden behind mud nests. I cleared out the dried mud and tried the pedals. Some notes were stuck still, and others would not play. Mud had gone into the reeds themselves and had to be taken out.

I found the wire reed hook hanging inside the case and, one by one, pulled the reeds out and cleaned them. I tested each one by blowing on it. It was like blowing on a French harp, but I could make only one sound at a time, and I could feel the thin metal sounding strip against my tongue. Each one tested, I put them in a bucket and took them out in the sunlight to brush them with a rag.

I knelt behind the organ with a bucket of reeds beside me and did not know how to put them back. I could see that the big ones belonged at the bottom, the little ones at the top, but that was not enough. The letters printed on them did not help. All I had to go on was sound, and I did not know *do* from *mi,* or anything about chording.

I started with the biggest and worked up, going as fast as I could, knowing that I would be in trouble if they came and found I had been fooling with the organ. At last the reeds were in—some of them sounding wrong when I tried them. I switched them around and tried them again. No matter how I changed them, they still sounded wrong. When it was too dark for me to see I closed the organ up and pushed it against the wall.

The others came in but nothing was said about the organ. After dark, Aunt Nellie came with Willie and Myrtle to eat supper with us and spend the night. The girls looked better. They had their color back, and enough hair to comb.

"You look right peart now," my grandmother said to them.

After supper, she wanted them to play and sing, but they shook their heads.

"We ain't sung none since the fever," Willie said. "We're plumb out o'practice."

"No need to practice up for us none," my grandmother said. "We wouldn't know the difference, just so's you make some music."

When they seemed about to give in, my mother took a lamp to the other room and set it on the organ.

"I don't know about this old organ," she said. "Dirt daubers is been at it all summer."

"It'll sound good enough," my grandmother said, "once it gets started."

When the right amount of begging had been done, so that she would not be thought to be showing off, Willie seated herself on the organ stool and pumped up and down on the pedals. A low hissing of wind in the bellows sounded through the room. She tried some chords, and then turned to my mother.

"It don't chord right," she said. "Listen. I'm playing C chord, but it's F where it ought to be G."

My mother tried a song on it and had to stop.

"It's mixed up all right," she said.

She looked at me and I think she knew who had mixed it up, but she said nothing. I kept quiet and half hidden in the corner behind the organ.

"I can straighten it out all right," my mother said, "but it'll have to wait for daylight."

Willie tried it again and found that by remembering the notes out of order she could play the C chords.

"We'll have to sing everything in C," she said.

My grandmother laughed.

"I wouldn't care if it was X,Y,Z, as long as it's music."

She had her way and they sang a song they had learned in Oklahoma. It was a Civil War song, but it was about the boys in blue, not the boys in gray. It was a sad song and, in their high wailing voices, they sang it with enough sadness to bring tears to the eyes.

> There was an old man,
> And he was bent with age,
> He landed in this village
> After dust was laid.
> "Is this the express office, sir?
> I'm looking for my son.
> They tell me that the train was due
> This place at half past one."
>
> "Oh, you have made a sad mistake—"
> His voice was meek and low—
> "This is an express office, sir,
> And not a train depot."
> "But you don't understand me, sir,"
> The old man quickly said,

"He's not coming as a passenger,
He's coming to me dead.
He's broken his dear mother's heart,
Likewise mine's broken, too.
I told him that he'd come back dead
When he joined the boys in blue."

The song ended, but the old man stayed in the room with us, his sadness a sadness for us, the lesson of his son a lesson for us.

"He shore oughtn't to a gone off that way," Aunt Nellie said.

He was a Yankee soldier sent home by a Rebel bullet, but we were not thinking of Yankee and Rebel. We were thinking only of the man and woman, and a boy dead in a coffin.

When Willie and Myrtle were resting from singing, Aunt Nellie looked at them.

"I want you to show Alice what you learnt in school."

They put it off by telling us about the school they went to in Oklahoma. It was a one-room school out on the prairie, where most of the people lived in dugouts and the children came to school as dirty as they lived at home. The teacher was a young man who knew more about reading and arithmetic than he did about making the older boys behave. His method was to make them spend their days memorizing, all from the same book, and saying by heart before the whole school the lines they had learned.

"Willie, you keep a-going as long as you can," Aunt Nellie said. "Myrtle'll help out if you get stuck."

The two girls stood side by side with the lamplight on their faces, with their hands pushed against their thighs. Willie started in a flat voice.

> The Browns have become illustrious by the pen of Thackeray and the pencil of Doyle within the memory of the young gentlemen who are now matriculating at the universities. Notwithstanding the well-merited but late fame which has now fallen upon them, any one at all acquainted with the family must feel that much has yet to be written and said before the British nation will be properly sensible of how much of its greatness it owes to the Browns. . . .

She rushed on, sliding over strange names and strange words.

> These latter, indeed, have until the present generation rarely been sung by poet or chronicled by sage.

Aunt Nellie held up her hand to stop her.

"Gentlemen," she said. "I'll put this up agin anything for jaw-breaking words. Start it up agin, Willie. I want them to hear."

Willie went on till she was out of breath, and then Myrtle took it up.

> In the first place, the Browns are a fighting family. One may question their wisdom or wit or beauty, but about their fight there can be no question. Wherever hard knocks of any kind, visible or invisible, are going, there the Brown who is nearest must shove in his carcass. . . .

She had to be stopped, too, while she was still giving the good and bad about the Browns, because Aunt Nellie wanted to get something else off her mind.

"You ever hear of anybody like them?" she asked. "I'd as leave live next to a bunch o' Choctaws, and I know what I'm talking about when it comes to Choctaws."

Myrtle started again, ran out of breath, and dropped down on the organ stool, leaving Willie to say words as she had learned to say them in an Oklahoma schoolhouse.

> O young England! Young England! . . . Why don't you know more of your own birthplaces . . . All I say is, you don't know your own lanes and woods and fields. Though you may be chockfull of science, not one in twenty of you knows where to find the wood-sorrel or bee-orchis which grows in the next wood or on the down three miles off. . . .

She came to the end of all she had learned.

"I quit school and didn't go no further," she said.

"I seen what he was learning them and took them out," Aunt Nellie said. "I just wanted you to see the foolishness of it."

My grandmother did, but my mother wanted to know more about the book. They knew it was called *Tom Brown's School Days,* but they had never read past the part they had memorized. When they quit school, they left the book behind, and we would never know what happened to Tom Brown and the other Browns.

Aunt Nellie wanted to tell my grandmother about the Choctaws. The ones she knew hated work and liked revival meetings.

"They can go on singing all night and all day," she said. "You know that old song we used to sing at Pin Hook? I'll bound you I heard Ma sing it a thousand times. I can hear her now starting up singing 'I Have a Father in the Promised Land.' "

All of us knew the song, and knew it had belonged to Missouri Ann, and that she was a part of it:

I have a father in the Promised Land,
I have a father in the Promised Land,
And I know some day we will all meet there,
Away over in the Promised Land.

"You ought to hear the Choctaws shower down on that one,"
Aunt Nellie said.

"Can you sing it?" my grandmother asked her.

"I don't know. I ain't sung none since Bessie died."

They begged her some and she said, "You play it, Willie, and
I'll give a try at it."

Willie played C chords. Aunt Nellie stood by the organ and
sang in a rough, hoarse voice:

I have a father in the prog no long,
I have a father in the prog no long,
Nee rasha nay and a nay she goes about,
Go sheruby in the prog no long.

"I learnt the words by heart, listening to them," she said. "I
ain't about to take time to learn Choctaw."

She had other things to say about Choctaws, things she whispered to my mother and grandmother when I was on my pallet
trying to stay awake, things that made me glad we did not live close
to Choctaws and see them eat their meat raw.

Linden was a good school, but soon after Christmas we were
staying home again, cutting sprouts, burning brush, working at
anything we could to get the land ready for planting. We had not
stayed in school long enough to get promoted, or to get report cards,

but that could not be helped. We were renting the land, and we had to make it pay more than the rent. All of us had to go to the field. My little brother was staked by a pallet, in the shade near the turnrow, in the sun when we were working in the middle of the field.

It was a long, hard summer and when the cotton was picked, the corn gathered, my mother knew we had made a mistake moving to the Womack place. When the shares of cotton and corn had been given up for rent, there was little to show for a year of work. The only way to get ahead, she said now, was to work your own land.

Aunt Nellie, giving up her shares to us, said the same thing: better to starve to death working her own land at Novice than paying rent on ours at Blossom.

So it was settled that after crops were in she would move back to Novice and we would go back to our place at Blossom. She was going back with less than she left with when she went to Purcell. There had been bad luck all the way. Everything she had could be put on one wagon, and she had to borrow a mare from my grandmother to make up a team to pull it.

While we waited for the move, Cleaver and I went back to school. We could not go to Blossom till we were back in the district. My mother decided we should go to Walnut Ridge. We might be a little ahead by going to Walnut Ridge.

It was a long walk, more than three miles across fields and through woods, and no other children to join us on the way. We started out at sunup and got home when dark was coming on. On the way, there was plenty of time to get the look of cloud and sky, the feel of the earth, the color of limb and leaf, the sound of a bird.

Walnut Ridge was a two-teacher school, with the grades up through the third in one room, the higher grades in another. With nothing to show from Linden, I went to the little room, in something like the third grade. Miss Era, the teacher, was young and thin, and in her first year of teaching. She was having trouble with the big boys, and had little time for two more pupils. She had me share a desk with a boy sixteen years old and six feet tall.

His name was Thummon and he could not read the third grade reader. Miss Era stood him in front of the room and kept him there while he spelled out each word and then said it. After half a page she gave up.

"You read next," she said to me.

The page she gave me was one I had studied at Linden. I read it through without missing a word.

"You ought to be ashamed o' yourself, Thummon," Miss Era said, "letting a little boy like that read better'n you."

Thummon said nothing.

My mother soon knew she had made a mistake sending us to Walnut Ridge. We were studying reading and spelling we had passed at Linden. She took us out of school and kept us out till we moved back to Blossom.

We had no report cards, nothing to show what grade we were in at Walnut Ridge. My mother decided that we should go to the fourth grade room in Blossom.

Christmas came and went, with all of us at home and no one to visit us. There were a few packages of firecrackers for noise at night on Christmas Eve, and fruit and cake to show that Christmas Day was not like any other day. In the quiet of being alone there was talk of other times, other places.

My grandmother talked about "Old Christmas"—the twelfth night after our Christmas—when the horses talked at midnight and cows walked on their knees, when things never seen by daylight could be watched clear as anything in the blackness of night. She had never stayed up herself to see and hear, but she had heard tell of people who had. It was something to be believed. She had heard it in Arkansas, from people who knew about it long before they came to Arkansas. She could not make the sound of a horse talking, but she had heard it sounded like a man talking deep in his throat.

"Some say it's a night for ghosts to walk," she said. "All I know is, it's not a night I'd want to take the shortcut to Blossom."

We knew what she meant. The shortcut was on a road that went through a Negro cemetery. By day it was a quiet place in the woods with scraped patches of earth and a few whitened stones. By night, anyone could tell us, white ghosts had been seen rising from the ground up into the open air above the treetops. The ghosts had to be white, they said. Colored people always turned white at death. No one we knew had ever seen one, but this was what they knew.

As the talk went on, I wanted to see for myself what would happen on Old Christmas. I believed what I had heard, but believing was not enough. I wanted to be in the barn by myself at midnight.

When the night came, I stayed up to put out the lamp and cover the fire after all the others had gone to bed. Slowly the old clock on the mantel ticked. Slowly the hands moved toward midnight. I rubbed my eyes and shook myself to keep awake.

When the fire was only a reddish glow through gray ashes I heard the click of the hammer rising to strike the spring. Five minutes to twelve. In five minutes the clock would be striking midnight. I put on my coat and went out into the clear, cold starlight night, walking without a sound, straining my ears to hear the things I had never heard before. Ahead I could see a dark line of trees. Under them lay the Negro graves. I looked above them for ghosts, but saw only a night sky whitened by white stars, and shapes of white light reaching into treetops, changing shape with every step I took till they seemed to be flying, up and down, in and out.

A little less afraid of the sky, I opened the barn door and slipped inside the horse stall. It was too dark to see anything, but I could feel warmth from the horses and breathe a smell that never changed. The noises I heard were the same I remembered from any night of late feeding. Old Maud and Old Fan were sleeping side by side, standing on their feet, hanging their heads down almost to the ground. I nudged them gently, but they only sighed in their sleep.

I went past them to the cow stall. Old Reddy was lying down asleep, with her calf beside her. She should have known it was Old Christmas and midnight. I gave her a quick kick in the ribs. She grunted, got up on her front knees, and stood up without taking a step. The calf got up and started to suck.

I waited in one stall and then the other. It was no use. The horses kept on sleeping. The cow kicked the calf away and lay down. No matter what they said, Old Christmas was no different from any other night in the year.

Shivering with cold, I went out of the barn. The sky was

whiter, and the whiteness glowed on the trees over the graveyard. This was not the night, but there had to be a night when I would walk there by myself. Still shivering, I took off my clothes and crept into a bed warmed by my brothers.

The two should never have been separated. They say animals grieve for each other just the way people do. Old Maud and Old Fan had pulled double so long together that they started and stopped, geed and hawed like one. One never slacked traces on the other. When they cropped grass, they cropped together. Old Maud belonged to my mother, Old Fan to my grandmother. Sometimes my grandmother put a sidesaddle on Old Fan and went to town or for a visit. When she came back, the two old mares nickered to each other and stood neck to neck for hours at a time.

Then my grandmother let Aunt Nellie have Old Fan for a full crop year down at Novice. It was not easy for her, not when Old Fan was her way of picking up and going when she felt like it, riding sidesaddle the roads from Blossom to Pin Hook to Novice, her black skirt pulled down over her shoe tops, a white woolen shawl around her shoulders, a white bonnet pushed back from her face. Now the cloth and leather sidesaddle was left hanging on the front porch and my grandmother said, "I'll go only when I feel like going footback and walking."

Old Maud was the first to get sick, to change from a look of grieving to one of suffering. My mother and grandmother looked for signs of blind staggers, a disease that began with weaving and falling and ended in death. Old Maud stood with stiff legs and bloated belly, her head hanging down, the whites of her eyeballs showing.

"You can see it's her belly," my grandmother said. "Nothing to do but drench her."

It was night and they had to work by lantern light. They mixed Epsom salts and warm water in the white milk pitcher. My mother and Monroe held her head up, her mouth open. My grandmother poured the drenching down her throat. She flinched and kicked, but they did not stop till the dose was down. Then they took turns sitting up with her, the way they would with the sick.

Before daylight, my grandmother woke us with the light of the lantern.

"She ain't no better," she said. "It ought to a scoured her, but it didn't."

"You got any notion?" my mother asked.

"Locked bowels."

My mother began to cry. That was almost as bad as blind staggers.

"I don't see how we could stand to lose her," she said.

The horse doctor was needed, but there was no money to pay him. Nothing to do but wait and see. They waited till up in the day and she was worse. Then Monroe went to find the horse doctor to ask him what to do. No harm in asking, and it would be cheaper than having him come.

It was dark when he came back.

"Did she scour?" he asked.

"No sign of it."

"The doctor said she's got to. He showed me how to help her."

We went to the barn again, my grandmother carrying the lantern, Monroe with a dish of lard. It was cold and dark in the barn, and I had to hold up the lantern for light. My grandmother tapped Old Maud's swollen belly.

"She's nigh about to bust," she said.

Monroe rolled up his sleeve and greased his hand and arm. With a set look on his thin boy's face, a look that said there was nothing else to do, he worked his hand deep inside her body. My mother held her head but did not need to, for she stood still, with all four feet solid on the ground.

All done that could be done, we waited. They sent me to the house to bed, but I could not sleep. Toward midnight my mother came to the house to warm. She stood with her back to the fire and lifted her skirt to let the heat reach her body. She was crying, and I knew she had given Old Maud up.

While she stood there, Monroe and my grandmother came in. "She's dead," Monroe said. "She just laid down and died."

My mother cried harder.

"What'll we do," she asked, "with only a pony to make a crop?"

My grandmother was past crying.

"Make it with a hoe," she said. "It won't be the first time a crop's been made with a hoe."

My mother said nothing more to her, but she did to us. Times were not like they were right after the war. No need in people having to work the way they did after the war. My grandmother could ask for Old Fan back from Aunt Nellie, but she did not. Aunt Nellie, with only girls to help her, needed her more than we did.

The next morning Monroe hooked the pony to Old Maud and dragged her off to the woods and left her to the buzzards and possums. I went to see her that day and the next. When I saw that strips of hide had been pulled away, I could not look any more. I watched the buzzards in the treetops and knew what was going on down below.

Then, when it was early summer, there was a letter for my grandmother from Aunt Nellie. I brought it from the mailbox and read it to her. It was short and full of grief. Old Fan had swelled up and died from eating a bait of green corn.

My grandmother began crying.

"Now both o' them's gone," she said.

My mother, coming in, heard what she said.

"No more'n anybody'd a expected, once she got out in green corn."

My grandmother had nothing to say to that. She did go to the wash pan and start washing her face.

"I've got to go see Nellie."

"Walking? It's a good ten miles."

"I'd go if it was twenty. I cain't stand to think o' her down there, grieving all by herself. It ain't right if I don't go, and right now. No need trying to wait to catch a wagon."

She went, and I went with her to keep her company. She wore a gray chambray dress that touched the ground with every step and a white sunbonnet with a ruffle on the tail. My white waist was buttoned to knee-length pants and my feet and legs were bare. My straw hat, the one I wore in the field, was stained red and blue with plums and blackberries.

There was no time for fooling along on this trip. My grand-

mother was too much in a hurry, and if I dragged behind I had to
trot to catch up. We could have followed roads all the way, but they
wound around farms and went out of the way to cross creeks where
crossing was easiest. With nothing but the sun and what she could
see to guide us, my grandmother cut through woods and across
fields. When a road was in our direction, we followed it. When it
turned to right or left, we took to the woods or fields.

Once we found ourselves in woods that had never felt the saw
or axe. The trees, mostly oak, stood tall and close, and the leafy
limbs shut out the sky. My grandmother stopped long enough to get
her direction and then went ahead.

"Keep your eye on the moss," she said. "It grows on the north
side o' the tree."

We kept to the north among the oaks and through thickets of
huckleberry growing wherever the sun shone through. It was hot,
and there was a heavy smell of dead leaves and damp mold. Our
voices sounded as if they had been shut up in a box.

"Mek keest," my grandmother said when I got behind. "You
get lost, you'll never get out."

She did not slow down. I had to keep up.

We came out of the woods when the sun was straight above us,
on a road that came within a mile of Aunt Nellie's house. We kept
on walking and found Aunt Nellie in the field, working her corn
with a hoe.

Their meeting was one of hugging and kissing, sunbonnet to
sunbonnet, and of crying out loud, over the loss of Old Fan.

"I never hated anything as much in my life," Aunt Nellie said.
"We tried everything in the world but nothing done her no good. I
don't know what in the world we'll do without her."

"I don't either, with Old Maud dead. Where is she?"

"Out'n the woods there, what's left of her."

Aunt Nellie sent me to the mulberry tree to pick mulberries for
myself and they went across the field to the woods, two women
walking together, slow as if they were walking to the graveyard.

They went, and came back to the house, to eat in the kitchen
and talk on and on. From their talk I knew how much the loss had
been, and what the chances were, raising crops with a hoe. It would
be better if we lived close together. Then we would be able to swap
hoeing and plowing.

Aunt Nellie did not want to move again. She was on her own
place. Better for us to move near her, to a place with enough land
for us to work. It meant moving away from Blossom, away from

school, but they could not see that school had been of much help to any of us. We could read and write. That was enough for farm work.

"I been thinking about the old Addison place," Aunt Nellie said. "It's been laying out a long time. Planting it would be just like planting newground. I'll bound you it'd make about a bale to the acre."

The Addison place was on the road between Novice and Pin Hook, and only a mile from Aunt Nellie's house. I had never seen it. I did not see it then, but my grandmother and Aunt Nellie walked over it before dark and told each other it was the right place for us. We could rent it, third and fourth, and be a heap better off.

That night I lay on a pallet in the hall listening to them talk.

"It's always been a curiosity to me about the Addison boys," Aunt Nellie said.

"Me, too. What ever become o' them?"

"Nobody knows for sure. They say they had to move on, running from the law, but they must a cleaned up here while they were at it. I used to see them riding the road, all four of them, on their fine horses and saddles trimmed in silver—them and others with them, young men like them, going out on a raid they say, or coming back to lay low till it blowed over. Some say they rustled cattle."

"They wasn't like the James boys," my grandmother said.

"Nothing like the James boys. Nobody ever heard of a Addison giving anybody a nickel. I reckon they seen people as poor as anybody, but they kept their money to themselves, or buried it. They say they had to leave out so fast they did not have time to dig it all up."

"You believe it?"

"I don't know. Some people do. Ain't no trouble a-tall to find signs o' digging."

When we knew that our next move was to the Addison place, nothing was right with the place at Blossom. The land was too thin, and there was not enough of it. The house was too small and too far from neighbors. The school was good, but no good to us when we had to spend all our time working for enough to eat and for clothes good enough to wear while we worked. My mother, believing in books as much as ever, gave in and let us move away from school. She even kept me out of school to work. Everything had to be ready when the time came.

The move took place in December, close to Christmas, and took several days, first for the corn and hay from the barn, then the hogs and cow and chickens, with Dewey left at the new place to take care of them. On another day they loaded the things from the house on the wagon, everything except a feather bed and quilts, an iron cooking pot full of boiled backbone, and a skillet for baking bread over the fire. My grandmother was to stay behind to clean the house. It was nothing but right to leave a place clean enough for somebody else to move right in. She wanted me to stay with her to carry water and keep her company.

With the washpot full and the fire going, I walked to Blossom to get my grandmother a piece of chewing tobacco. When I came out of the store it was late recess at school. I could see the boys and girls on the playground and hear them laughing and shouting. All at once I knew that I did not want to leave Blossom and school. Nothing at the Addison place would make up for what I would miss at the Blossom school.

I walked across the railroad track toward the Womack store.

Long before I reached the footbridge across to the school ground
the bell for books rang and the boys and girls went inside. I walked
close to the schoolhouse, but not up to the door. I had already left
anything that went on inside the door.

Slowly I crossed the footbridge and railroad track. I wanted to
be out of sight when school let out. I crossed to the sidewalk and
went slowly past the drugstore, the dry goods store, the racket store,
looking at them with the feeling that I would never see them again.

When I got home my grandmother had scrubbed the floors and
set her corn-shuck scrub brush by the fireplace to dry. She had made
down a bed for us on the floor and had supper cooking on the
hearth—the backbone in the pot, bread baking in the skillet, and
sweet potatoes roasting in the ashes.

By the time I got in wood for the night, it was dark and time
for us to shut ourselves in. My grandmother nailed the windows
shut and buttoned the doors with the big wooden buttons. She
jammed sticks of wood under the doors and hammered them in
with the axe. Then she put the axe on the floor by her side of the
bed.

"No telling who might come around here tonight," she said.
"It ain't too far to nigger town."

Shut in for the night, with flames leaping on the dark window-
panes and throwing shadows on the bare walls, we sat by the hearth
to eat our suppers. My mother had left us plates and spoons, but
fingers were better for backbone. We broke the pieces apart and
sucked out the marrow. The potatoes were soft and sweet. The corn
bread tasted of smoke and long cooking.

While we ate, my grandmother talked to me of what it was like
to be hungry. She had seen it in the war and after.

"I'll tell you about the Yankee soldier," she said.

It was at the end of the war and Missouri Ann had taken her
children to the field to make a living. One day a Union soldier, a
straggler, maybe a deserter, came out of the woods close to where
they were working—thin, dirty, his lips blistered by the sun, his face
swollen, his eyes feverish. They could see he was starving.

"You got anything to eat?" he asked.

It was after dinner and all they had left was a pint fruit jar of
black molasses. Missouri Ann gave it to him. He put it to his lips
and did not lower it till he had drained out all that would flow.
Then with his tongue and finger he cleaned the inside of the jar as
far as he could reach. When there was nothing left, he thanked
them and went back to the woods. He was so weak a woman and

children could have captured him. They did not. They thought he was on the long walk back to his home up north.

"When I get so hungry I cain't stand it I think about him," my grandmother said.

Alone with me, she took time to talk, not of what would be but of what had been, not of the Addison place and Addison boys but of growing up on the Ouachita.

"You ever see Jesse James?" I asked, knowing the story she would tell.

Her eyes had a faraway look.

"Many a time."

"What'd he look like?"

"Tall and slim, and he had a heavy head of hair and beard. His eye was black like all the James'. I recollect the first time I seen him. We lived on a farm close to Camden after the war and I was a young girl. I was named Alice James, but they sometimes called me Allie. It was fall of the year, cotton picking time. One night a man come up on his horse and asked if he could stay all night. Ma let him come in, and I could tell the way they talked there was more than he was letting on. He asked for a job picking cotton and she give it to him, when we didn't have more'n we could pick ourselves and needed all the work we could get."

"Did he tell you he was Jesse James?"

"No, but Ma told me after he was dead. I recollect that night clear as anything. He was at the table eating and I was waiting on him when he said, 'What's your name?'

" 'Allie James,' I said. 'What's yourn?'

"Quick as anything he said, 'James Allie.' He stayed with us two weeks and we never called him anything else."

"Did he ever come back?"

"Off and on for a while. Sometimes he would come at night, bringing some of the others with him. Sometimes he would be gone again before we woke up in the morning."

It was like being close to Jesse James to be with someone who had sat at the table with him and picked cotton beside him in the field. She had seen him ride away to hold up a train or rob a bank. She had heard of the widows and orphans helped on their way by the twenty dollar gold pieces he had given them. Banks and railroads took land and money from the poor people. She had seen Jesse James when he was carrying on his fight against the rich.

"After a while he stopped coming," she said, "and they told us he was dead, shot in the back by Robert Ford. When Ma got the word, she set down and cried like a baby for her kinfolks."

I thought of what they said about him at school.

"They say he was wrong," I said.

She looked at me hard, and the fire was in her eyes.

"Whatever he done wrong, they made him do. They drove him to it. I'm here to say one thing: Jesse James was a good man. I'd be thankful if you'd grow up to be as good a man as Jesse James."

Long after we were under the quilts and she was sleeping, I lay watching the light and shadows on bare walls and ceiling, thinking of Jesse James, glad that I could call him cousin.

When Monroe came the next morning we piled what was left of our things on the wagon. My grandmother climbed up to the springseat with him. I sat in the back, between the Georgia stock and turning plow, with my back against a chair that had been turned upside down over a washpot. It was a cold gray morning and I wrapped a quilt around me to keep warm.

It was time to go and I did not want to. I had looked forward to the Addison place and told myself that I would be the one to find the buried money, but this was home and it was not. I looked at the house, shut up and silent, the walnut tree by the well, our rope swing still tied to a limb of a big red oak. The wagon started on the shortcut through the woods. I stared back at the house as long as I could see it through the bare trees and then covered my head with the quilt and cried.

It was a long day, a long trip over roads of wet sand, muddy clay. At the long hill down to Baker Creek Monroe had to brake the heavy wagon by chaining the back wheels to the axle so they would not turn. By the Novice Church we stopped long enough for the horses to blow. Then we went on, over a road I had never seen before.

We came to the Addison place late on a gray afternoon and I stood up to see my new home. The house was set back from the road on a rise in a bermuda grass pasture, and looked like houses I had seen before, but more run-down. It had two front rooms with an open hall, a shed room behind one of the rooms, and a porch across the front. It faced west, to the road, and there was a big oak to shade it from the sun. The south room was of hewn logs, the cracks between daubed with white mud. The north room, added later, was of pine boxing planks, with a door to the hall and no windows. The roof, made of hand-split oak boards, roughened and curled out of shape with weathering, sat like a bonnet pushed too far down.

Aunt Nellie had said it was a big house. It was bigger than the one at Blossom, but ramshackle, no better than the houses Negroes lived in. Mud had run from the cracks where the rain hit; the stick-and-dirt chimney had crumbled at the top. The barn, to our right as we turned in from the red clay road, was no better than the house. The Addison boys had lived in the house, and stabled their horses in the barn. Nothing like the James boys. The James boys would never have lived in a house like this.

I slid down from the wagon and carried my quilt with me to the house. The log room was crowded with beds and chairs only half straightened out. A small deadwood fire burned in the fireplace, making patches of dim light and broad shadows in the windowless room. I went on to the shed room at the back, where I found the stove set up and my mother leaning over it, cooking supper.

"How you like your new house?" she asked.

I burst out crying and hid my face against her waist. It was an ugly place, and we both knew it, ugly and run-down. Maybe the Addison boys had kept it up. No one else had. I looked out the back door at the gray bermuda grass pasture, stretching down a gentle slope to a line of gray trees along a branch. Not a sign to show where the money might be buried.

"We have to tote water," my mother said. "I've been waiting for you so you could fill up the buckets."

She handed me two buckets from the shelf at the back.

"Go back the road you come till you see a road fork off. Take it till you come to a house with nobody living in it. It's about a mile.

The well's in the back with a rope and pulley. You'll have to draw with one of the buckets."

Before I had seen the other room I was on the road again, carrying a bucket in each hand, walking on the leaves at the side of the road, out of the mud, knowing that twice a day or more I would be going for water. I found the house and the well. It was too dark for me to see the water, but I could feel changes in the rope as the bucket turned on one side and sank. Hand over hand I pulled on the rope, and my hands were dripping before I touched the bucket.

The water was soft and sweet to the taste, coming over the rim of a bucket, and I had let the bucket down enough to know it stood deep in the well. I did not like carrying it. With rests on the way, my shoulders and legs got tired, and the bucket bails cut my fingers.

When I got back the wagon had been unloaded, the horses unharnessed and fed. There was still work to be done—beds set up for the night, sticks to be picked up to keep the fire going. In a gray turning dark I crossed the road to a patch of blackjack oak. No one had gathered wood there in a long time, and there were plenty of dead limbs in the leaves on the ground.

Dark came, and there was no more we could do that night. When supper was ready we took our plates and sat on the floor in front of the fireplace. The Addison place, we all knew, was not what we wanted, but we had it and had to make the best of it. There was work to be done: the chimney had to be rebuilt and firewood cut. The land had to be cleared of sassafras sprouts before the time for ploughing.

They had seen the land and knew it would raise good crops. I had not seen much of anything but the long walk to and from the well.

36

My older brothers slept in the room across the hall, three in a bed, with no fireplace, and no light when the door was shut. They stayed in the other room as late as they could at night and ran back first thing in the morning to put on their shoes in front of the fire. As long as it was winter, the other room could be used only for sleeping. The organ was in it, closed up, never touched.

One morning Dewey did not come in with the others. The cold he had caught at Christmas was worse. It had settled in his chest and he was burning up with fever. My mother and grandmother stood over him a while and then came back to the fireplace room to get warm. A norther had come during the night and the room he was in was freezing cold.

"Sounds like pneumonia," my mother said.

It was enough to make us look at each other and draw in closer together. Pneumonia was the worst disease of winter; few people who got it managed to pull through.

"It wouldn't surprise me none a-tall," my grandmother said. "We better go get Nellie."

The day was cold, and a gray whiteness in the clouds made us look for snow before night came. Dewey had to be kept warm. He had to be moved to the fireplace room, but that meant taking him across the open hallway where a chilling wind whipped through. My mother, knowing she had to move him, started making a bed for him by the fire.

Aunt Nellie came and went in to see him.

"You cain't bring him out in the cold," she said. "It'll kill him shore as the world."

My mother went ahead making the bed.

"He cain't stay where he is," she said. "He's all choked up with cold now. It'd be a heap worse by morning."

Aunt Nellie shook her head.

"I'll just warn you. If you move him, you dassen't let him get chilled."

With Monroe to help her, my mother nailed up quilts on both sides of the hall, shutting out the wind and light, making a passage-way from one door to the other. Then they wrapped him in quilts and carried him through to the fireplace room. When they put him in the bed by the fire I could see him, his dark hair hanging over his forehead, his thin face flushed, his eyes bright with fever. He was breathing hard and saying things that did not make sense.

"He's out'n his head already," Aunt Nellie whispered to my mother over the cookstove. "If you don't have a doctor by night, he could go into congestion. That'd kill him shore as the world."

My mother began to cry. She had no money to pay a doctor, and no promise of money till the cotton could be planted, raised, picked, and sold. The weather was bad and getting worse. No doc-tor would want to come out on bad roads in bad weather, without much hope of getting paid. She knew Aunt Nellie was right. If the doctor did not come, Dewey would die. There were only two doctors who might come: Dr. Reeves at Pin Hook or Dr. Bishop at Spring Hill.

It was my grandmother who sent Monroe for Dr. Bishop.

"Tell him to come and I'll work it out," she said. "Tell him I'll work it out any time he calls me."

Monroe bridled up one of the ponies and went off bareback to call Dr. Bishop, and we all felt better at doing what could be done.

"It'll be a hard night tonight," my grandmother said, looking at the heavy clouds. "Some's got to watch, some's got to work."

My mother and Aunt Nellie did the watching. My grand-mother took me with her to get in enough wood to last out the storm. We had to go farther and farther from the house picking up sticks. We had to scratch them out of the dead leaves, break them in fireplace length, carry them to the house, and stack them on the front porch. Fear of weather, fear of freezing if the fire went out, made us walk fast when we had a load, trot when we didn't. It was getting colder and our faces and hands were raw from the wind. My grandmother tied a wool shawl around her head and pinned it over the lower part of her face. Her breath came through it in clouds, and moisture froze on the wool.

"Mek keest," she shouted at me, coming and going, "it'll get dark before you know it."

Late in the day the gray-white clouds turned into swirling, drifting flakes that covered the leaves. Scratching out sticks was harder and took longer. Still we went on, slowed to a walk but not giving up. Dewey had to be kept warm. That was something I could do.

Monroe came riding through the snow, too cold to knock away the snow that lodged on his clothes and on the pony's mane. He told us that Dr. Bishop was coming and went on to the barn to take care of the pony. My grandmother, with less worry in her face, went inside to help get ready for the doctor.

When the gray whiteness was turning to gray blackness Dr. Bishop came down the road in his double buggy. He had wrapped his large body in coats and lap robes, and let the snow cover him over. Inside our gate, he rolled out of the snowy robes and climbed to the ground. He looked at me, still holding the wire gate open, and handed me the reins.

"Hold my horses for me," he said. "They might get skittish in the snow."

Alone with the horses, where the blackness of night, the whiteness of snow made all shapes look different, I watched the front door open for him to go in and close quickly behind him. I wanted to go inside and watch, but I had to hold the horses. I turned my back to the north wind and tromped the snow under my feet.

After a long time of waiting, when my bones had been chilled to the marrow, Monroe came out and took the reins from my hands.

I brushed the snow off in the kitchen and was sent to stand by the door to the fireplace room. I could tell how sick Dewey was by their faces. My mother was on one side of his bed, the doctor on the other. Aunt Nellie held the lamp for the doctor to see. My grandmother was folding a piece of sheet for a plaster. There was a smell of mustard and of steam from the iron teakettle on the hearth.

With his saddlebags open on the floor beside him, the doctor was mixing medicine on the stand-table at the head of the bed. He measured white powders from glass bottles in a heap on the table and mixed them with a stone rod. Then, holding the long end of a capsule like a biscuit cutter, he set it down on the powder over and over till it was filled. Then he capped it with the short end. As he worked he talked.

"You can see the dose we gave him's a-beginning to take

effect," he said. "You can see he's breathing easier. That's the way it is with pneumonia. If you can catch it in time, the medicine works fast. It's a good thing you sent for me when you did."

"I was never so glad to see a doctor in my life," Aunt Nellie told him.

"If you keep up the treatment, you'll see a great change by morning."

He had my mother write down the treatment. Then he closed up his saddlebags and went out into the night for the long cold ride home.

"Gentlemen, he's a good one," Aunt Nellie said.

My grandmother looked at my mother.

"I told you he'd come if I sent for him."

Knowing that he was better, we ate our supper of middling meat, corn bread, and milk, standing around the kitchen stove, keeping quiet to let Dewey sleep. My grandmother dipped her slices of meat in her milk.

"It takes away the salty some," she said.

Late at night, when Dewey had gone back to sleep after his second round of medicine, we sat around the hearth, with only the fire to light the room. We could not all sit up all night—turns had to be taken at sitting up—but no one wanted to go to bed yet. It was good to be there, sitting close together, knowing the medicine was taking effect.

Aunt Nellie looked out the kitchen door at the snow and came back to the fireplace.

"I got that sugar I brought," she said. She looked at my mother. "If you've got the milk and flavoring we could have snow ice cream."

"Milk'll taste as good now as at breakfast," my mother said. "I cain't churn anyway. It's too cold for the milk to turn."

Monroe took a bucket and filled it with heavy wet snow from the smokehouse roof. From it my mother filled the bowls and rounded them on top. Then she added vanilla and sugar, and poured on milk in which tiny spines of ice were floating. We stood close around the kitchen stove, eating ice cream, warned that head pains come from eating too fast, eating too fast, laughing at each other because we all knew better.

Then I had to stand in front of the fire, warming myself through, getting ready to dash across the cold hall to the other room, where I could sleep till I felt like waking up.

37

On Monday of the New Year Cleaver and I started to school again. The Addison place was in the Pin Hook district but Pine Creek was between us and the schoolhouse and the shortest way, through the woods, would take us across it on a footlog. My mother did not want us to have to cross it when the rains came in the spring and the creek got out of banks.

"Many a time I've seen it overflowed so it looked like a river," she said.

So she sent us to the Spring Hill school, three and a half miles by road and no shortcut through the woods. There was no question in her mind about the grade. If we were good enough to be in the fourth grade at Blossom, we were good enough to be in the fifth at Spring Hill. The fifth was taught by a man and, to her way of thinking, we were ready for a man teacher.

Almost the same height and weight, dressed in the same kind of knee britches and long black stockings, carrying one shiny dinner bucket between us, we started out for school walking on a road part of which we had never seen before. It passed along one side of Aunt Nellie's place but out of sight of her house. Then it went for a long stretch through woods of blackjack and post oak, with no fence on either side, winding around big trees, narrow where it cut through sand knolls, wide in the flats where wagons made new ruts when old ruts got too deep in mud. It passed houses and farms and the Novice Church, and the crossroads where a fork of the Paris road went down to Slate Shoals on the Red River. Another stretch of woods and at last we came to the Spring Hill schoolhouse, which was also called Medill.

It was a two-room white frame building set off the road in a broad clearing. It was backed up to the woods, and big trees had been left around it to shade it in the hot days of spring. Nearer the road the playground was open for running games like wolf over the river.

Books had taken up and we went slowly across the silent playground, with Cleaver in front, the oldest, knowing he had to go in first because he was the oldest, with me walking on his heels because I did not want to be left behind. We knew which was the door to the big room, but Cleaver went all around the schoolhouse and came back to it before we would go in. He did not knock. He opened the door, we sidled in, and he shut it behind us.

The teacher, a thin, dark-haired man in a blue serge suit, was at the blackboard working a problem in arithmetic. He stopped, dropped his piece of chalk in the tray, and came toward us. I knew at once that I was afraid of him. The other boys and girls turned to stare at us but they did not make a sound.

"We're starting to school," Cleaver said, keeping his back to the door.

"Well, come on in," the teacher said. "I'm Mr. Jessee."

He took our names and wrote them on the board for the others to see.

"What grades are you in?"

"Fifth," Cleaver said and I could feel him trembling against me.

Mr. Jessee looked at me and then at him. He was three years older.

"Both of you?"

"Yes, sir," we both answered.

"Let me see your report cards."

"We ain't got airn."

"Where have you been going to school?"

"Blossom. We moved down here and didn't get our report cards."

No report cards. No books. Nothing to show what grade we belonged in. But we were there and he had to do something with us. There were five rows of desks, one for each grade from the fifth through the eighth, and one for the older boys and girls who had finished the eighth grade and were coming back to review, some with the aim of getting teaching certificates. He seated us at the back of the room in the fifth grade row and told us to sit there while he heard the other lessons.

Grade after grade he took the boys and girls through arithmetic, reading, and history. I had never seen anyone who knew so much, or who could go from one thing to another without ever looking tired. He was not a tall man—some of the older boys were taller—but his flat stomach and straight shoulders made him look taller. His face was dark and narrow, and stern through all the lessons. His eyes were brown with enough yellow in them to make them catlike. He was my first man teacher and I began to see how easy the women teachers had been on me. At the same time I wanted to be like him. He had left my name on the board. I tried to copy it the way he had written it.

Mrs. Jessee taught the little room. Some of the pupils were afraid of her and we knew why when we saw her. Her hair was red: Red-headed people are hot-tempered. The pupils said Mr. Jessee was strict, but Mrs. Jessee was stricter. She looked it, standing on the playground, silent, unsmiling, watching some little girls playing house.

Mr. Jessee came to the door and rang the bell. Standing straight as a ruler, he watched us get in line.

"They say he wears corsets and braces to be as straight as that," a boy in line whispered.

"Don't let him hear you say that," someone else said. "He'd as leave lick you as look at you."

In the afternoon the fifth grade had grammar and he sent me to the board with a sentence to parse. It was written in his hand and stretched from one line in the blackboard to the next: "Is it I who am accused?" With no softness in his eyes he told me to write the words in a column and opposite each the part of speech. I had not studied the parts of speech and did not know what he was talking about. To give myself time, I began writing the words in a column: "Is . . ."

One by one I wrote the words, making them look as much like his writing as I could. Then I looked at my brother for help. It was useless. He knew no more than I did about the parts of speech. At last Mr. Jessee sent me to my seat and diagrammed the sentence to show what he meant, and why "am" was the correct verb. It was no help for us. We had never heard of pronouns and verbs.

He talked of sending us back to the little room but did not. He did tell us to listen to the others saying their lessons and try to catch up.

It was a long day and I was glad when it was over. On the way home we walked with other boys as far as the Novice Church. Then we had to go on alone through the long stretch of woods when the sun had set and darkness was coming on. The next day would be longer if we wanted to get to school before books took up.

My grandmother met us at the door with the lamp.

"It took you a whet to get back," she said to Cleaver, who was in front of me.

"We kept on hoofing it—"

"You'll have to hoof it faster or get in wood and water after dark. It's done this time but it won't be when work starts in the field."

That night we had to sit in front of the fire and tell the others about school.

"You like your teacher?" my mother asked.

"I reckon. They say he's strict."

"I hope he is, and I'll tell you what I've told you before. You get a licking at school, you'll get a licking at home. You hear me?"

We nodded our heads.

"He sure stands up straight," Cleaver said. "They say he wears a corset."

At this my older brothers began laughing.

"He must be some man, wearing a corset."

"It don't bother me what he wears," my mother said. "What did he teach you?"

Both of us shook our heads. There was nothing we could put in words.

"Didn't he teach you nothing?" my grandmother asked. "Didn't he try to teach you nothing?"

"He sent me to the board," I said. "He tried to make me diagram a sentence but I didn't know how."

Not any of them had gone far enough in grammar to study diagramming. It was as funny to my older brothers as wearing a corset, or a red-headed woman teacher.

Before I went to bed I wrote my name several times the way he had written it on the board. Then I wrote "Is it I who am accused?" and thought it looked the way Mr. Jessee had written it.

The sentence stayed with me through the night and on the long walk to school the next morning. I had books now, a speller and a reader, and my mother had said she would send to the store when she could for a geography.

At reading that day I was ahead of most of the boys and girls in the fifth grade, but not at grammar. Mr. Jessee gave us each a sentence, reading them out of a notebook, and sent us to the board to diagram them. He went on with another class, leaving Cleaver and me to stare at each other after all the others had left the board.

Lemmie Williams, one of the girls reviewing to be a teacher, saw the trouble I was having and moved to a seat near me. Mine was a simple sentence beginning with "the."

"Adjective," she whispered. "Write 'adjective' by 'the.'"

She followed with "noun," "verb," "adverb," and I wrote them down, still not knowing what they meant. She did the same for Cleaver and we went to our seats.

This time Mr. Jessee took a new sentence from his book and wrote it on the board. Then, word at a time, he explained the parts of speech and showed on a diagram how one followed after the other. This was something I wanted to know and I listened to every word.

When he went down the board grading our sentences he stopped at mine. The parts of speech were right, but there was no diagram. Taking time with me in a way that made me feel he had all the time in the world, he diagrammed the sentence and told me the meaning of subject and predicate. Before he moved on to the next sentence I had made up my mind to memorize everything there was to know about grammar.

"I want you to take some sentences to study," he told us at the end of the lesson. "You can copy the ones you want from the book."

There were one hundred sentences in the book and I copied them all, not knowing that in them he had brought together all the rules of grammar he thought we ought to know.

That night in front of the fire I started doing what I knew I had to do: diagramming the sentences one by one and naming all the parts. No one had asked me to study this hard before and I did not know enough to finish the first sentence. I began learning the sentences by heart. Next day Mr. Jessee would show me the diagramming and I would learn it the same way.

38

It was the same with reading. I wanted to learn everything I could about reading. Mr. Jessee divided us into two kinds of pupils: the ones who still had to learn to read and the ones who knew they had to read to learn. Both groups read from the same book, the Elson *Grammar School Reader, Book Two.* The ones learning to read took their turns before the class, standing up, stumbling over the words, waiting for the teacher to help on the hard ones.

This is how I heard my first lines of "The King of the Golden River," read by a boy who saw nothing but words on a page, who said each word separately and looked at the teacher to see if he had said it right. He did not see a story; he saw only the lines set for him to read that day. He came to the end of the line and sat down.

I had to read on, but not then. Half a dozen other boys and girls had to read the same lines aloud. I listened and waited. Then the book was in my hands when the teacher went on to another class. I turned to "The King of the Golden River" and read through without stopping, not hearing the sounds in the room around me, knowing only that I had to read fast to get through before "books" was over.

The story ended and I was left in a world of my own. School out, I walked home by myself, not wanting to talk to anyone, wanting only to take myself again and again through the story. Without having it said to me, I knew that reading was more than saying the words one after the other.

As the days passed I had my own lessons to learn from this book—lines from "The Story of Achilles," lines from "The Story of Ulysses," now and then a verse from a poem:

> Have you seen an apple orchard in the spring?
>   In the spring?
> An English apple orchard in the spring?
> When the spreading trees are hoary
> With their wealth of promised glory,
> And the mavis pipes his story
> In the spring!

I had not, but I had seen an apple tree in bloom and knew what the poet meant.

At times Mr. Jessee gave me verses to learn to read. I wanted to learn the whole poem by heart, and often did. I copied them down in my tablet and read them over and over on the long walk home from school.

I hardly knew when reading changed to saying out loud. It may have been when Cleaver dropped out of school to work in the field. I was lonesome in the woods and to keep myself company I would start saying something aloud like "Abou Ben Adhem, may his tribe increase. . . ." or "Blessings on thee, little man, Barefoot boy, with cheek of tan. . . ." Mr. Jessee liked to give us poems that taught a lesson:

> Dare to do right! Dare to be true!
> You have a work that no other can do...."

Or:

> I'll find a way or make it.

Or:

> Heaven is not reached at a single bound....

He once had me recite the whole of "A Psalm of Life" in class and then he talked to the boys and girls about the lesson in the last verse:

> Let us, then, be up and doing,
> With a heart for any fate;
> Still achieving, still pursuing,
> Learn to labor and to wait.

There was one he passed over, "Horatius at the Bridge." It was too long and the words too hard. I liked it best of all, for the story and for the sound of the words. I did not try to memorize it, but many words stuck in my mind, so that when I was walking through the woods alone and wanted to be Horatius I could say as I thought he said it:

> O, Tiber! father Tiber!
>   To whom the Romans pray,
> A Roman's life, a Roman's arms,
>   Take thou in charge this day.

The other boys and girls were laughing at me. I found out when I heard them calling me "Wild Bells" behind my back. I had stayed in at recess because I wanted to, and they knew I wanted to recite all of "Ring Out, Wild Bells" to Mr. Jessee. They could see me standing near the desk where he was working. They could hear me saying:

> Ring out, wild bells, to the wild sky,
>   The flying cloud, the frosty light;
>   The year is dying in the night:
> Ring out, wild bells, and let him die.

They heard him say, "Go on and play now. I don't have time to hear any more."

They laughed at me for trying to be teacher's pet, for the clothes I wore, and for not knowing the things they did. They had been to Paris. Some of them went to Paris nearly every Saturday. Anybody who had never been to Paris was behind the times.

Before then, I had not thought much of going to Paris. The talk I had heard had been of going to Purcell or Dallas, unless it was to sell a bale of cotton or buy a wagon. Paris was fifteen miles or so from Spring Hill, on a dirt road over red clay hills that turned to red wax in rainy weather. In dry weather the clay packed down into hard wagon tracks. A fast-stepping team could make it to Paris and back in a day, with time left over for hanging around on Bonham Street or taking in a picture show.

"You been to Paris, Wild Bells?" one of the boys asked.

I had to say, "I ain't been."

It was something to laugh at, that I had never been to Paris. My mother had, and my older brothers. That was not enough to keep them from laughing.

"You ever seen a moving picture show?" the same boy asked.

I had never seen a moving picture show. Neither had anyone in my family.

"No, I ain't never seen one."

"I seen one Saturday. It was so real you'd have to see it to believe it. It was some cowboys trying to catch a gang o' rustlers. They come up on them on the side of a mountain and chased them all the way down the hill, shooting as they went. You could see the smoke and purty near hear the guns go off. You ain't never seen nothing like it till you seen a moving picture show."

With nothing to go on but what he told me, I saw what he had seen, and it became real for me. On my way home that day I thought about nothing but the moving picture show.

"Can I go to Paris?" I asked when I got home.

"When?" my mother asked.

"Next time somebody's going."

My grandmother was listening.

"From the amount of work we've got to do," she said, "that'll be a whet."

To the south of our house, across a wide bermuda grass pasture, we could see a small log and lumber house with one room, an open porch on the front, and a shed room at the back. In the daytime we could see smoke from the chimney. At night a lamp burned late in the window. It was a Negro house and we were not likely to know what it looked like inside, or more than we were told about the people living in it. We were white; they were black. They had their place; so did we.

We knew the house belonged to an old Negro preacher. We saw him on Sundays, riding his mule, going back into the woods to Galilee to preach. The Negroes called him "Pahson" Perry. To his back, the whites called him "Possum" Perry and made fun of him for carrying a Bible when he could not read or write. He lived in the house with his wife, Betty, who had got too old to work out for white folks. She was not too old to take care of Negro children left with her when there was no other place for them to go.

On my way to and from school I passed close enough to see them on the porch or in the yard. When I went to the well for water I sometimes heard their voices, but I did not go near enough to speak to them. They were beneath us, I had been told, and knew it. The problem was to keep them knowing it, and there were ways. I was to speak to Negroes I met on the road and the ones who came asking for work, but I was to call them only by their first names unless they were very old. Then I could call them "Aunt" or "Uncle." Going to their houses to get them to work was all right. Going to visit would bring the white down as low as the Negro. I wanted to go. It was hard not to on the days when "Old Betty," as we began to call her, working outside around the washpot, showered down on "Swing Low, Sweet Chariot" in a voice that cut through woods and fields and a thin white skin.

I did go, on a Saturday when I had chilled myself through rambling up and down the creek banks, and needed a place to warm myself without being given a job to do. Coming up out of the bottoms, I saw the smoke rising from Parson Perry's chimney and knew I had to go in. If my mother found out she would not like it, but that was a risk I had to take.

From the front gate I looked through the open door and saw that Parson Perry was weaving a basket in front of the fire. Baskets hung from the porch roof to dry. There was a pile of fresh-split white oak withes on the porch floor. With whites, I would have called "Hello" and waited for the answer, "Come in." Not sure this was right with Parson Perry, I lifted the gate latch and went inside the yard. He saw me at the steps and stood up with the curling withes in his hands.

"Yo' mumma want me?" he asked.

"No, I wanted to get warm."

"Well, come on in, child. We working here, but we can square around enough to give you some o' the fire."

Old Betty was on the other side of the fireplace carding cotton, with the carding combs in her hands and a pile of lint in her lap. Without getting up, she nodded to me and walked her chair back. He kicked a hickory-bottomed chair toward me.

"I has to take up mos' o' the room," he said. "Making baskets takes a heap o' thrashing around."

"Don't let me stop you," I said. "I wasn't meaning to keep you from nothing."

Old Betty was back at her carding, not even a bat short because of my coming. Old Parson went down on his knees again and began weaving the withes in and out. Close up, without his black hat, he looked older, his dark skin more wrinkled, his woolly hair whiter—much older than Old Betty, whose brown cheeks were smooth. She had "wropped" her hair in pigtails with red and blue rags that hid the color of her hair.

Old Parson, too old for farm work, not paid much for preaching, could make baskets, everyone knew—feed baskets, cotton picking baskets, handled baskets good enough for a white woman to carry on Sunday. The baskets drying on the porch were feed baskets, made of rough, heavy withes with some of the bark left on. The one he was working on was for carrying clothes on a washday. The withes were thinner, finer, and he smoothed off rough edges as he worked with a piece of broken glass.

"How come you can make baskets so good?" I asked him.

"Old massa lernt me when I was a boy back in the old country. He says to me, 'Come on, boy, me and you is going to the woods.' He took me to the woods and showed me how to pick out the straight young white oaks—them that ain't got no knots so's they'll split easy with the grain. Old massa never split a log in his life but he showed me how to hold the froe and maul and rive out the withes not too thick and not too thin. He stopped right there. I had to pick up the rest from the old men that wove old massa's baskets."

I began feeling sorry for him. He had been a slave with a good home and somebody to take care of him, and the war had ruined everything for him. I knew what the war had done to the slaves.

"You were a slave?" I asked him.

"Born a slave, back in the old country, close to Tupelo, Mississippi—me and my old woman both."

"You'd a been better off staying slaves," I said.

I knew I was right in saying it. All the white people I knew said the same thing. Slaves didn't have to worry about anything. They got everything furnished when they needed it, and were taken care of when they got old. No call for a worn-out slave to work the way Old Parson and Old Betty were working.

Old Parson wound a withe under his arm and held it there. His hands, free, came toward me, the palms hard and yellow, the fingers rubbed gray white with the weaving.

"Don't say that," he said. "You don't know what you saying. Somebody else done said it and you believed 'em."

His voice trembled and there was a sad look in his eyes. He believed what he had said to me. So did Old Betty. She kept on

carding and her voice was not much louder than the sound of wire
teeth on lint.

"You tried it?" she asked.

"No."

I would have said "No'm," but she was colored.

There was something wrong in what they said. My grandmother had lived through the war. She had seen how slaves had felt
when they were taken from their masters. Maybe Old Parson and
Old Betty had been too young to feel it.

"You must a been mighty little when you got freed," I said.

They looked at each other and I knew I had said something
that hurt them. I would have left then but he would not let me
go.

"Don't believe what they tell you," he said. "It wasn't right,
being a slave, with nothing o' yo'self to call yo' own. I was old
enough to know all right. We got married while the war was going
on, and nobody knowed what'd happen to us. We seen some mean
times before it was over, ain't we?"

Old Betty stopped carding.

"Worse'n we ever seen since."

"We could tell you," Old Parson said, "but no needing to. It
all passed when the war was over. We took up and left for Texas
and been right here might nigh ever since, plugging along, nobody
telling us do or don't do."

He leaned closer to me than I had ever been to a Negro before.

"Don't let them tell you nothing about slavery," he said. "You
don't know nothing about being a slave till you been one."

The house was close and I was warmer than I wanted to be. I
stood up and sidled toward the door.

"Much obliged for letting me warm up," I said.

Old Betty nodded and smiled. Old Parson got up and, holding
the withes to keep them from curling and tangling, came to the
door.

"I reckon we won't be missing what you used up," he said.

When I was on the steps he stopped me.

"Yo mumma marked her hogs yet?" he asked.

I looked at him, thinking he ought to know better.

"Signs ain't right yet," I said.

He laughed.

"Ain't I know that? I said that to myself, seeing them shoats
y'all got penned up in the lot. I said to myself, 'They's work to do

there when the signs gits right.' You go tell yo' mumma. Tell her I'm coming to see her, asking c'n I mark her hogs. I reckon she ain't got nobody big enough to do it."

I told her, and he came the next day on his way from church, riding his mule, wearing his black hat and suit, and carrying his Bible in his hand. My mother and grandmother had figured out what to do. They could not ask him to come on the porch, but if he got down off his mule they would have to ask him. They told me to watch for him. I saw him coming and opened the wire gate at the road for him.

"Ride on around to the back," I told him. "I reckon they can talk to you from the kitchen door."

I went through the house and was with them at the kitchen door when he rode around. He stopped facing us but did not offer to get down.

"Good e'ening," he said.

"Good e'ening."

He was friendly; they were not.

"I was just passing by on my way from church."

"I heard you might be coming in."

My mother was friendlier. She wanted the work done, but she did not want Old Parson to feel that he could get dressed up and come visiting on Sunday. Her face was red. It was not easy to talk to a man about marking hogs, even when he was old and black and a preacher.

"I heard you wanted some work."

"I'm asking c'n I mark yo' hogs when the time comes. I don't charge no money. It's pay enough for me to take the leavings."

My mother's face was redder.

"You're welcome to the leavings," she said. "I couldn't a paid no money."

"I ain't asking none. You c'n count on me. I'll come when the signs is in the hoof."

He tipped his hat and rode off around the house. I opened the gate for him and closed it. Then I watched him down the road. The leavings he would get would be pig's tails and the parts of ears cut off to make our mark: underbit in the right, crop off the left—what we would throw away anyway.

40

In the warm days of March my older brothers went to the fields before sunup and came back after sundown, too tired for anything but to eat supper and crawl into bed. The land was good—they knew it was good—but it had not been worked in so long that breaking it was like breaking new sod. Sassafras and persimmon stood in thickets. Roots ran shallow in the sand. They had to be cut with a coulter bolted to the beam of the turning plow. Once they were cut they had to be pulled out by hand and piled with the brush for burning.

Cleaver had dropped out of school without complaining. He had been kept home so often that he could never keep up with the class anyway. When the days were long and warm there were more and more jobs to keep him at home, and then he did not go at all. It was not so easy for me to drop out. Whatever it was in other ways, school was for me a place of books. With a book in my hand I could forget most of the things around me. I was memorizing a poem by Whittier, with the stanza:

> Still sits the school house by the road,
> A ragged beggar sunning;
> The sumacs still around it grow
> And blackberry vines are running.

It was in a book that I could not take home from school and I copied down verses as I could.

When I had most of it by heart my mother told me one morning that I was to bring my books and things home from school. It was Friday and a good time to stop. Monday morning I could go to the field and do my share of the work.

All that day I packed into my head what I could, studying with the feeling that this was my last time to study. I had seen what had happened to Monroe and Dewey, and was happening to Cleaver. They were not in school now. They would never be in school again. All the talk of school was lost because we had to work too hard to make a living.

Without telling Mr. Jessee that I would not be back on Monday, I took my books and left my desk bare. Then, not wanting to tell anyone that I had to quit school, I walked home by myself.

The sun, bright and warm, was behind me all the way, casting my shadow ahead of me when the road was in the open, in the woods losing it in the shade of new-leafed oak trees. Blackberry vines along the fencerows were white with clusters of flowers.

"And blackberry vines are running," I said the poem over and over as I walked, and this line stayed in my mind, even after I had left the road and was crossing the bermuda grass pasture. It stayed with me and I began trying to make verses of my own about blackberries. Whittier's poem had a story. I could think of no story. All I could think of was how the vines looked loaded with flowers and then berries that were first green, then red, then black. I never got a line of verse. What I was trying to say got lost when I thought of a riddle:

"Why is a blackberry green when it is red?"

There was no time to go back for another look at the blackberry vines. I had to get home for my share of the work.

On Saturday I was in the fields all day, and again on Monday. For the first time in my life I had to be a full field hand, doing any of the work that had to be done except the plowing. I was still too light to hold a plow to the ground. When I tried, the blade rose and barely skimmed the top.

Then school was out. I knew because my report came by mail with "Retained" in red ink written in Mr. Jessee's hand. School that year was a hundred and twenty days. My report card showed that I had been there less than a third of the time.

41

The dog days of August came, hot, dry, and dusty. In the middle of the day the sun shone white hot in a dust-blue sky. At sunset it glowed blood red through dust that hung in layers, thin high up, thick like clouds above the treetops. Water in the creeks and sloughs dried up. The few holes left were covered with green scum, the water too rotten for cows and horses, the kind of water that mad dogs ran to. Stories of mad dogs traveled the road—of dogs shot because they whined in the heat or went into running fits. It was a time for staying close to the house, in the shade of hall or porch. The ones who had to go out carried clubs.

On a Saturday at sundown Monroe came home from work at the sawmill carrying two long fish in a white floursack. He was sweaty and tired and his duckings were wet to the thighs, but he did not seem to mind. With all of us watching he went straight to the back porch and laid the fish on the wash shelf.

"Grinnel," he said. "You never tasted no fish till you've tasted grinnel."

"Where'd you get them?" my mother asked.

"Caught them myself. Muddying. They stopped work after dinner and we all went down to the slough on the other side of the sawmill. We muddied till everybody got all the fish he wanted. Them two'll make more'n we can all eat for supper."

"I never cooked grinnel," my mother said, "but you clean 'em and I'll get the fire jounced up. They won't keep till morning."

My grandmother took up the biggest fish and bounced it on her hand.

"It'll weigh three pounds if it weighs a ounce," she said. "It looks good enough to whet anybody's appetite."

I went back with Monroe when he went to clean the fish. I watched him skin and gut, but I was thinking about muddying.

"A lot o' trouble to muddying?" I asked him.

"Not when the water's low. You just wade in and you c'n see the mud boiling up with every step. In no time a-tall you c'n see catfish whiskers come to the top. The little ones gape on top. The big ones stay under, but they get so sluggish you can lift them out with your hands. You've got to walk hunkered down so you c'n go in with your hands when you feel something with your legs."

It sounded easy and I knew that at the first chance I had to slip off I was going muddying. I knew a good slough close to Pine Creek. I could bring home as good a grinnel as anybody.

When the fish were washed and cut up, my mother took the pieces and rolled them in cornmeal. Then she put them in a skillet of hot lard. First there was the sound of frying, and then the smell of fish frying. My mother stood over the stove. The rest of us sat on the back porch listening to my grandmother tell how she and her oldest brother caught a big catfish in the Ouachita.

"Ain't nothing better'n fishing," she said. "'I've been laying off to go for a long time. It'd do me good to wet a hook."

They talked of deep holes farther down Pine Creek. They even talked of going down to the river—of getting enough people together to have a fish fry down at Pine Bluff ferry.

I got the first piece out of the skillet, a round piece with no bones but a backbone. With corn bread and buttermilk it was enough for supper. I begged and got another piece. Then I was sent to bed on a pallet in the hall, where I could smell fish frying and hear them talking and laughing.

Late at night they were still on the back porch, singing songs, talking in low voices, sometimes laughing at the words of a song. It was the kind of night I liked. There would be another one like it when I brought home my grinnel, not Sunday—no chance to slip off on Sunday—but maybe Monday, or some other day. I could go to sleep thinking about Monday.

It was Wednesday before the chance came. I took the stick my grandmother carried for mad dogs and, keeping out of sight in the line of trees along the branch, went at a trot toward Pine Creek. It was hot and still, and the air was full of the smell of wilting, drying leaves. My face was wet with sweat and then my clothes, and my skin stung rubbing in the wetness. I kept going, pushing deeper and deeper into the woods.

I came to the dry bed of Pine Creek and turned up it till I came to a narrow scum-covered slough. The water was low and there was a wide bare bank between it and the button willows hanging over it.

I stuck the stick up in the mud at the edge, hung my clothes on a button willow, and waded in. The bottom was ankle-deep in soft blue mud and rotting leaves. As I churned with my feet, blue mud boiled up through the yellow water and green scum, and the smell of fish and souring water rose in the still air.

I bogged my way down the slough once and back, muddying as I went. When I turned to go again I could see black catfish whiskers wiggling on the surface, and then the fish themselves, too many to count, the size of tadpoles and the blue black of the mud. Another time through and the big ones could be ready to catch.

In my hurry I forgot to keep my feet sliding in the mud. I stepped hard and felt the burning pain of a catfish fin sinking deep into the arch of my foot. I jerked my foot up and the fish came with it, a thick, wiggling mud cat, dangling on a fin. I grabbed him and pulled him loose. Then I threw him as far as I could into the woods. He was too little to keep.

The fin had left a hole that oozed blood and burned like a hornet sting. I slid along on one foot to the bank and sat down. The pain was enough to make me cry, but I was in the woods by myself. No one would hear me. There was nothing to do but wait for the pain to ease itself enough for me to walk.

I watched the water, the catfish whiskers on the water, till I saw a stirring that made me think a big fish was near the top. My foot felt feverish, but, when I stood up, I found I could bear my weight on my heel.

Slowly I slid my feet into the water and worked my way along, hunkered down with my hands in deep enough for my fingers to work the soft mud. If a fish was there I would get him.

I felt him first when he brushed my leg, a long fish moving sluggishly. It had to be a grinnel to be that long. He was moving toward the bank, with a gentle stirring of the water. I kept after him, with my legs apart, my hands grabbling for a feel of him. Where the water turned shallow I brought my hands together and grabbed him tight in the middle. Then I jumped clear of the water to the bank with him in my hands.

It was a big black water moccasin, twisting in my hands, his cottony mouth open close to my bare body, close enough for me to see the fangs and springlike tongue. I looked, landed, and threw him. He hit the ground and slid out of sight under the muddy water.

Shaking, crying now, with a feverishness in my foot and stomach, I got my clothes and, watching the ground before each step, I went away from the slough and out of the woods.

It was sundown when I crossed the pasture and went up past the smokehouse to the back porch. I was afraid to face them, and I knew better than to tell them what had happened to me.

But my mother had been watching me.

"I seen you limping," she said, "like you had a sore foot."

I kept my foot down to keep her from seeing the swelling around the hole.

"I stepped on a thorn," I said, "but it come out easy."

"I'm glad it's no more'n that," she said. "I thought you walked like you had a stone bruise."

They never knew any more. They did not know how feverish I was through the night. They did not know why I cried in my dreams.

42

The water was sweet, the well deep, but it was not ours. We could use it only till someone moved into the house and made the well his own. This was bound to happen, we knew, for anyone looking for a place to live would look for a good well.

People before us had dug wells on the Addison place and filled in the dry holes, after they had found not veins but seeps in the red clay. A water witch had come, they said, walking over the land with a forked peach tree limb in his hands. He had tried and tried, but the end of the limb never dipped. No use to dig again, they said, when a water witch could find no signs.

My brothers dug anyway—two wells—one in the backyard not far from the smokehouse door, the other down by the branch, on a sandy strip that was under water in the floods. For the first they set up a windlass they made with a pole, a rope, and a homemade crank. One worked in the hole, throwing out the dirt, a shovelful at a time, as long as he could reach the top of the ground. Then they tied a bucket to the windlass rope. One dug and filled the bucket; the other cranked it up and emptied it.

Hour after hour they worked, and they became the color of the clay they dug in. At night they dug till they could no longer see, and studied the last diggings for signs of moisture. In the morning they went out early to see if water had broken through. All of us went out with them, hoping for water, with me hoping hardest, for I was still the one who carried all the water. When they were down as far as they could dig enough water seeped in to sink a bucket, but it was the rust red of clay and gravel, and minerally to the taste. We knew then the water witch was right.

They filled up the hole and dug the second well. At twelve feet they struck a strong seep and decided to stop digging. The water was all right for the stock, but it tasted of mud, and soap in it left a whitish scum and no lather. I knew then that as long as we lived on the Addison place I would have to carry water.

One day the house at the well was empty; the next, someone had moved in, after I had carried the water for the day. They moved in and sent word that we would have to find another place to get water. We did not see them or ask them why, when the well never got lower even in the middle of the drouth. It was theirs to say, and we did not want to be owing to strangers.

The next morning my mother handed me two buckets.

"You'll have to try down at the Swindles," she said. "Tell them we'd be much obliged to them if we could get water at their well. Tell them we'll find a way to make it up to them."

The Swindle house was a mile from ours down the Pin Hook road. We had not visited them and they had not visited us, but we knew them. Their children went to school at Spring Hill, the five old enough to go to school, riding to and from in a one-horse buggy, with sometimes a ride for me if one of them was out sick. The three oldest—Jesse, Eva, and Oma—were reviewing to take the examinations for teaching certificates. Alma was in my class; Pat in the little room. Two more were at home—Lois and Dahlia. We saw Mr. and Mrs. Swindle passing on the road. When we worked in the fields we saw them working, with only a narrow strip of land between.

I did not like to ask the Swindles for water. I was used to the road to the other well. It was sandy and easy walking in any kind of weather. The other road went down a red clay hill, with clay that stuck like wax when it was wet and dried in clods and ridges sharp enough to cut. It crossed three branches that had to be waded in wet weather. It passed a Negro house—a shack half falling down—lived in by old Henrietta and her children and the other children "staying with her." They had a well and would laugh at a white boy carrying water.

I hated to go, but I had to—bareheaded, barefooted, swinging two buckets by the bails, saying to myself that I would bust a nigger in the head with a bucket if he laughed at me. I had to say something to keep myself going.

When I was crossing the first branch I saw two Negro girls come out of the woods, and turn up the road toward me. One of them was old Henrietta's Idabel, and they were both older and taller. They were pushing each other from one side of the road to the other and laughing at something funny.

I looked at the woods on either side. Better to stay on the road. Let them get off if any getting off was to be done.

I kept to the middle of the road and walked fast. They stared at me and laughed harder. They stopped pushing each other but they did not stop laughing. I would have to pass between them when we met.

"Get off the road, niggers," I yelled when I was close to them.

They stopped laughing and took to the ditches on either side, with Idabel closer to me—so close that I could see her eyes roll white and her fists clench.

"I ain't no nigger," she said, her voice low, sullen.

"Me neither," the other said.

They were close enough for me to bust either one with a bucket, but I did not. I wanted to run, but I had to hold my ground.

"Show me a nigger if you ain't," I said.

Idabel spoke flatly.

"The devil's a nigger."

We met and passed without coming any closer. I had the middle of the road. They had the ditches. I had scared them enough to make them give me the middle of the road.

"Niggers," I said again.

I heard and pretended not to hear when one said to the other:

"It makes me so mad—a white boy calling me nigger."

I walked straight ahead down the road and past old Henrietta's house. She was sitting in the door shelling dried butter beans.

"Good e'ening," she said.

I could have said "Good e'ening" but I did not. No need in speaking to an old nigger woman in a sunbonnet.

I did walk faster and soon came to the Swindle house. It was a fine white house set back from the road with trees and rosebushes in the front yard and a plank fence to keep out the cattle. The well was on one side at the front. I could see the rough oak curb and a galvanized bucket hanging from a galvanized chain. I could have filled my buckets and left without being seen, but I knew someone would hear the chain in the pulley.

Hating it, I went to the gate and stood close to it. The top plank level with my eyes, I stood on tiptoe and took a good long look at the clean-swept yard and the house—at the two front rooms, the hall between, and the porch across the front. It was a lot of house in front, and more behind.

"Hello," I called.

Mrs. Swindle came to the door of the fireplace room and looked out. She looked older than my mother, and taller, but not so fleshy. She had combed her hair, black with streaks of gray, away from her face and knotted it on top of her head. Her skin, sallow over her high cheek bones, darkened almost to blackness around her dark eyes.

"I know you," she said when she saw me looking over the gate. "You live up the road a piece. Open the gate and come on in."

She looked friendly and sounded friendly. I opened the gate and walked in, holding the buckets close to my legs.

"You want something in the buckets?" she asked.

"Yes'm. Water. We want to draw water from your well."

She came to the front steps.

"Draw all you want. It's never been dry yet."

I remembered what my mother had told me to say.

"We'll be much obliged and make it up to you somehow."

"No need'n making up for water when we've got so much." She came close enough for me to smell cooking on her clothes.

"You gave me a turn," she said, "standing there at the gate like that. You look so much like the little boy I lost. He died before we moved here from Alabama. I've passed you on the road and said how much you looked like him. He was just your size when he died. I cain't see anybody with blue eyes and curly hair without thinking about him.

I thought she was going to pat me on the head but she did not.

"I was making tea cakes," she said. "You go draw your water and I'll bring you a tea cake."

I said "Much obliged" and went to the well. The chain rattled when the bucket went down, the pulley squeaked when it came up. Thirsty from the long walk, I put my lips to the rim of the well bucket and drank. It was good water and cold, better than any I had ever tasted. I filled my buckets and went back toward the gate.

Mrs. Swindle was on the yard side of the gate with two pale-brown tea cakes in her hands. I set my buckets down, took them, and ate them both without stopping. When I looked at her again she was smiling.

"Much obliged," I said again and picked up my buckets.

"Come again. Maybe Pat'll be home next time and you can stay long enough to play."

She went back to the porch and I started up the road, glad that I had gone to the Swindle house for water. The road was long, the buckets heavy, but there would be times when I could stop long enough to play. There might be another time for tea cakes.

Old Henrietta was still sitting in her front door. She had pushed back her bonnet so that I could see her crinkly white hair and the frown on her black face.

"I knows what you said to the guhils," she said.

I kept on walking. I could not run without spilling water from the buckets.

"Stop," she said. "You stop and lissen to me. If'n you don't, I'll go right straight'n tell yo' mammy on you."

I stopped but I did not set the buckets down.

"You ought to be ashamed, saying what you said."

I could not believe what I was hearing. Ashamed of saying *nigger* to a nigger? I knew I was afraid but I was not ashamed. Everybody said *nigger* to a nigger.

"You ashamed o' yo'self?" she asked.

I shook my head.

"You ought to be, and you will be if'n I ever hear anything like that from you agin."

I started up the road and she did not stop me. When I was at the branches again, where nobody could hear me, I said *nigger* out loud.

"I'll say *nigger* when I want to," I said. "What do they think they are if they're not niggers?"

At the same time I knew I would never let old Henrietta hear me. I had to pass her house twice a day carrying water.

43

All year there had been talk of tearing down the old chimney and building a new one. Dirt had washed off the top, leaving oak timbers of the frame showing. In the dampness of spring the back of the fireplace caved in, and the hearth crumbled till building a fire was dangerous. It was not our house but we had to do the work or move out before winter. We did not want to move. It was good land and we had made a good crop. Nothing to do but take time out from the gathering and build a chimney.

"Better do it in dry time," my grandmother said. "The mud'll never harden if it's wet."

The old chimney was stick and dirt. The new one would have to be the same. The man who owned the land would not buy bricks, and we could not. Lucky for us, Uncle Charlie knew how to put a stick-and-dirt chimney together, and we could pay him back in work.

"It's got to be done," my mother said. "It won't be easy, living with a hole in the wall, but we've got to put up with it."

Monroe began tearing the old chimney down, sitting astraddle the roof pole at first, punching out chunks of clay, prying pieces out of the oak frame. The others of us worked on the ground, shoveling away the pile of dirt, stacking the old timbers on the woodpile.

When the work was done and there was nothing left but a

hole in the log wall, Uncle Charlie came with his hammer and square and a plumb line long enough to reach from the rooftop to the ground. He looked at the hole in the wall and in his slow, quiet way of saying things began talking of the jobs to be done: the lumber to be brought from the sawmill, the post-oak clay to be dug, the grass to be pulled.

"Brown sage is better," he said. "You c'n fill out with crabgrass if you have to, but brown sage holds better. You maybe c'n find enough if you follow along the fences."

He and Monroe went to the sawmill. The rest of us took our cotton sacks and hunted for bunches of dry brown sage on the fencerows and in ungrazed patches in the pasture. The bunches, knee-high and higher, were brown close to the ground and reddish brown at the top. The stems were hard to break and cut like wire when they slipped through our hands. We knew it was good for holding. We knew we would not use crabgrass in our chimney.

We saw the wagon go and come. We heard the sounds of saw and hammer. When we took in our first load of grass the four tall uprights were in place and Uncle Charlie was fitting in the frame that would be the back of the chimney.

"He is bodaciously slow," my grandmother said, where he could not hear her.

"Slow but careful," my mother said. "I never knowed nobody to take such patience."

When there was enough sage grass, the clay had to be dug. Uncle Charlie went with us to pick out the spot.

In the woods a good mile from our house he found a flat place where scrub post oaks grew, and nothing else. I had seen the place in spring, when it stood in water, and I had waded in it for the jellylike clumps of black frogs' eggs and the black tadpoles wiggling out of sight under rotting leaves. In summer the water dried up and the leaves blew away. Now it was grayish-white earth too hard to grow grass and weeds.

Uncle Charlie rubbed some of the dirt between his fingers.

"I never seen any better for making cats and bats," he said. "It'll dry hard as e'er a rock."

It was already hard as a rock, but it had to be dug up, the clods pounded out, and hauled to the house. It was slow work and we had to keep digging to get two loads a day.

Each trip back to the house we could see that the frame was getting higher. Uncle Charlie looked down on us, and my grandmother kept her grumbling to herself.

When the dirt was piled high and Uncle Charlie said we had enough, we dug a mixing vat in the hard-packed earth between the house and smokehouse. Then we hauled water from the creek and filled the tubs and washpots.

Uncle Charlie was the only one among us who had ever seen cats and bats made. He had us fill the vat with dirt and then add water. Then we waded in barefoot and mixed clay and water till we had something as heavy and sticky as biscuit dough and a dirty gray in color. Uncle Charlie showed us how to take up a wad of clay, mix sage grass through it, and shape it. Our feet and legs were muddy; so were our hands and arms, and then we were like mud people from head to toe. But we learned how to mix and shape the cats and bats so that they would hold together until Uncle Charlie worked them in and around the wooden frame.

Uncle Charlie had started the day in clean clothes and wide gray stetson hat. Before he got the first piece of clay he put his hat aside. Before he had shaped the hearth and jambs he was the color of post-oak mud, but he could not stop. If he let the mud dry, cracks would come at the places of joining. Working steadily, sometimes inside the chimney, sometimes out, he laid on layer after layer of cats and bats till he had covered the top of the frame. He was careful but he was not slow. The drying mud kept him moving.

The top finished, he had us mix a smooth paste of clay. Inside the house, he smoothed it and shaped it to hide all the rough places in the fireplace and hearth.

When he was all finished, before the clay began to harden, he took a nail and scratched in the strip under the mantel, "C. Kitchens." That was the only writing he knew how to make.

44

The chimney built, the cotton fields scrapped for the last bolls, Cleaver and I could start to school again, weeks after the opening, to pick up what we could. "Some schooling's better'n no schooling a-tall," my grandmother said. "I wisht I'd a had the chance you've got."

The first day was not easy. The Swindle children in their buggy passed before we got out on the road. We walked the long way alone and came up to a schoolhouse with all the doors shut. Books had taken up and we would be the last to go in.

Mr. Jessee saw us at the door and came to meet us. He took us to the back of the room, to the last two seats in the fifth grade row, and left us with nothing to do till he heard another fifth grade lesson. There was plenty for me to see. The fifth grade this year was the fourth grade of the year before. At the left of my desk bookshelves had been built in and there were books on the shelves, close enough for me to reach them without leaving my seat. On the wall over the blackboard there was a war poster with a German soldier's bloody boots walking on the bodies of the dead and dying.

We knew about the war, but not much. Without newspapers, we had to depend on what we heard from people passing on the road. I stared at the poster for a time and then began reading the poem Mr. Jessee gave me, "The Barefoot Boy."

Before the first recess of the first day we knew that Mr. Jessee had planned an all-day Thanksgiving Program with dinner on the ground. He had ordered a book with Thanksgiving songs and poems and given them out to the boys and girls. We were too late to

have a separate part, but we could sing with the whole room "The
Corn Song," to the tune of "Old Lang Syne."

The words were by John Greenleaf Whittier and I found them
in an Elson *Reader*. Cleaver wanted to be left out of the program. I
did not. When the time came for practicing singing, I was at the
front of the room with the others, singing as loud as I could:

> Heap high the framer's wintry hoard,
> Heap high the golden corn;
> No richer gift hath nature poured
> From out her bounteous horn.

And then:

> Let other lands exulting glean
> The melon from the vine,
> The orange from its glossy green,
> The apple from the pine.

It was a pretty song and I liked it—more after Mr. Jessee told
us about pineapples and where they grew. I was in the song but I
wanted to be in something else. When I asked Mr. Jessee, he shook
his head. There were no more parts. When I begged, he let me look
for any short poem about Thanksgiving. I looked through all the
books in school, but the poems I found had already been given
out.

On the way home I knew I had to find a part. We had ordered
new clothes from Sears, Roebuck, and my brothers met the mail
carrier every day. I would have new clothes and I wanted to stand
by myself in front of the crowd and be seen in them.

Cleaver went ahead. I lagged behind, trying to put words together to make my own Thanksgiving poem. I had memorized parts
of "The Barefoot Boy." I thought of things to be thankful for, like
corn in the field and the blackberries I picked in the woods along
the creeks. I tried blackberries first and soon gave up on them.
Whittier could say "purpled over hedge and stone." I had never
seen a hedge and the only stones around us were the pieces of gravel
in creek beds. It was even harder with things like "apples of Hesper-
ides." I wanted to do what he had done, but nothing would fit
together.

The bundle from Sears, Roebuck was there when I got home,
unopened, kept for the time after supper when, the work for the
day done, we could try on our new clothes together.

Before supper I told my mother about the Thanksgiving Program.

"We'll all go," she said. "I won't mind going, all of us in new clothes."

"I don't have a part," I told her.

"How come?"

I told her we had come too late and all the parts had been given out. I told her about looking for a poem, but not about trying to make one up.

"I'll make you one up," she said. "Give me till morning and I'll have you one made up."

The package was opened by the fireplace and the room was filled with the smell of new clothes—of cotton, wool, and leather. My mother took out the clothes piece by piece. My grandmother had to feel the stuff of each one.

"It feels good," she said. "How much did it cost?"

My mother would check the piece against the order and tell her.

"That sounds like a heap o' money," she would say.

My brothers and I were not worried about the money. We wanted to try on our clothes. We did, and I walked back and forth, feeling new leather soles slippery on the bare floor, feeling soft cotton and rough wool on my skin. My mother felt my shoulders and then my toes.

"Good fit," she said. "You look good enough to say a piece anywhere."

So did Cleaver, but he did not want to say a piece. He looked forward to dinner on the ground, but not to singing songs and saying speeches.

Once the clothes had been tried on, they had to be put back in boxes and sacks and put away for Thanksgiving.

The next morning my mother had a piece for me—a poem about how happy and thankful we should be on this Thanksgiving Day. It sounded like something out of a song book, but it would do. It would not get a laugh like the one with the words "I could eat a bear fried in spit with claws and hair" but it was a poem and it was about Thanksgiving.

Mr. Jessee wasted little time reading it.

"If you can learn it by heart, you can say it," he said.

In the few days left I learned it by heart, saying it at night in front of the fireplace, with my mother and grandmother telling me how to bow coming and going, how to stand, and how to sound out the words.

"I'll put you up against any of them," my grandmother said

the night before Thanksgiving. "You say it through once or twice after breakfast, you'll know it all right."

There was too much to do after breakfast. It was Thanksgiving Day and we were all going to the schoolhouse, dressed in our new clothes and taking dinner on the ground just like anyone else. The two trunks had to be emptied of clothes and packed with chicken and ham, cakes and pies, jelly and pickles, and some hard red candy still in the sack. The trunks had to be carried to the wagon. We had to get in ourselves.

My grandmother, in a black dress and black sateen bonnet and with a white wool shawl over her shoulders, sat on the springseat with my mother. My mother had on her blue worsted skirt and white waist, on which she had pinned the mother-of-pearl pin that had belonged to Missouri Ann. Monroe, looking older in suit and hat, sat on the dashboard and drove. The rest of us sat flat on a quilt in the wagon bed.

"You stay down," my grandmother told us. "We ain't wanting nobody to pitch head fo'most out'n the wagon today."

At the Novice Church we saw other wagons ahead of us.

"Looks like everybody and his brother's headed for the dinner on the ground," my brothers said.

The schoolhouse looked the same, but not the school ground. Wagons were lined up all around the edge, the teams unhitched but still in harness. A long table had been built in front of the door and was ready for the women to spread their tablecloths. Dr. Bishop's car was near the table. The children were being sent to the little room to wait for their turns for speeches. Men and women, older brothers and sisters, went through the front door to the big room where the program would be held.

When I got inside the little room it was time for the program to start. Mrs. Jessee had lined the boys and girls up around the room to wait their turns.

"Be quiet," she whispered. "Mr. Jessee's going to say a few words."

We could hear his voice but not what he was saying. When he stopped, she pushed the girl at the head of the line through the door. We could not hear her but we knew when she finished by the handclapping. She came back white and shaking—enough to make any of us dread going through that door. Mrs. Jessee pushed a boy through the door and the line moved up. Too late now to be scared.

I was in line behind Pat Swindle and having a hard time

remembering my poem because I could hear him whispering, "I could eat a bear fried in spit with claws and hair." The line kept moving up till he had been pushed through the door. I could hear him, but it did not sound like him. The voice was too high, too quavery to belong to him. The people began laughing before he finished. When he came through the door, as white and scared as any of the others, he left behind a room full of laughing, clapping people.

They stopped clapping when I went through the door, but they did not stop laughing. There was no stage, only a platform at the front of the room. I went to the middle of the platform and stood with my back to the blackboard.

"Thanksgiving Day," I said without waiting, and the sound was not my voice.

The laughing stopped. I had been told to keep my eyes on a spot on the wall near the ceiling. I could not. I could only stare at the smiling faces, looking for someone to help me. I had forgotten every word. Then Mr. Jessee, sitting at one side, started me off. With eyes half closed I went through to the end as fast as I could go, forgetting every sound, every movement of my hands that I had practiced, even the bow to mark the end. I just turned and stalked out.

I could hear the handclapping as I went. I could also hear a man near the door laughing and saying, "fried in spit with claws and hair."

"The Corn Song" was next. While I was still shaking, Mrs. Jessee put me in line with the others and marched us back in. I was on the front row but not alone. It was easier to follow along with the others:

> We better love the hardy gifts
> Our rugged vales bestow
> To cheer us when the winter drifts
> Our harvest fields with snow.

The song was like the piece I had said.

The program over, the people went outside for dinner on the ground. The men brought the trunks, tubs, and boxes of food. Women put on their best tablecloths and set out the food, more than I had ever seen at one time before. Then we had to wait for an older man to ask the blessing.

I had been told enough times what to do. First I had to take a helping at my mother's table. Then I was to go to each table there, ask for something for my plate, say "Much obliged" and something good about the cooking.

"Don't you dast slight nobody," my grandmother said.

I did not. I went to every table, but each time I came back to my mother, proud that she was there, glad that we were taking part just like everybody else. My mother was friendly to all the people who came to taste her food. My grandmother felt the goods in women's dresses.

"How much did you pay for it?" she asked.

There was time for visiting, time for the boys to run themselves breathless in a game of wolf over the river. Then it was time to pack up the grub left over and go home, rattling along in a wagon in a long line of wagons.

Christmas that year was a time of pies and cakes and fire-crackers, with something in the stocking for every one of us, of rest from work in the fields and woods. Amos Sutton, who was Monroe's age, came from Blossom on Christmas Day, walking alone down the road, carrying a bundle of clothes, enough to last for two or three days. He had many things to tell, sitting in front of the fire, the firelight touching red in the beard he was growing.

Days, he and my older brothers roamed the woods. Nights, they played dominoes and forty-two and he talked of the places he had seen bumming around looking for work. He had taken to smoking cigarettes and every time he made one we all stopped to watch. In his vest pocket he carried a sack of Bull Durham smoking tobacco with a round tag with a bull on it hanging out. He also had a thin packet of cigarette papers called LLFs—Loafer's Last Friend. He would hold a paper curved in his fingers of his left hand and fill it with tobacco. He had a way of holding the sack in his right hand so he could pull it open and shut with his teeth. When the bag was back in his pocket, with the bull showing so we would remember jokes about it and laugh, he would roll the cigarette and seal it by drawing his tongue along it. Then he would h'ist a leg and strike a match on his tight pants.

This was what I liked most to see. He would stretch his duckings leg till the blue was almost white. Then he would draw the match toward him, barely letting the head touch the cloth, and it would flame up a reddish yellow. He would hold the match still till the flame was clear yellow and then light his cigarette. He let me try it, but I did not get my duckings leg tight enough and the match stick broke.

My grandmother saw me and told me not to try it again.

"Boys that play with matches wet the bed," she said.

She had said this before, not only of matches but of coals of fire in the fireplace. So had my mother. I could build fire but not play with fire, and the matchbox was kept out of my reach.

I did not try it again then, but I watched him every time he did it and learned why I had failed. A longer leg was needed, or pants tighter than mine.

On a clear, cold day Amos walked back up the road. My older brothers already at work in the woods by the branch, I went with him a ways to keep him company. My grandmother had gone the same way on a visit to Aunt Niece, but earlier. When we had passed Parson Perry's land he stopped to roll a cigarette. The wind was high but he kept the tobacco in the paper and had to use only one match. Old Betty came out of her house and went poking along the fence for pieces of wood.

Amos went on up the road, letting out puffs of smoke that hung around his head for a moment and then disappeared in the wind. I kept up with him till it was time for me to turn back.

"C'n I try to strike a match?" I asked him.

He stopped and took a handful of wood matches from his pocket.

"Try all you like for all of me," he said.

I lifted my leg and brought a match up hard. The stem broke, the head fell to the ground, blue and white in the reddish sand.

Amos laughed.

"You've got to get more English on it," he said.

Afraid to ask him what he meant, I tried again and wore the white tip off a match without getting it to strike.

"I've got to get hoofing it," Amos said. He put the matches in my hand. "Here. Keep on trying. You'll get the hang of it."

I watched him out of sight and then went slowly down the road. The wind was colder, cold enough for me to feel the chill through my duckings and jumper, cold enough to blow away any warmth from a bright sun far to the south. I stopped and tried to strike a match on my leg. It broke. I struck the head end on my shoe sole and lit a pile of leaves in the road. Before it burned out, I had warmed my hands and feet. With little fires I could keep warm all the way home.

At first I was careful to light these fires in the middle of the sandy road, where sparks could not leap to the dead leaves and grass in the fencerows. Then I came close to Parson Perry's lane and Old Betty saw me.

"Don't you be striking no matches," she told me.

Without answering her or looking at her I went on down the road, past their lane and even with the Roberts meadow. It was a big meadow, running all the way from the road to the woods close to Pine Creek, with our place on one side, Parson Perry's on the other. Ungrazed, it stood waist-high in broom sage, a reddish-brown sea waving like ripe wheat.

That'd make some blaze, I thought.

I wanted to stick a match to it and let it go, but I was afraid to. At the same time, I could not keep from trying. I struck a match on my shoe and stuck it to a bunch of grass at the edge of the road. It burst into flame like powder. Scared, I stomped the fire out and started on down the road. But Old Betty had seen me and was running down the lane.

"You white young'un," she yelled, "you put out that fire. I'm gonna tell yo' mammy on you. You stop it right now."

She made me mad. I had never been ordered around or threatened by a Negro in all my life, and I was not about to now. I was white. No nigger was going to tell me what I could or could not do—and I dared a nigger to tell my mother on me. She was two hundred yards away from me and old and fat. It would be easy to show her. I pulled my duckings leg as tight as I could and rubbed a match back and forth against the cloth.

The match burst into flame, only to fly from my hand and light in the dry grass. Before I could catch my breath flames rose around

me high as my knees. I stomped at the blaze and felt the heat
through my shoes. Old Betty was coming closer, screaming.

"Stomp it out. Help. Stomp it out."

I was stomping as hard as I could. There was nothing between
the meadow and our place but a dry rail fence. The fire would go
right through our house and barn. I kept stomping till my feet were
hot and blistering, but the fire was spreading.

Old Betty turned back, running down their lane, yelling,
"Pahson! Help! Oh, Pahson!"

When I saw that the fire was spreading faster than I could
stomp it, I started to cry. Then I started to run as hard as I could, to
the house to get help.

Before I got there, the fire had crossed the fence into the
meadow and gray-white smoke was beginning to roll. Help had to
come fast.

My mother was in the kitchen when I got to the back door. She
saw me and ran toward me.

"What's the matter?" she asked.

"The meadow's on fire," I said, and my throat burned. "Old
Betty set the meadow on fire."

My mother ran to the front door and then out to the backyard.
By then the flames were running across the grass as fast as a horse
could run, red flames running and leaping, leaving blackened stubble and smoking patches. The wind was right to bring it straight to
our house and barn. Her face went white and her eyes were afraid.

"Go get Monroe," she cried. "Down by the branch. I'll wet the
sacks we've got and find what I can to beat the fire with."

I went past the smokehouse and down through the pasture,
through grass well grazed but still ankle-high. No way of stopping
fire in it. Before I got across the pasture my brothers came out of the
woods at a run. They had seen the smoke. Now they could see the
flames.

Without a word to me they went past the house and to the
barn. When I got there, Monroe had hitched the pony to a turning
plow to plow a firebreak between us and the meadow. My other
brothers pulled down a piece of rail fence to let him through. My
mother came running with sacks and hoes.

With a grim look on his face Monroe set the plow in the sod
and clucked to the pony. She stepped to one side and the other, but
would not go ahead. When he slapped her with the reins, she still
would not go. My mother broke a limb from a tree and thrashed her
on the flanks. She only turned back and tangled herself in the

traces, and galloped toward the barn, dragging them both, when they unhooked her. They put her back in the lot and fastened the gate.

"We've got to set a backfire," Monroe said. "Keep it out'n the fence if you can. If you don't—"

With a bunch of burning sedge he ran down the meadow side of the fence setting a strip of flame that widened fast behind him. We followed him, beating out the flames on our side of the line with sacks and hoes. The wind was rising and flames leaped as high as treetops and broke into pieces that floated a moment and then disappeared. Gray smoke rose above them and drifted in heavy clouds across the meadow and woods. Our backfire, moving fast, looked slow against the speed of the coming flames.

They tried to save all of the rail fence, but they could not. Before they could get half the length with the backfire, the other fire swept across it and dry rails, dry grass burned in flames that wrapped around the tops of sweet gums in the fencerow.

The only thing left was to tear the fence apart and pull the rails back to make a wide gap. The fire crossed to our own pasture, and we had to fight to keep it from cutting back to the house and barn. It was easier to fight in the short grass, easier to turn the fire back to the high grass of the meadow.

We were out of breath and our hands and faces were burning from the heat, but we could not stop. Where the meadow grew into the edge of the woods the grass and weeds were higher than a man on horseback. When the fire reached that, sparks would rise and drift, nobody knew how far.

By late afternoon we could breathe easier. Our house and barn had been saved, and we had not lost enough winter pasture to hurt. The fire roared on through the grass and weeds of the meadow, and burned itself out in the damp leaves and mold of the woods.

While we were putting out the spots that started here and there, my grandmother came running across the pasture with her skirts flying in the wind. She had seen the smoke from Aunt Niece's and was sure our house and barn had burned. When she saw that we were safe, she began crying and catching her breath. Her legs gave out and she sank down on a pile of rails.

"How'd it catch?" she asked.

My mother looked at me and then back to her.

"Old Betty must a set it. She was seen out by the road, plain as day."

Afraid they might ask me more, I ran down through the lower

pasture, where my brothers were still fighting the fire that blazed and crackled in short grass and leaves. They beat at it slowly, wearily, knowing they could put it out but too tired to be in a hurry. They looked at me, but not one asked me how it started.

At sundown, when the last spark had been beat out, we went slowly up to the house. The meadow was a black patch of earth from which a dying wind swept soot and ashes. The trees on it were bare and black, swept clear of leaves and small branches. It would be that way till spring.

When we got to the house my mother and grandmother were waiting for us in the yard.

"I'm gonna give Old Betty a piece o' my mind," my grandmother said.

My mother looked at me.

"I'm going with her. You're coming, too."

Without another word we went up the road and down Parson Perry's lane. Now I'll catch it, I thought. Old Betty'll tell on me and I'll catch it. I could see the switch; I could hear them telling me to take down my duckings and stand up straight.

Old Parson and Old Betty must have seen us coming. They were standing on the porch side by side when we came up to the gate.

"Good e'enin'," Old Parson said.

My mother said, "Good e'ein'," but the rest of us kept silent. He did not tell us to come in. He knew my mother and grandmother would never darken his door. The gate latch was handy, but they did not lift it.

My grandmother raised her hand toward Old Betty.

"You got little enough to do," she said, "going around setting fires."

Old Betty shook her head angrily.

"I didn't do it," she said. She pointed a finger at me. "Ask him who done it. He'll tell you I didn't do it, if he'll tell the truth. Just ask him."

I felt my mother's hand on my shoulder and heard her whisper for me to keep quiet.

"I asked him and he said you—"

"He said me?"

"You heard me."

"You believing him? You believing him when I seen him with my own eyes striking matches on the road? You putting his word before mine?"

"Yes."

Old Parson spoke up.

"I'd never a thought it."

"I'd never a thought lots o' things," my grandmother said. "You have to see to know. Come on," she said to my mother, "I've said all I need to say, when I say I don't ever want to see it happening agin."

We went out the lane and down the road. I thought they would say something to me, but they did not. Neither did I. I knew that my word was better than a nigger's any day, but I did not feel very good about it.

My grandmother looked across the black meadow.

"Nothing lost but some winter grazing," she said.

I trailed behind them and went to the barn, where my brothers were shucking corn and talking about the fire. It was too dark for me to see their faces. They did not ask me any questions. They did not say anything about it to me then, or ever.

46

One day in early spring, when I had been kept home from school to work, I watched a truck come down the road and stop in front of our house. A man got out and came toward our gate, walking slowly, looking at the house, the barn, giving the whole place a good once-over. He was a large man, dressed in a good gray suit and a white stetson hat.

By the time he got to the gate I was there to open it for him.

"You all got a piano?" he asked.

"No, sir. We got a organ—"

"I'd like to speak to the lady of the house. I want her to see the piano I've got there on the back of the truck."

There was something on the back of the truck, boxlike, covered with a wagon sheet, the shape of a piano, though I had not seen one since I left the Blossom school.

He went to the front door. I went to the back, to give my mother and grandmother time to get ready before they went to the door to meet him.

"Tell him we ain't got time to talk," my grandmother said.

My mother shook her head.

"Won't hurt none to talk to him."

She took off her apron and wiped her face and hands on a towel. Then she went to the front door. My grandmother followed her, close enough to see and be heard, but not be seen.

The man took off his hat and bowed.

"It's a pleasure to see you, ma'am."

My mother got red in the face.

"It is my understanding that you don't have a piano in your home."

My mother got redder, at this one other thing she did not have. The man waved to the driver to bring the truck up to the porch.

"I have a fine piano to show you," the man said. "You won't know how fine it is till you see it. My man'll back right up so's you can see."

The driver backed the truck up so close that I could walk from the porch to the truck floor. The man pulled back the wagon sheet and showed the shiny wood of the top.

"Mahogany," he said. "I'll bound you never saw anything prettier in your life."

"No," my mother said.

"The tone's even prettier."

He held the wagon sheet and lid up with his right hand and played some chords with his left. My grandmother came out on the porch and we all three stood looking at him. From the look on my grandmother's face I knew she was ready to send him packing.

"You ever hear a better tone?"

We had not.

"You cain't tell till you hear all of it," he said. "If you'll let me set it on the porch—"

"Will it cost anything?"

The man laughed.

"To try it? Of course not."

It was time for my grandmother to speak up. She did—not to the man but to my mother—in a voice meant for the man as much as for her.

"You've got about as much use for a pyanner as a hog has for a sidesaddle."

Without showing that he had heard her, the man took the wagon sheet off and we could see all of the piano.

"It won't cost a thing to try it," he said. "We could try it right here, but it needs walls around it to sound its best."

He was going to swing an end of the piano toward the porch but my mother would not let him.

"I cain't say nothing till I talk to the boys."

She started me to the field to call them but they were already on the way to the house to see why a truck had been brought inside.

They came through the hall and stood looking at the piano.

"Here, give us a lift," the man said.

Without asking anyone why, they went to help. The piano was heavy and it was all they could do to lift it over the gap from the truck to the porch.

"Which room would you put it in?" the man asked my mother.

"The north room."

They rolled it through the hall, lifted it over the doorsill, and turned it so the light from the door made a mirror of the mahogany and glowed on the white keys. The driver brought the stool from the truck and set it in front of the piano.

The man sat down at the piano and let his fingers run up and down the keyboard with the speed of lightning. The sound was enough to make shivers in the backbone and draw us close around the piano. He let his right forefinger glide up the keyboard and then popped it at me with a sound in his throat. The others laughed at me but I would not move back.

He closed his eyes, set his body to swaying slowly, and began playing something I knew I had heard before. Soon I knew it was "Over the Waves," a waltz that Uncle Charlie played on the fiddle. Uncle Charlie knew only one part. The man played this part with his hands all over the keys. He played the other parts, all of it by heart, his hands light at times, at times heavy on chords that made the walls rattle. He stopped and bowed his head over the keys.

"That's the prettiest music I ever heard," my mother said. "I'd give anything to be able to play like that."

Without looking up, the man started another piece. With his

left hand he began runs on the bass notes, soft at first and then with the roll of thunder.

"That's 'The Storm,' " the driver said from the hall. "He might nigh always play 'The Storm.' "

The thunder rolled louder and louder till it crashed on our ears and echoed from the woods—enough like a storm to make us think of dark clouds and the flash of lightning.

"Man, cain't he make it talk," the driver said.

The storm came close, reached its peak, and began moving away. Then we heard a tune like the crying of a lost child or a hurt animal above the low rolling thunder. It was enough to make my throat hurt and tears come to my eyes. I looked at my mother and brothers. Their faces looked the way I felt.

Then there was no more of storm and thunder—only a soft happy tune of clearing skies.

"That's the shepherd," the driver said. "Hear the shepherd."

We heard but we did not want to talk about it. We only wanted to listen till it was all over and his hands stopped, and be sorry they had to stop.

"You play good," my mother said. "Do you ever sing?"

"Sometimes, but not so good."

"Could you sing something?"

"Have you heard 'Ehren on the Rhine?' "

When my mother shook her head he began singing a sad song about war—a love song about a boy and girl separated by the war. He played low, full chords, and his voice was full and low, and sad as he told of a dying soldier's last words:

> Oh, say to my love, be true,
> Be only, only mine,
> My life is o'er, we'll meet no more
> At Ehren on the Rhine.

My grandmother came in from the hall.

"You have a good singing voice," she said. "Can you sing 'The Ship That Never Returned?' "

He let his fingers pick up a tune.

"That's it," my grandmother said. "I'd know it anywhere."

She took a chair over by the piano so she could watch his face while he sang.

> It never returned, no, it never returned—
> The ship that never returned—

When he had finished, the man went over and raised the lid to

our organ. He set some stops and tried the pedals. Without a word
he sat down and began playing "Over the Waves." He could make
the organ sound good, but nothing like the piano. The piano was
light, the organ reedy. He stopped and looked at my mother.

"Do you play?"

She would have said no, but my grandmother did not let her.

"She plays good," my grandmother said. "I never heard nobody
play better for singing."

"What kind of pieces do you play?"

"Songs from the songbook."

"Try something."

"I don't know. I never tried a piano."

"It ain't too different from the organ."

My grandmother brought the songbook from the organ. My
mother turned through it till she found "When the Roll Is Called
Up Yonder I'll Be There." She sat on the piano stool and put both
feet on pedals. She pressed the keys lightly and pumped up and
down on the pedals. The sounds she made were soft and beautiful,
and the man hummed the chorus with her. I never wanted to see
the piano taken away again.

My mother played the song through once, and then again.
Then the man asked Monroe to try.

Monroe had learned enough chords to second Uncle Charlie on
the fiddle. He did not have a tune to play, but he could play the C
and G chords, with one note in the left hand, three in the right.

"You could learn to play good," the man said.

Not on the organ, we knew, from the way he said it. It had to
be on the piano. He looked around at us and knew we wanted the
piano. Even my grandmother had stopped talking against it. Then
he said something that left my mother and grandmother without an
argument.

"It's a good thing to keep a family together with, at home."

"How much does it cost?" my mother asked.

"Only three hundred and seventy dollars, and the stool thrown
in. That's a low price for a fine piano."

"I ain't arguing that," my mother said. "I just don't see how we
could ever pay for it."

"I'll take part in trade." We went to the hall and looked
toward the barn. "I'll take a cow or a hog, or anything you could let
me have on it, and the organ can be the down payment. You
wouldn't owe me nothing again till cotton picking time. Let's just
set down and do some figuring."

While they were figuring, I went to the piano and touched a note. It sounded loud, but they did not stop me. Then I picked out a tune I had learned on the organ. When no one stopped me, I played it again and sang the words:

> Papa had a billy goat,
> He was old enough to butt;
> He chased me up an apple tree
> And this is what he said to me:
> "I like coffee,
> I like tea,
> I like the girls
> And they like me."

When I came out again the trade was done and the piano was ours. The man and his driver shook hands with all of us. Then my brothers helped them load the organ on the truck and brought the black heifer from the lot. They pulled and pushed her up the front steps and into the truck. Then, while they held the gate open, the driver turned around and the truck was gone, with the heifer bawling.

When I got back to the house they were all in the north room, around the piano, taking turns at trying it out. Monroe was playing chords. My mother had the songbook open to another song. It would be a long time before I got my hands on it again, but I had to do something.

I ran down the front steps, between the house and barn, and climbed the rail fence into the meadow. A fine coat of green grass covered the blackness left by the fire, soft to my feet, easy to run on. Before I knew it I was trying to see how far the piano could be heard. Monroe was still playing C chord, with a steady beat, and I was running to it—farther and farther till I could hear only a soft, low thumping.

Then I saw Parson Perry coming across the meadow toward me at a half-trot. He was bareheaded, and there was a curious look on his wrinkled face.

"Your mummer got a new gittar?" he asked.

I laughed because he did not know better.

"No. We got a new piano."

He stopped and cupped his ear toward our house.

"You ever seen one?"

"No, I ain't."

"You ain't seen nothing till you do. It's ten times louder'n a gittar."

"I hadn't heard your mummer was thinking about no piano."

"She wasn't. A man come by with it on a truck and she bought it."

The sound changed. I turned and ran back across the meadow, the sound getting louder with each step I took. My time would come, and I did not want to miss a minute of it. I had forgot to try to make the sound of thunder.

47

Revival time came at the Novice Church in late August—still in the heat and drouth of dog days. Word of the meeting was passed up and down the road: Old Brother Cummings would do the preaching, and only at night. It was too hot and dusty for people to come out in the middle of the day, and the men could not take enough time off from work to build a brush arbor. Benches from the church could be brought out and left out. The organ could be carried out and back every night.

Brother Cummings would "stay around" and the ones who wanted him for a meal or the night could send word to one of the deacons. Brother Cummings would tell the people when they could expect him.

We did not have room for him to stay all night, but my mother sent word that she would be glad to cook supper for him any night he wanted to come.

"He won't come," my brothers said. "He'll know it'll be slim pickings. He'll know to set his feet under a stronger table. He knows who'll be able to put the big pot in the little 'un for him."

My mother sent word anyway. She had two boys big enough to be grown and not yet converted. It would be a chance for Brother Cummings to convert them. They knew how to do right, but that was not enough. They had to confess their sins in public. Then they had to be baptized. She could talk to them, but not the way Brother Cummings could.

The meeting opened on Sunday night and we did not go, only because there had been so much work that nothing was ready.

"I sure hate not to go," my mother said, "but I'd hate it worse, going looking the way we do."

Then on Monday morning word came from Brother Cummings: He would eat supper with us that night. We could expect him before sundown and he would go with us back to the church.

My mother had meant to wash that day and starch and iron the white waists and shirts, getting ready for going to meeting. There was no time for washing. The floors had to be scoured with homemade soap and a corn-shuck brush. The chickens had to be killed, cleaned, and fried, the black-eyed peas picked and snapped, and boiled all day, a cake baked.

"Corn's hard enough for grit bread," my mother said. "I'll bound Brother Cummings won't have grit bread unless'n we make it for him."

Monroe made the gritter. He took half a molasses bucket and drove it full of nail holes. Then he nailed it to a board with the rough side out, with enough space between for me to put my doubled fists.

Making meal was a job I could do. I went to the corn patch and up and down the rows looking for ears with the outer shucks beginning to dry. When I found one that looked right, I pulled back the shuck and tested a grain with my thumbnail. If it had milk, it was not ready. If my thumbnail cut in and no milk showed, it was ready. Grains too soft or too hard would not grit.

I took the corn and gritter to the back porch. It was hard work, pushing the ears back and forth over the rough tin, and slow. When my arm got tired I let my fingers rest in the soft meal. When I got hungry I held raw meal in my mouth till it turned from the taste of corn to the sweet of sugar. When there was enough, I watched my mother mix it with buttermilk and put it in the oven to bake. Then she sent me to the gate to watch for Brother Cummings.

When the sun was still a hand high I saw him coming down the road, kicking up a little cloud of dust as he walked, his long black coat open down the front, his broad black hat in his hand, his white hair and whiskers hiding all but the upper part of his face. I ran back to the porch.

"He's coming," I yelled.

That would give my mother and grandmother time to put on their shoes and clean dresses.

"He's might nigh about to the gate."

Then I ran back to the gate and opened it for him.

"That's a good boy," he said when he passed through.

I had never seen a man like him. He was hot and tired, and reddish dust had settled on the sweaty patches on his coat. I could not see his mouth, but I could see his eyes. They were dark under white eyebrows and white forehead. When they looked at you, you had to listen.

My mother and grandmother met him at the front steps and set a chair for him in the hall, where he would feel the first breeze stirring. My mother brought him a dipper of water.

"I don't want to put you to no trouble," he said.

"It ain't no trouble, having the preacher come."

"I'd a told you last night, but I didn't see you at meeting. I said to myself, 'I'm bound to go see them first.' It wouldn't be right, missing a chance to say prayers with widows and orphans."

Monroe and Dewey came around from the back porch, where they had been washing up. Brother Cummings shook hands with them.

"You been saved?" he asked them.

They shook their heads. He looked at my mother.

"It's time, Sister," he said. "Time to let up on work for a week and look to their souls. Nothing like now to begin talking it over."

My mother was ready for this.

"We could go inside," she said.

We took our chairs and went from the bright light of the hall to the dusk of the windowless room. Brother Cummings sat near the door. My mother took the sheet off the piano, turned the stool down a turn, and sat with her back to the keyboard.

"I always like to start a service with a song," Brother Cummings said.

My mother turned her back to us, getting ready to play, but he did not wait. He leaned forward, with his arms outstretched, his face raised toward the rafters, and began in a voice worn from preaching and singing, in a voice that started off sounding old and tired and then louder, stronger.

> I will arise and go to Jesus,
> He will embrace me in His arms;
> In the arms of my dear Savior,
> Oh, there are ten thousand charms.

While the sound of the last word, soft and sad, still hung in the heavy hot air, he sank to his knees, saying, "Let us pray."

He prayed for widows and orphans, a prayer made up for us, not naming our names but telling who we were in such a way that we knew when he went from one to the other. It was a long prayer, long enough for the grain of the rough floor to leave stripes on my knees. Then it was over and he was asking my mother to sing and play a song.

She played the Do chord and then started the words of the first verse of "When the Roll Is Called Up Yonder I'll Be There." We sang with her, but Brother Cummings did not. He sat with his head bowed, his beard covering his breast.

At the end of the song he handed my mother his Bible, for he could not read or write.

"Read us a Scripture, Sister," he said. "Something from the Psa'ms. I've always been partial to the Psa'ms."

She went to the door and held the Bible up in the light. She turned a few pages and began reading in her high clear voice, "O, Lord our Lord, how excellent is Thy name in all the earth. . . . Out of the mouths of babes and sucklings hast Thou ordained strength. . . ."

I followed the words in her voice and on his lips. He knew them by heart and said them with her under his breath.

The Psalm ended, he asked for another song. My mother handed him the Bible and went back to the piano.

"You got a favorite song?" she asked.

"I'd be partial to anything you wanted to sing."

She played some chords—chords that belonged to a song she liked. Then, looking up, where dark was gathering in the rafters, she sang, and we sang with her.

> Life is like a mountain railway
> With an engineer that's brave;
> You must make the run successful
> From the cradle to the grave.
> Watch the turns, the grades, the tunnels,
> Never falter, never fail—
> Keep your hand upon the throttle
> And your eye upon the rail.

"It's true, Sister, so true," Brother Cummings said when the song was over. "It has been a blessing to be with you. Let us pray."

After the prayer we took our chairs to the kitchen. I had to wait for the second table, sitting on the edge of the back porch, where I could not see but I could hear.

I could hear Brother Cummings returning thanks. Then I heard my mother and grandmother passing things to him, the chicken, the black-eyed peas, and then the grit bread.

"Soft bread," I heard him say and knew he was glad to see it. "It's been a long time since I've seen soft bread. I recollect when I was a boy making meal for soft bread."

It was after sundown when Monroe hitched the ponies to the wagon and drove up to the front steps. He and Dewey were taking Brother Cummings to meeting. It was too late for the rest of us to get ready for that night.

Brother Cummings shook hands with all of us and then climbed up to the springseat. He put on his hat and, once the wagon had turned, we could no longer see his face.

We stood on the front porch till the wagon was out of sight.

"He's one good man," my mother said.

My grandmother sighed.

"I reckon you won't find one better."

He was gone, but there was still work to do. My job was to fill the water bucket.

"Take one bucket," my mother said. "If you'll gallop a little you c'n make it while it's still light."

I took one bucket but I did not hurry. Better not to hurry, dark or no dark. Better to think about Brother Cummings and all the things he knew. Better to walk slowly saying out loud, "O, Lord our Lord, how excellent is Thy name in all the earth. . . ."

By the next night it looked like a baptizing all right. When Brother Cummings gave the call for sinners to come to the mourner's bench, grown men and women went and knelt close together, praying out loud, not to be converted but to be brought back into the fold. They were the ones who had strayed, the backsliders, brought back now by fear and the song the people were singing:

> Come home, come home,
> Ye who are weary come home.
> Softly and tenderly Jesus is calling,
> Calling, "Oh, sinner, come home."

It was a night of tears and prayers, of clapping hands and shouting when a sinner on his knees before Brother Cummings said he was ready to turn his back on the past and look to a new Promised Land.

It did not end for us when we left the church. Our wagon was like another meeting place with songs and prayers and talk of the

need to be converted and then baptized. Converting had to come
first—with a public confession. Without it, baptism was a blas-
phemy, a sin that could not be pardoned.

The next night, when the call to the mourner's bench came,
Dewey got up and went, leaving a bench full of boys behind him,
going to the bench where the deacons waited to put their arms
around him and talk to him. He was tall and awkward and shy, and
they did not have to work on him long till he was ready to ask for
the right hand of fellowship. When he did, on his knees before
Brother Cummings, my mother clapped her hands and cried. One
of her sons was ready for the baptism.

Then they worked harder on Monroe, the deacons going back
to the bench where he sat to talk with him and pray with him. He
listened to them, staring straight ahead, not showing how he felt,
only holding back when they tried to start him toward the mourner's bench. Night after night they tried, but they never got him to
go.

At the same time they were working on a man who lived up the
road from us, a cocky little man who always had a joke and a laugh.
At every revival meeting for years the preachers and deacons had
worked on him, but he held back, "hardhearted, stiff-necked,"
Brother Cummings said in a prayer made only for him, "without a
hope of seeing the Redeemer face to face." Then one night he went
to the mourner's bench, and the preacher, the deacons, the sisters,
and brethren went with him, to kneel over him, to cry and pray
over him, and fan him with palm-leaf fans, and to sing over him in
tear-wet voices, "Come home, come home, Ye who are weary come
home." And then, "Almost persuaded now to believe; Almost persuaded Christ to receive." When they were tired and hoarse and wet
with sweat he came through, still kneeling, with his hands up, reaching for Brother Cummings' hands. The singing and praying stopped.
People leaned against each other and wept that the long hard fight
was over, that one they had counted for lost would be washed clean.

The baptizing was after dinner on Sunday in a pool in a cow
pasture, a hole of yellow water with cow tracks in the mud at the
edge. The people had to leave their wagons at the road, crawl
through a barbed-wire fence, and walk across dried grass to the
pool. The men to be baptized wore white shirts and dark pants.
The women wore loose white dresses with skirts down to their
ankles. To keep their skirts from floating up in the water, they had
tied them down below the knees so the steps they took were short,
hobbled.

They gathered at the side of the pool for songs, prayers, and a sermon. Then it was time for the baptizing. The people were singing.

> Oh, think of the home over there
> Beyond the portals of light
> Where the saints all immortal and fair
> Are robed in their garments of white.

Brother Cummings, in his dull black suit and white shirt, took off his shoes at the edge of the water and waded in till his gray beard was just touching. Two of the deacons came to the edge of the water and waited.

From the women's side two sisters came with a girl between them leaning heavily on their arms. The singing went on.

> Over there, over there,
> Oh, think of the home over there. . . .

They took her to the deacons, who took firm grips on her arms and moved her slowly out to the preacher. She stopped, clasped her hands on her breast, and looked up to the hot blue sky. He gripped her hands with his left hand and put his right behind her neck.

> Over there, over there, over there,
> Oh, think of the home over there. . . .

Still gripping her with his left hand, Brother Cummings lifted his right and said in a loud voice:

"I baptize you in the name of the Father, the Son, and the Holy Ghost."

With his right hand behind her neck he lowered her out of sight in the water and raised her again. With water and tears running down her face, she came out of the pool and, met by the women, wrapped in a quilt, went behind the singers, who had again come to "Oh, think of the home over there."

One by one the women were led down, some of them hard to hold in their happiness, some of them shaking, scared at going into deep water. They were led out again and, in a group across the pasture and road to the church, to put on dry clothes, powder their faces, and comb their hair.

The men came next, wading in slowly, quietly, without help from the deacons, and stood in line, with bowed heads waiting to step up to Brother Cummings, to hear the words, to feel the water cover them. The greatest convert of them all was in the line but he did not bow his head. He stood stiff-necked as ever—maybe as hard-hearted. Baptizing would be easier, everyone knew, if he would be a little limp-legged.

His time came and he stepped forward with his clasped hands pulled tight against his chest and his head up. Brother Cummings gripped his hands and said the words to end the fight hard won: "I baptize you in the name of the Father, the Son, and the Holy Ghost." Then he tried to push his head down, but the man pushed back. Brother Cummings took a new grip and got him under water up to his chin. A tin snuffbox popped out of his shirt pocket and floated on the water. With a look of sadness for this proof of sin, Brother Cummings grabbed the box and flung it out to the dry grass. Some of the people laughed, some looked on in anger, a few sighed. They knew it would not be easy for him to give up his sinful ways. Brother Cummings got another grip and pushed harder. He twisted and turned, but went down, not out of sight but far enough for Brother Cummings to say a loud "Amen."

The baptism was soon over, but not the talk about it. Some said he would have to be put down deeper than that to wash away his sins. Some said only the devil himself could have kept him from going under, Brother Cummings pushing as hard as he was. There were other questions: Had he been baptized? Could he go to heaven no more baptized than that? Would he be kept from sinning next time crapshooting came around?

On our way home in the wagon Dewey had nothing to say about the baptizing, but my mother spoke to the rest of us:

"I won't be happy till I see the last one of you come up out of that watery grave."

48

Peanut digging came while the days were still dry and hot. It had to be over before frost blackened the tops and spoiled the soft peanuts underground. We knew the thrasher was coming down the road our way. Then word came that the thrasher would be in our field and we had to be ready. We had to stop picking cotton, with only part of a bale picked. We had to stop stripping the sorghum and leave rows of leafless canes waiting to be cut and hauled to the molasses mill. The peanuts had to come first—not the peanuts but the thrasher.

At the blacksmith shop Monroe got a steel blade made that could be bolted to the feet of the cultivator. Up and down the rows he went, the blade slicing under the rows, loosening the dirt and cutting the taproots of the peanut vines. We followed after him, each one making his own cloud of dust, shaking dirt off the vines and piling them in windows. They dried fast in the hot sun, and we hauled them in the wagon to a place easy for the thrasher to get to. It was hot, dusty work. After an hour of dust and sweat we were the color of dirt from head to foot.

There was not time to stop. In the mornings we were in the field while the stars were still shining, in the time before daylight when shooting stars raced and burned across the sky. We ate in the field in the middle of the day, in the shade of the wagon. At night we worked till it was so dark we had to feel for the vines.

The thrasher came—two wagons, one with the thrasher, the other with a gasoline engine—and we were ready. The man and his boy set it up in the field by the stack of peanuts. There was work for all of us to do. The vines had to be lifted on pitchforks and piled in the hopper. The peanuts came out of one spout, the leaves and stems out of another. The peanuts had to be sacked, the thrashed-out vines loaded on the wagon for hay. Once the engine was going, with a clap, clap, clap that echoed from the woods, we had to keep up with it no matter how much the dust burned our eyes and clogged our noses.

The crop was good, better than we had thought it could be. We had bought sacks, but not enough. Something would have to be done with the overflow. At night, working by lantern light, we built a wall higher than my head on either side of the hall. Nothing to do but live with the peanuts till we could get more sacks or get rid of them.

The thrasher went on, hour after hour, and the pile of peanuts in the hall got higher and higher. When we slept, we slept with the smell of drying peanuts around us. What we ate tasted of peanuts and dust.

When the peanuts had started spilling over the wall the thrashing was over and the wagons moved on down the road, leaving us with time enough to wash up, rest up, and talk about what we would do with the money when we sold the peanuts.

There was talk of taking a load of peanuts to Paris to sell at the market square. From the time I heard it, I knew I had to go. My older brothers had all been to Paris. It had to be my turn next. When I asked my mother she only said for me to work hard and she would see.

One day when I came back from the well I found Monroe and Dewey scooping peanuts into the wagon bed. Dewey would be on the way to Paris before daylight.

"Who's going with him?" I asked.

My grandmother came to the front door.

"I been laying off to go," she said.

"Cain't I go, too?" I asked.

"You're too little to be any help to him. I reckon the wagon's got enough weight without you."

When I asked my mother, she sent me to feed and water the hogs. I shucked corn and carried water. When I came in again I brought a load of wood for the kitchen stove. She said nothing about going to Paris.

All through supper there was talk of what Dewey was to do and how he was to do it. The wagon would have to be driven up on the scales. He would have to watch the weights. People had been

cheated not watching the weights. He had to do his own multiply-
ing to see that they paid him the right money.

After supper we sat on the end of the porch in bright moonlight and listened to my grandmother talk of the places she had
been: Purcell, Dallas. It was nothing to go to Paris after those
places. It would be hard for a shirttail boy to get lost in Paris.

My mother went to the kitchen and began ironing one of my
white waists.

"What for?" I asked.

"To wear to Paris. I won't have you going dirty to Paris."

She said it without a show of feeling. I took it the same way,
but I knew how I felt inside.

"When we going?"

"Before daylight."

"Anything you want me to do?"

"You better get corn for the horses. Nobody thought about
corn for the horses."

I went out the kitchen door and passed the others on the porch
without a word. They knew I was going to Paris. They all knew
before I did. In the dark corncrib I shucked sixteen good ears of
corn and put them in a tow sack. I put the sack in the wagon, ready
to be taken out when we went to the wagonyard. I had never seen a
wagonyard but I knew what it would be like with wagons and
teams and people—some of the people staying all night, sleeping
in their wagons.

Not ready to go back to the house, I cut across a patch of woods
and came out into the bright moonlight and the plowed ground of
the peanut field. The ground was soft and cool under my feet. The
moon was high in the sky and bright enough to read by, if there
had been anything to read. Without thinking what I was doing, I
started running as hard as I could across the field. The moonlight,
the thought of going lightened my feet and I ran like something
wild.

When my clothes became hot and binding, I pulled them off
and ran naked in the pale light. Looking down, I could see my
white knees and thighs pumping up and down. My breath began
coming fast and a prickling of needles was in my thighs. Not able to
stop, I kept going till I could run no more. Then I threw myself
down on the soft earth and dug in as close to it as I could get, glad
for the cool dewyness on my hot skin. After a time I got cool, and
then cold. I slid my hands and feet under the outer layer of sand

and found a warmth left from the sun. It was like putting my hands under warm covers on a cold night.

I lay in the sand and thought of what I would do. The next day I was going to Paris. Some day I would go to Dallas. After that, I would go on and on till I had reached the outer edges of the world. Nothing, nobody would ever stop me. I made my mind up to that.

When the moon was straight overhead, when I had worn thin the thoughts on going, I found my clothes and pulled them on over my sand-covered body. Then I went quietly through the woods and up to the house. All was dark inside, and lulled with the smells and sounds of sleep. I found my pallet and eased myself down.

"Where'd you go?" my mother asked from her bed.

I could not say I had been running in the peanut field.

"I thought I heard cows in the corn. Somebody had to go see."

"Did you find any?"

"I didn't see none."

"I reckon you better get to sleep. No need'n staying up all night. You'll be long on the road at daylight."

While the moon was still white in the sky we were on the road, with Dewey on the springseat holding the lines, clucking the horses along. I lay on the loose peanuts behind him, less than an hour out of bed, sleepy but not wanting to go to sleep, with the smell of drying peanuts in my nose and the taste of soda biscuits and flour gravy in my mouth.

The load was heavy. I could have walked faster than the horses traveled. The sun came up while we were passing the Novice Church. It was warm on my back and shoulders before we turned up the Paris road at the crossroads. From there on it was a new road to me—a road that wound through miles of post-oak flats and then came out on the open land of Shockey's Prairie.

We passed through Faught with its church and store and cluster of houses and came to the red clay hills. The clay of the road had been packed hard and smooth. The going was slow uphill, fast down. There were no houses—only the red of the road and the rusty brown of scrub oaks.

The peanuts shifted under my weight, making hollows the shape of my body. With nothing to keep me awake, I went to sleep and slept through the rest of the red hills.

A grinding noise like that of a steel blade on a whetrock woke me. My first thought was that the wagon had not been greased, that the thimbles were dry and the wagon would break down before we got to Paris.

"What's wrong?" I asked, sitting up.

"Nothing. We hit the gravel." Dewey had been over the road many times before. "We just come on the pike."

I knew about the pike, but no one had told me about the sound of wagon tires in gravel. I looked back at the road. We were not leaving a track in the gravel. Only the sound showed we had passed.

On one side of a fence the grass was dry and brown, on the other, watered and green. On the green side there were big shade trees and sprays of water turning slowly in the sun. It was the prettiest pasture I had ever seen. Men were walking in it, but I could not tell what they were doing.

"What's that?" I asked Dewey.

"Golf course. They're playing golf."

This was something new to me, a game that took enough room to make a cow pasture. It took us a long time to go past, and I watched and asked questions. Dewey had seen it before but only from the road. I watched the men but could not tell what they were doing. From what I could see, I thought they might as well be working.

"Town folks," Dewey said. "They don't know much about work."

We left the golf course behind and went past houses with gardens and corn patches too small to feed a family of any size.

"I'd as lief live in the country as live here," Dewey said.

Suddenly the grinding of the gravel stopped and the wheels rolled as smoothly as they would on a floor. Dewey swung the horses around to the right and we were on a paved street.

"Lamar Avenue," he said.

There had never been anything like it. It stretched ahead as far as we could see, a smooth polished floor with white houses and trees on either side, with green grass in the yards and beds of petunias bright in the sun. My throat hurt and I had nothing to say. All I wanted was to look. Paris. Lamar Avenue. Houses and trees and cars. Sidewalks for people going from house to house, people on a weekday in clothes better than most had for Sunday. It was what I had thought it would be, and more than I thought it would be. How could I know that any place would be so beautiful.

Dewey kept the horses to the side of the street, clucking them along, in a hurry to sell the peanuts.

Riding high on the wagon, I looked in windows and doors, liking the way town people lived, the way they looked. My white waist and blue duckings were dusty from the peanuts. I dug my bare feet down out of sight. They were too rusty to be seen by the people along Lamar Avenue.

We turned off on a side street and went past the market square to a peanut plant on the south side of town.

"Don't get out'n the wagon," Dewey said. "They can weigh us both ways."

A man came out, saw the peanuts, and motioned for us to drive on to the scales. It was like going on a bridge, but when the wagon stopped the scales kept on in a gentle swaying. Dewey got down and looked at the scales and the figure the man wrote in a book.

Then he drove under a suction pipe like the one in a gin. The suction picked the peanuts up and they went rattling through the pipe out of sight in the building. My job was to push peanuts out of cracks and corners to the suction pipe, and it was a new thing for me to feel the pull of the wind on my fingers.

The wagon empty, we went to the scales for the second weighing. Again Dewey checked weights and figures. He counted the money twice before putting it in his pocket.

I had not been out of the wagon. I did not get out till we were inside the wagonyard, in a walled-in lot where there were wagons and teams but only a few people. He paid the wagonyard keeper a dime. Then he left me to feed and water the horses while he went to buy the things he had to buy.

"Don't you go off," he said. "I don't want to be running around hunting you." I was afraid to go off, but I did go outside the big gate. I walked on the concrete sidewalk and saw people on their way to the square. It was close enough for me to see a line of stores on one side but I did not go closer. There was enough to see where I was to keep me busy.

Toward sundown he came back, hitched the horses to the wagon, and drove out of the wagonyard. He kept on back streets till we came out on Lamar Avenue. Then he opened a paper sack and took out cheese and crackers. Sitting beside him on the springseat, I ate my supper and stared at the houses we were going past. This was my first time in Paris, but not my last. I knew I would come again when I would not have to stay in the wagonyard.

49

The letter was there when I came home from school. It had been there since mail time, read and reread, with sadness, with worry. It was the call for Monroe to go to the Army. On the morning of November 8 he had to report to the courthouse in Paris. From there he would go—"Only the Lord knows where they will send him," my grandmother said. "Only the Lord knows when he will come home again." This from my mother, who had already made up her mind that he would be a long time gone.

Monroe had read the letter as often as my mother, but not in the same way, his face showed. It was a way to get out. They were saying that it was a sad thing for two widow women to lose the one man they could count on. He listened but did not answer back. No matter what they said, he was going, but he did not tell them he was glad to be on the way. He kept that for talking in bed in the north room.

There were things to be done before he went: clothes to be sewed and washed and packed, plans to be made for the winter and spring, talk, hours of talk, to set him on the right way, to save him from the wrong. Then there had to be a way of saying good-bye.

"I'm going to give a party," my mother said.

Not since we left Pin Hook had she given a party.

"If it's the last thing I ever do for him, I'm going to give him a party the night before he leaves."

My job was to tell the neighbors that there was going to be a farewell party for Monroe. On the pony, riding bareback, I went up the road toward Novice, down the road toward Pin Hook as far as Pine Creek, stopping at all the houses, telling the people to come to a party at our house: everybody invited, nobody slighted. I rode right past old Henrietta's and Parson Perry's.

On the night of the party, when I came home from school, there was a good fire in the fireplace and they had taken down the beds in the north room. Monroe's clothes were ready. If they wanted to, the people could stay till he had to leave in the morning.

Before dark Aunt Nellie came walking down the road in a Sunday dress. My mother and grandmother met her at the door and they had a good cry together. No one else had time for crying. Monroe looked too happy to cry if he wanted to. He went to the north room and played chords on the piano. He would have to do the seconding when Uncle Charlie came with his fiddle.

At dark the people began coming in buggies and wagons and on horseback. We had never seen some of them. Word had gone on down to Pin Hook and to people we had never heard of. We were glad they had come, even when the rooms were full and men and boys stood around in the dark of the hall and porch. I tried to keep count, but there were too many. When it was solid dark they were all over the place.

The people from Pin Hook asked my mother if they could play snap and she said she didn't care. In Novice, snap was a game to be played in the middle of the room in front of everybody. A couple stood up holding hands. Another couple chased each other around them till one or the other was tagged. This was what my mother expected, and she asked the people to stand back for a game of snap. This was not the way the people from Pin Hook played it. A couple went outside to hold up hands in the darkness behind the big oak tree. A boy snapped a girl and went out to chase her around the couple.

I watched from the end of the porch and they never played the game right. The couple did not hold up hands. There was no chase, no snap. The second boy stayed out with the first girl and the others went back to the house. He held her hands a long time, but he was too close to her for the game the way I had seen it, and the other girl waited a long time before she came back with another partner.

By the time Uncle Charlie came with his fiddle there were snap games going behind the oak tree, out by the smokehouse, and down by the front gate. I watched them all, close up. My grandmother went out to the porch but it was too dark for her to see anything.

From the darkness I heard the fiddle and then the piano, the tuning up, followed by sawings and chords, the slow movement to the tune to be played and the key it would be played in, all done without music, with only the feelings of the fiddler and the seconder. The first tune they came to was "Lorene," a love song, a waltz good for dancing or singing. Sounds in the house and hall stopped. People were listening to the music, some of them singing to themselves:

> Give me your answer, Lorene, today—

The music sent me leaping through the dark, out to the meadow, where all I could hear was the music, where the air was heavy with the smell of fires burning in November woods. Monroe was there, playing. Tomorrow he would be gone. Nothing would be the same when he was gone. I did not feel like crying. I went around the house, across a field, through a patch of woods, hearing the tune, not the words, wishing I was old enough to be drafted.

After the fiddle stopped I went back to the house through the kitchen, where my grandmother and Aunt Nellie were talking about the people from Pin Hook.

"It takes a fast girl to play that kind of snap," my grandmother said.

Aunt Nellie shook her head.

"You wouldn't catch a girl o' mine out'n the dark like that."

I worked my way through the north room, to the corner where the end of the piano was pushed close to the wall. I was out of the way there, but close enough to watch the fiddle and bow as Uncle Charlie played "Red Wing," "Soldier's Joy," and "The Eighth of January," close enough to feel the piano shake with the chords Monroe played.

When Uncle Charlie put his fiddle back in the case, my mother had the snap games stopped. It was time for singing, and they all had to be inside to hear the singing.

Bessie Haley said she would sing "I'll Be All Smiles Tonight" if Monroe would second for her. She was a tall pale girl from Pin Hook, not as good-looking as some, and not snapped the minute she came in from a game. She could sing and, to me, she was pretty when she was singing, and the song was as pretty as anything I had ever heard:

> Though my heart may break tomorrow
> I'll be all smiles tonight.

The song left them sad and with not much to say. Monroe was going to be a soldier. They talked a little about it and wondered where he would be the next night and the next. Aunt Nellie came from the kitchen.

"Jessie," she said to my mother, "you know what I'd like to

hear? I'd like to hear you sing 'The Drummer Boy from Water-loo.' "

This was one of my father's songs that she sometimes sang to us. We liked to hear the story. I liked the way her voice rose high and clear and fell back to a minor note that left the song unended when the words were over. I could already hear her singing:

> When battle round the warlike band
> With courage loud the trumpet blew,
> Young Edward left his native land,
> A drummer boy from Waterloo.

My mother looked at Monroe, sitting on the piano stool.

"It cain't be chorded," she said. "If it could, I couldn't stand to sing it tonight. I'd be bound to falter."

There were other songs sung, and then talk of going home. Some had many miles to go. Monroe had to be up early. My grand-mother went over near the piano.

"I want you to sing a church song before you go," she said. "I'd feel a heap better if you sung a church song."

This time my mother let herself be brought to the piano. She sat down and opened the songbook to "In the Sweet By and By." Monroe held the lamp close for her to see. People came in till there was no more room for standing. Those standing close enough to see sang the verse through with my mother and by the last line they were singing all together:

> We shall meet on that beautiful shore.

The party broke up with the people who were leaving saying "You all come to see us some time." Long after they had gone, we could hear wagons going through the Pine Creek bottom and the sound of singing.

My mother and grandmother still had things to say to Monroe. They said them in front of the fire, with me listening from bed till I went to sleep.

When I woke up in the morning there was a good fire going and Monroe was putting on his clothes in front of it. My mother brought him fried eggs and hot biscuits and he ate while he got ready. I watched her slip a piece of cake and a piece of corn bread in with his clothes.

Before daylight a wagon came up the road and he was gone almost before we knew it, with no kissing or shaking hands. He just picked up his bundle of clothes and ran for the wagon, leaving my mother and grandmother crying in the gray light.

The day was not like other days. School and work were there, to be got through with, and not much more. It would be that way till we heard from Monroe and knew what he had gone into.

In the early dark we heard the wagon coming back down the road. We thought it would stop, and there would be some word of Monroe. When it stopped we heard someone jump to the ground and then Monroe yelling, "I'm home again." By the time he got the gate open we were there to meet him.

"How come they sent you back?" we asked.

"It may not be for good. They told me to come home and wait three days. Then I got to go again."

"It don't seem right," my grandmother said. "It does look like they could make up their minds and keep them made up."

My mother was different. We had three days and they were to be made the most of. She gave us supper and the cake with it. After supper she let us parch peanuts in the fireplace. It was almost like another party with Monroe telling us the things he had seen and done in Paris.

The day was bright and cool, the kind we often got in November, after the first frost and before the first norther. Monroe had been home three days and it was time for another call. He was packed and waiting, and getting all the work done he could. If it was not done now, no telling when it would be done, and some jobs can't wait, like steepling up the fence where the cows got out.

My mother had come down to the lot to see how the job was coming along.

"There comes Pat Swindle," she said.

He was coming up the road at a trot, his cap on backward, his freckled face red from running.

"The war's over," he yelled from the gate.

"How do you know?" my mother asked.

"News come up from Woodland. They got it over the telephone. They say the armistice has been signed."

It was a new word to us, and not easy to say, but it meant the war was over, that now Monroe would never have to go.

While we were standing there, word come down the road the other way, from a man on horseback who said he had heard the church bells ringing in Paris and knew the war was over.

We had no church bells to ring. We could have hammered on a sweep, but we did not. Monroe went on steepling up the fence. It was down and had to be got up again before dark.

Pat and I went around the barn and over the rail fence into

the meadow. The sage grass, a purplish brown in the sunlight, was knee high and dry, good for running in, good for rolling in. We ran till our tongues were hanging out and then we rolled, falling over each other, tussling but not wrestling. It was too good a day to be wrestling. A great thing had happened. We did not understand it, but we knew it was great.

When it was near sundown Pat went down the road home. Not ready to go in yet, I waded through the deeper grass at the lower side of the pasture—grass so deep that I could see nothing but grass and green-blue sky. No one had said enough about the armistice. I was staying out in the pasture, trying to find out how to say it to myself.

There was a poem I had learned by heart and I said it out loud:

> With mingled sounds of horns and bells
> And a far heard clang the wild geese fly,
> Storm sent from Arctic moors and fells
> Like a great arrow across the sky.
> Two dusky lines converged in one,
> Chasing the southward flying sun.

It was the kind of poem I wanted to make, but I did not have enough to go on. There had been no horns or bells—nothing but quiet talk that the war was over. Whittier had wild geese. It was time for them, but I had not seen them. Where I walked there was sky and sage grass and I could not make them say the war was over. Maybe there would be something at the house.

When I got to the house they were sitting down to supper and it was like any other day in the week.

50

The war was over and Monroe was restless. My mother and grandmother blamed the draft. It was the draft that got him thinking about leaving home. He was not wanted for the draft, but he wanted to leave home and strike out on his own. My mother tried to keep him from going, but there was no stopping him, and he went up the road, wearing his Sunday clothes and carrying some work clothes in a bundle.

We heard from him first at Purcell. He was working at odd jobs on farms, looking for a steady job as a farmhand. My mother felt better. If he had to be away from home, it was better for him to be close to kinfolks.

When we heard from him again he was in the Oklahoma oil fields, roughnecking it, moving from Drumwright to Oilton to any other oil town where there was work. At times he sent money and at Christmas, for the first time in my life, I had a whole dollar to spend—a dollar my mother gave me from the money he sent—and I spent it all on firecrackers.

After Christmas there were no more letters from him, and the letters my mother wrote him came back. Through January she wrote to him two or three times a week, and met the mail carrier every day.

"I'll bound he's dead," my grandmother said. "He could be dead and buried and we never know it."

My mother did not give up hope. When Dewey wanted to go find him, she cried at the thought of losing them both, but let him go.

"I don't know why you let him do it," my grandmother said.

"We'll be here by ourselves, two women with three young'uns, and niggers passing the road."

Dewey went anyway, taking the money we had left. With a few clothes in my grandmother's old suitcase he went up the road.

It was the same with Dewey as it had been with Monroe, a few postcards from Drumwright and Oilton, and then nothing. He had not found Monroe, and then was lost himself.

My mother took it hard, my grandmother harder. It was time for plowing and soon would be time for planting. We had to have a crop or starve. My mother would have to go back to the plow if they did not come home. My grandmother looked at us. I was barely thirteen, Cleaver sixteen, and Roy seven.

"It'll be a slim crop if you ain't got nothing better'n them to depend on," she said.

Worse, she began worrying about anybody passing on the road, day or night. She started taking an axe to bed with her, bringing it in at night, walking out backward with it in the morning, taking it out exactly the way she brought it in. It was bad luck to bring an axe in the house if she did not.

Then she worried about noises she heard at night, in the yard, the barn, even the house. It could be haints—haints of the Addison boys. It could be niggers, prowling where they had no business going.

On a dark Saturday night in March my mother called us to the front door to listen. Someone was at the mailbox, raising and lowering the flag, opening and shutting the door. Then there was the sound of footsteps, of someone running down the road—too solid sounding for a haint.

"Somebody playing pranks," my mother whispered.

"It don't sound like pranks to me," my grandmother said. "It make me uneasy. Too many niggers passes this road."

My mother looked at me.

"Too bad we don't have one o' the older boys at home."

Then there were sounds from the fields and woods, like faraway voices talking and laughing—no telling how many. My mother and grandmother shut the doors and pushed the dresser against them. My grandmother got down the old muzzle-loading gun and set it by the axe on the hearth. It would not shoot, but it would scare anybody looking in. They kept the lamp burning. Better light than dark if anybody tried to break in.

The sounds of voices stopped, long enough for my mother to put Roy to bed, and for my grandmother to get started on telling what it was like at Camden when Yankee soldiers walked the road at night.

She was stopped by a wild laugh up the Novice road.

"What was that?" they asked each other.

They looked at each other, listening. When it did not come again, my grandmother moved the lamp out of line with the window and they stood close to the door. When we were listening to nothing but our own breathing, the laughing came again, closer.

"It's a man," my mother whispered. "It sounds like a man—"

"A heap closer—no piece up the road now—"

Again silence, long enough for him to pass the house if he kept walking, but it did not last. In front of our gate, standing in front of our gate, he sang words from a song we had never heard, and laughed so loud the echoes came back from the woods.

"We got to get shet o' him," my grandmother said.

"I don't see how. Two women and not a man in the house."

My mother was crying.

"Make it look like we got a man."

My grandmother pushed me to one side and slipped Monroe's old coat over my shoulders. She took his old hat from a nail and stuck it on my head. She took the corncob pipe from her own mouth and stuck the stem between my teeth.

"Here. Set here," she said.

She set me on a stool in front of the window, in plain sight of the man on the road. Then she put the muzzle-loader in my hands.

"Make out like you're loading it," she whispered.

I worked the ramrod up and down the empty barrel. Anything to stop the laughing in the road. My grandmother brought the axe and, holding it ready to strike, stood beside me. The laughing got louder.

My mother was at the door, with her ear to a crack.

"Sounds like a nigger," she whispered. "I never heard nothing sound more like a nigger."

I pushed the ramrod up and down and sucked on the pipestem, drawing bitter tobacco juice into my throat. I coughed once.

"Don't do that," my grandmother said.

The man left the road and circled through the woods and across the field, singing and laughing and yelling, going farther away, in the direction of Galilee.

"I hope he don't stop," my mother said.

By the time she said it he was coming back our way, making a big circle through the field, and coming almost straight to the house through the woods. He crashed through the brush and crossed the road. We could hear him stumbling in the dark. Still laughing, but not so loud, he opened the front gate and came toward the front door.

My grandmother stood by the door with her axe raised.

"Jessie," she said, "get the poker."

My mother grabbed the poker and stood on the other side of the door, the dresser between them. I aimed the gun barrel across the window.

We heard shoes on the doorstep. Then there was silence. I looked at my mother and grandmother. They were ready for a shoulder to hit the door.

"Aw, come on and open the door."

We knew the voice and the laugh that followed.

"Monroe," my mother cried.

Axe and poker hit the floor. They pushed the dresser back and jerked the door open. Monroe was standing in front of it, laughing and slapping his thighs.

"I could just kill you," my mother said, "playing a trick on us like that."

She threw her arms around him and brought him inside. He looked at me with the gun and corncob pipe and doubled over again. My grandmother patted his shoulder.

"When'd you get back?" she asked.

"Tonight."

"Well, I do think you might a let a body know."

"Where's Dewey?" my mother asked.

"I ain't seen him."

"I sent him after you."

She began crying.

"He'll come back," Monroe said. "I did."

He was back and it was not too late for plowing and planting. Over a cold supper he talked about what had to be done in the fields.

51

Then one day the land we had cleared of grass and weeds and sassafras sprouts was no longer ours to work. We had rented it long enough to feel that we owned it, but the owner came and said he wanted the place for someone else. We could stay to the end of the year, but no longer. My mother talked to him of the work we had made on the land and place, and asked for another year. It was no use. The trade had been made and somebody else would move in as soon as we could move out. So much we had done we could not take with us.

"It's always the way when you rent," my grandmother said.

The place had been rented from under us, not for doing too little but for doing too much.

"I'm a good mind to go back to Pin Hook," my mother said.

She looked at other places to rent, but it was late in the year and the ones she could find had poor land, poor houses.

"Not fitten for a nigger," she said of some of the shacks.

Soon there was nothing left but to go back to Pin Hook, to our own land, where we would have to work harder to make less, but where we would not have to pay rent and the things we did raise belonged to us. We knew that in a way it was giving up. We had left Pin Hook to get close to a better school. Now, seven years later, we were going back, and with little to show for our move. Monroe, who had stopped in the fifth grade, would never go to school again. Dewey was off rambling, nobody knew where. Cleaver, at sixteen, was still in the sixth grade. The Pin Hook school was not very good, but maybe good enough for what use we would make of it.

To me it had two advantages. It was only half a mile from our house and the teacher was Mr. Jessee, who had moved from Spring Hill. The free school book law had come in, and the books at Pin Hook would be the same as the ones at Medill.

In the fall, while we were picking cotton and gathering corn, we watched Mr. Jessee go by in the morning riding his bay pony. At sundown he came back. At times I went for water when I knew I would meet him on the road.

"I'm going to Pin Hook school this year," I told him. "We're gonna move back to Pin Hook, when our house gets empty. We'll walk to Pin Hook till we move."

"You starting soon?"

"The cotton's got to be scrapped over again. Then I can start."

It was November before Cleaver and I could start to school. The path we took was through our pasture and then through the woods along Little Pine Creek. We crossed the creek on a log and went up through fields to a lane that ended at the schoolhouse.

Seven years since we had left Pin Hook, and changes had been made. The old school had been torn down. In its place a new two-room school had been built. It was a fine school, clean and white under the red and brown leaves of oak and hickory. The roof was of galvanized sheet iron. The same kind of sheet iron made a roof over a new cistern and a barrel fountain. We saw the fountain and knew that the bucket and dipper had gone, and that no one had to carry water.

At one side under the trees there was a brush arbor, left from the summer meeting. The sawdust on the ground was still fresh, the oak board benches still in place. Some of the older boys and girls were waiting on the benches for books to take up. The smaller children hung around the doorstep to their room.

Mr. Jessee stood on the little porch and rang the same bell he had used at Medill. The smaller children lined up in front of the little room and Miss Blanche Moore came to march them in. Cleaver and I lined up with the older boys and girls. The school had only eight grades that year. Miss Blanche had the first four, Mr. Jessee the rest.

When we had marched in, Mr. Jessee put Cleaver and me in the sixth grade and gave us the free books. They were the books I had been in the year before. I could say some parts of the reader by heart.

It was a day of another kind of learning for me. I was just fourteen and the youngest in my class—close to the youngest in the room.

The first thing I learned was that they hated and despised Mr. Jessee. He gave hard lessons and expected them to be learned. They hated the lessons and would not study. He kept them after school. He threatened whippings for the ones who did not study. I heard their talk but did not know why they hated him.

They were from fifteen to eighteen and had paired off, boy, girl, boy, girl. They were young men and women, full of talk of love. When Mr. Jessee turned his back, they passed notes up and down and across the aisles, notes that were stopped for peeks and giggles along the way. A note came over my shoulder with a girl's name on the outside. I opened it and read one word. At home my mother had washed my mouth out with soap and ashes for saying something not half as bad. I handed it to her. She read it, blushed a little, and started writing a reply.

At recess the older boys and girls paired off and sat on the benches under the brush arbor. It was like a party, a snap game, without the snap. Some of the girls sang old love songs, and the boys cut initials in the oak boards. Trying to be like them, I cut WAO, &, and then JM for June Moss, a girl who had been in my room at Medill. They asked me about her but I had little to tell them. I did tell them that I had once seen her brother Esker drink six cokes at a picnic.

Some of the younger boys hung around the cistern. I went up to them and tried to talk to them.

"Mr. Jessee's sure a good teacher," I said.

They laughed.

"We sure God ain't got no use for him. Too strict."

At home I had been told it was better to have a strict teacher.

"He ain't too strict for me," I said.

"You ain't had him a whole day yet."

When school was out, Cleaver and I went back through the fields and woods home. He wanted to talk, but I had nothing to say. It was all too new and strange to me, the saying of bad things to girls, the girls not getting mad at what was said. I had never thought that the things boys said behind the barn could be said in school.

At home, through supper and around the fire after supper, my mother tried to talk to me about the day in school. I could tell her about the books and drinking fountain, but I could not tell her what school at Pin Hook was like.

"You like the Pin Hook school?" she asked.

"Yes'm."

I was sure of that.

"You gonna learn a heap this year?"

"Yes'm."

I was thinking of more than the lessons in the books.

The day after Christmas we moved back to our homeplace at Pin Hook, to our own land. We were not renters; we would not have to move when somebody told us to. I went on the first load, to get in wood and water. The well, which my father had dug, was close to the house—a good well with all the water we could ever use. The woods were farther away, but close enough for me to carry in sticks.

It was middle of the day when we passed the Pin Hook store. We turned south at the store, passed the schoolhouse and graveyard, and went down the lane to our house, which was standing empty with the doors open. It was better than the house we had moved from, but not much. It had been a rent house for too many years. The front porch had pulled away at one side, the kitchen floor was wet from a leak.

One thing was better: Someone had papered the fireplace room with pages from *The Saturday Evening Post*. The minute I had a fire going I stopped to read. There was a story called "A Travesty of Justice." I found the beginning and end, but some of the parts were pasted on the underside of the pages. There were pictures, and I could imagine the stories that went with the pictures.

In two days we were settled at Pin Hook, but my grandmother was not with us. She had moved her things to Uncle Charlie's. After that, she would be with us only when she came for a visit, or when my mother sent for her to come.

52

The war was over but the sickness it left behind was a worse killer than the war. It was influenza and it spread from town to town, with newspapers carrying lists of dead on front pages. Then it spread to the country, along country roads, traveling from house to house, scattering death wherever it went. No one knew how to stop it; everyone tried something.

My mother tied up balls of asafetida gum in ragbags and hung them around our necks. We could hardly stand the smell of ourselves. When we were around the fire, the gum warmed and the smell hung heavy around us. Every morning before going to school I had to lift the bag and rub the part where the gum had seeped through around my mouth and nose to keep the germs out of my lungs. Then I had to sit in school alone in a double desk.

On a cold January day there was a letter from Dewey. He was sick and coming home. On the very next day he would be in Paris and wanted someone to meet him.

"He got the flu?" we asked my mother.

"I don't know," she said. "He wants to come home and I'd never say no to him. It could be smallpox and I wouldn't say no."

The next morning Monroe was on his way to Paris before daylight, in the buggy. It would be faster and easier riding than a wagon.

That night when I came home from school Dewey was there, sitting before the fire, looking taller and thinner than when he left. His face was flushed and there was a look of fever in his eyes. He did not seem to feel sick. He laughed and talked and sang a new song he had learned in the oil fields, "I'm forever blowing bubbles,

Pretty bubbles in the air. . . ." It was a new kind of song for me. So was another he sang: "Sweet summer breeze, whispering trees. . . ."

"Nobody up there knows the kind of songs we sing at Pin Hook," he said.

"Up there" was a great part of Oklahoma and into Kansas and Missouri. He had gone first to Purcell, and then on to oil fields around Drumwright, working by day, hunting Monroe when he could, but never finding him. At the end he went to Kansas City and studied for a little while at an automotive school.

When he was too sick to stay in school he came home to find Monroe there ahead of him, getting ready for spring plowing and planting. A letter could have saved him a lot of trouble, but he did not write the letter. He was too busy working and learning new things, some good, some bad. Now he wanted to write a book about the places he had been, the people he had seen. I looked at him as I never had before. He had been to far places, and was not the same.

There were days of sleet and snow, days when cold winter rain fell all day long. My grandmother came to see Dewey. At night, with nothing else to do, we sat in front of the fire. Monroe and Dewey talked of the new things of the oil fields; my grandmother told again her stories of Camden, Arkansas.

One morning my mother called me before daylight to build a fire. She felt chilled through and wanted a fire to warm the room. Half asleep, I sat on the hearth and raked together the few live coals left in the ashes. I put in small pieces of dry wood and blew on the coals till there was a good flame. Then I put on a backstick and built up the flame to light the room. My mother did not move in bed or look my way. The wind was roaring in the trees across the front and sleet rattled on the tin roof.

When it was time for my mother to get up, she only pulled the quilts closer around her.

"Somebody else'll have to fix breakfast," she said.

My grandmother came and felt her brow and counted her pulse.

"Fever," she said. "All the signs of a fever."

She put her ear close and listened to the hard breathing. Then she called us to the kitchen.

"It's the flu," she said. "I'll bound she caught it from Dewey."

I looked at Dewey. He knew as well as the rest of us what this meant. There was no sure cure for the flu. If she had it, there was not much chance she would get well.

"We've got to send for a doctor," my grandmother said.

There was a doctor in Detroit who had come to see patients at Woodland. His price was high, but there was flu in Detroit, whole families down with it, and he knew as much as anyone what to do. Monroe went to Woodland and sent word for him to come.

People along the road heard that my mother was sick but they did not come to see her or offer to sit up at night. They were afraid it was the flu—afraid of carrying it back to their homes.

All day long we waited, and no one came to make waiting easier. All night we waited, knowing she was getting worse by the hour. All of us knew she would die if we did not get help soon. Monroe went to Woodland to send word to the doctor again, told by my grandmother to wait for an answer. She also sent for Aunt Nellie.

"I've got to have me a woman to help," she said. "I cain't do it all by myself."

Aunt Nellie came late in the day, riding sidesaddle on a pony. Then Monroe came from Woodland. The doctor was coming our way and would be there some time in the night. There was sickness at nearly every house on the road from Detroit and he would have to stop any time he was asked.

Just before dark a cold, driving rain set in. We brought in wood and water and took turns standing by her bed, looking at her flushed face and closed eyes, listening to her choked breathing. Aunt Nellie made a mustard poultice for her chest. My grandmother wrapped heated bricks in flannel and put them at her feet.

When Aunt Nellie went to the kitchen to make a new poultice, I followed her. Her lips were set tight against her teeth. The pellagra spots looked whiter in the lamplight.

"Come over here."

Her voice, never soft, sounded harder when she kept it low. I went over and looked down at the mustard paste she was spreading on white flannel. She felt my forehead with her left hand.

"Your mammy's about to die," she said. "If the doctor don't come quick, there won't be a thing in the world he c'n do. Without'n help she cain't hold on long."

She began to cry, and all I knew about death rushed into my mind. My eyes burned but I kept my lips tight shut. Turning away from her hand, I opened the kitchen door and leaped into the blackness. It was bitter cold and rain beat on my face, but the feeling was nothing to the burning inside me. I went past the well and through a barbed-wire fence to a cow pasture. The ground under my feet was soft and squashy. In low places, water stood deep as my ankles. I felt what it was to be running in the wet, cold night—having to run from the fear inside me—running and willing that my mother would live. I ran the pasture, I ran the lane. If the doctor was coming, he would come by the lane.

When I could not run, I walked, my clothes water wet, my hands and feet numb, my face too cold for me to feel the crying. Then I knew I had to go back to the house, to the room where she was, to know from her face how close she was to death. I went by the front door, sidling in, to keep from opening the door wider. A man was leaning over her, holding her wrist, counting her pulse. The doctor had come. While I was running in the pasture, he had come through the lane.

Aunt Nellie saw me and handed the lamp to my grandmother. She took hold of me and led me to the kitchen.

"What you doing, going out'n the wet like that?" she asked. "Don't you know you'll catch your death o' cold? You'll get the flu and it'll kill you, sure as the world."

She made me take off my wet clothes in the corner behind the stove and rub myself down with a towel. Then she put me to bed with warm bricks.

"You stay there," she said. "The doctor's come. You c'n rest easy he'll do everything he can for your mammy."

"Is she going to die?"

"He thinks she'll pull through."

"Is it the flu?"

"The doctor says so. He says he smelt it the minute he walked in the door."

"We all going to get it?"

"Nothing to keep us from it. Now you go to sleep."

Warm from the bricks and feather bed, I settled down to sleep. I believed the doctor. My mother was going to get well. When Aunt Nellie left me, I drifted off to sleep.

My grandmother woke me at daylight laying her hand on my forehead.

"He's got fever," she said to Aunt Nellie.

"You might a knowed it, him running out in the wet and cold."

I felt the fever burning in my throat and the pain in my head. Flu. They did not have to tell me it was flu. I asked about my mother.

"She's better," my grandmother said. "The doctor stayed might nigh all night—till he knowed she was better. It's a good thing she's better. She'll be up to nuss the rest of us when we get down."

Aunt Nellie put a mustard poultice on my chest and gave me a dose of medicine the doctor had left for all of us.

"You've got to stay covered," she said. "You're sick enough as it is. You'll be a lot sicker if you get pneumonia."

It was February and corn planting time before the smell of flu and fever was out of the house. One by one the others came down with it, but with milder cases. With all of us just going to bed or just getting out of it, we were better off than many families we heard about on the way to Blossom and Paris. We were going to get well and strong again. In some families the last one was taken to the graveyard.

I was kept in bed longer than the others, weak and feverish and thin. Nothing they gave me to eat tasted right. Then they got me out of bed and helped me to a rocking chair in front of the fireplace. Hours at a time I would sit there, wrapped in quilts and staring at *The Saturday Evening Post* pictures on the wall. There was nothing new to read. The thought of reading made my head hurt.

Then one warm bright day my mother helped me on with my overalls and shirt and took me outside.

"Try walking a little," she said. "It'll do you good. You need something to make you want to eat."

The smell of spring was in the air and new grass made a sheen on the pasture. I started toward the woods on the other side. If it was spring in the pasture, it would be spring in the woods. I found purple four-petaled flowers standing inch-high in the grass, and reddish-green sheep sorrel coming up through the leaves. It was spring, and I knew I felt better.

Tired from walking so far, I lay down on dry brown leaves in a sunny spot in the woods. For the first time, with the sounds and smells of spring around me, with a spring sun warming me, I could forget the taste and smell of flu.

It was something to write about. There had to be words that would say how I felt when I knew my mother was going to die, words that said more than the fear and cold and fever I had gone through. Lying there in the sun, feeling more like myself again, I said out loud the words that came to mind, as they came and with no way to write them down.

Then I was hungry, and felt good at being hungry. It was a

long way back to the house, but I went, walking slowly, steadying myself when I could on tree and bush and barbed-wire fence.

The others were at work in the fields and the house was empty. There had to be something in the kitchen. All I found was a pan of cold corn bread and a jar of pickled hot peppers, not what I wanted but better than nothing. I took them to the fireplace and, sitting in the rocking chair, took first a bite of pepper and then a bite of bread till the bread was all gone.

My mother saw what I had done, and worried.

"Your stomach's too weak for anything like that," she said.

My grandmother was not worried.

"Ain't nothing better'n hot pepper to pull you back to strength," she said.

My strength back again, I had to go to school, but I did not want to. My shoes had worn out and I would have to go barefooted. We were down to corn bread for breakfast and I would have to take corn bread in my dinner bucket. The money we had saved up had gone for the doctor and medicine. Monroe and Dewey were at work in the woods cutting crossties for the railroad, but the money they made had to go for seed and to the blacksmith for sharpening sweeps. It would be corn bread for breakfast till more money came in.

It was bad enough to go back to school barefooted. It was worse trying to hide what I had to eat. As soon as the dinner bell rang the other boys and girls took their buckets and paper sacks and went to the benches under the arbor to eat and talk and sing "Oh, Bury Me Beneath the Willow." I would take my bucket, hide it

under my coat, and, going toward the privy and around it, slip out
of sight in the woods behind the school ground. There, hidden in
the bushes, I would cram down my corn bread and fried meat in a
hurry so I could get back for playing.

One day I was caught eating corn bread. The next day was wet
and cold and I did not take my dinner. The others would eat
behind the stove and I would not eat with them. When the dinner
bell rang, I told them a lie: that I had to go to the store to buy
something. I told it to them and to Mr. Jessee. He looked at my
bare feet and let me go, half a mile there, half a mile back.

"You won't have much time left for dinner," he said.

At the store I had to lie again and ask for something I knew
they would not carry. After I had asked, I stood around the stove,
where there were men sitting on nail kegs whittling. No need getting back before books.

While I was waiting, Mr. Jessee came in for a tablet and pencil.
He may have seen me, but I did not wait. I went out the back
door and toward the school.

Before I had gone halfway I heard Mr. Jessee on the road
behind me. He spoke to me about the muddy road and came up
beside me. I did not look up at his face. I looked down at his shoes
and knew why he talked about the mud. They were new and of fine
brown leather, so new that the white thread in the soles had never
been dirty. He walked beside me, so close that at every step I saw
my muddy bare feet and his new shoes.

Before we got to the school ground I knew what I was going to
do: I was going to be a teacher and wear good brown shoes every
day in the week. I did not tell him. I did not tell anyone else. My
friends would have no use for anybody who wanted to be a teacher.
Anybody would be a fool to be like Mr. Jessee.

Almost from the first day of school the boys and girls had
known they did not like him and did not want him to teach at Pin
Hook another year. He never gave time off on Fridays for basketball
games. He never gave time off from books for anything. He never
laughed at school, and he did not take time to visit around at the
homes in Pin Hook. The boys and girls knew he was not the kind of
teacher for them. Some of their parents had agreed from the first. By
spring, at the time when he could look for a new contract, people
were doing what they could to work against him. Once they had
decided he had to go, war was on between him and the boys and
girls, a war he could never win.

They had many weapons; he had only a few. One was the bell,

and we began to hate the sound of it calling us in from wolf over the river or any of the other games we played. For a long time we came when he rang it. Then when the days were warm some of the boys stayed in the woods. They had written words on the privy walls and left them for him to find. After school they wrote the same words on the girls' privy. The next morning Mr. Jessee went down the lane toward Pine Creek. When he came back he had a fresh load of brown birch switches. He stood these in the corner and rang the bell for books.

"I've been teaching a long time," he said when we were in our seats, "but I have never seen anybody like you boys and girls. It's Pin Hook. You don't want to learn. Nobody'll make you. It's the way people are in Pin Hook. They're not raising you to do right. They don't stop you from doing wrong." He held a switch in his hand. "The next one I catch'll get this. I don't care if it's a boy or a girl. I'd as soon whip one as the other."

This kind of talk from him was what they wanted. Nobody in Pin Hook wanted a girl to get a switching. That night the boys went to the schoolhouse. With sharp knives they cut deep rings around all the switches. Then they took the bell and propped it handle down on the front steps. One of the boys squatted over it and filled it full. Then they left it for Mr. Jessee, to let him know what they thought of him.

I was not with them on this trip, but I knew about it in time to be at school with them ahead of Mr. Jessee. We played wolf over the river, all of us barefooted to run faster, the girls also barefooted, and watching for him to come up the road. When we saw him we hid in the privies and in the bushes to watch his face when he found the bell. I was glad to be one of them, but I worried that this was going too far.

I hid in the bushes on the road from our house. He came up the road slowly, his horse at a walk, and I had never seen him look so tired. His blue suit was dusty and hair from his sweaty horse stuck to his pants. He tied the horse to a tree and went toward the front door. He stopped when he saw the bell, and I was glad I was not close to him. He said nothing, but every move he made was in anger. He grabbed the bell and with a sling of his arm emptied it on the ground. Then he drew water and poured on it till it was clean.

He must have known we were there, hiding. He stood on the front steps and rang the bell till it echoed in the woods. Then, still ringing it, he went down the lane for more switches.

The boys and girls in the little room lined up and marched in. We came out of hiding and went to our seats. We were afraid of what he would do, and dared each other to do more. One of the boys wrote a dirty word in a book and held it up for us to see. A girl marked her reader with a dirty word and passed it up and down the aisle. Then all of us were writing dirty words, some of them against Mr. Jessee, some of them about what boys and girls could do together in the bushes or under the schoolhouse.

Mr. Jessee came back and put his switches in the corner.

"It's all of you," he said bitterly. "If it was one or two doing things to be mean I'd know what to do. One's just about as bad as the other."

His voice was hard.

"I'll find out. I'll find out about the bell, and when I do—"

He did not have to tell us what he would do. We could see the switches and know that he would use them.

In the reading class he picked up a girl's book and read words that made a whiteness around his mouth. We knew what the words were. The book had been passed up and down the rows. He slammed it down on his desk and paced back and forth across the room.

"The books don't belong to you," he said. "I want all of them stacked on my desk now."

There was no time to erase words. One by one we faced him and laid our books on his desk. When we turned to go back to our seats, we looked into the white, scared faces of the others coming up. This was not what we had expected.

"The girls will stay in at recess," he said.

They stayed in all of recess. The boys waited on benches under the arbor and talked about what they would do if the girls got whippings.

"I gannies, I'll meet him in the creek bottom," one of them said.

The bell rang for books and we went back inside. The girls were in their seats, some of them crying.

One of them passed a note down the row.

"He's going to whip three of us after school."

We knew what for, but we still had to ask them.

"For what the boys wrote in our books."

At dinner time he kept in some of the boys. The rest of us sat under the arbor and watched the front door. Each one had his time coming.

It was nearly time for books when they came out. Mr. Jessee followed them with the bell in his hand.

"You gonna get it?" we asked the boys.

"This e'ening," one of them said. "He ain't about to wait."

"He thinks he's so big," one of the girls said.

A boy who had been at the middle of the trouble laughed.

"He can kill us but he cain't eat us."

That afternoon he let the girls go home but he kept three boys in. I waited in the bushes with some other boys, but we were too far away to hear what went on inside the schoolhouse.

When we were about to go on home, the boys came out and started along the road toward the store. They saw Mr. Jessee coming behind them on his horse and cut into the bushes, where we headed them off.

"Did he lick you?" we asked.

They pulled up their duckings to show the marks on their legs.

"Did it hurt?"

"It hurt like the devil, the old son-of-a-bitch."

"Did he say who's next?"

"He didn't talk about that. All he said was we're all in it and before he's through we'll all get it."

On the way home I could feel the whipping twice. My mother had always said that a whipping at school deserved another one at home.

The next morning a trustee was waiting on the school ground when Mr. Jessee rode up. They talked a long time, almost till time for the first recess. We could not hear what they were saying, but we knew it was about the whippings.

When the trustee had gone, Mr. Jessee rang the bell and marched us inside. All day long he kept us at lessons, talking only when he had to, with sharp words forced through tight lips.

"I'm the teacher in this school," he said once. "As long as I am, you'll do what I say."

That day after school he whipped three girls, the next, three boys, telling them each time that he would take more but he was afraid his arm would give out. He whipped the girls on their bare legs, and the next day everybody in Pin Hook was after him.

"You can fire me," he told the trustees when they came to the schoolhouse, "but you can't stop me from whipping them. As long as I am the principal, I will run the school. I'll show you the words they wrote. A whipping's coming to them and I'll see they get it."

They did not fire him. School had only a week or two to go, and they would have to pay him to the end anyway. They told him to lay off the whipping and went back to the crowd that waited at the store.

All day he sat at his desk and we sat in our seats. There were no lessons, nothing, but a day of staring at each other in hatred. With his bell he marched us out for recess and in again, but he did not speak to us. We knew it would be a bad day for whipping.

Still without a word, he rang the bell early, letting us out before the time of the last lesson. Without a word he went to his pony and rode off toward home.

The next day there were no lessons. At the end of the day he kept three boys in and whipped them.

"Your time's coming," they told us after he had gone home. "He said so. He said he ain't stopping till he's tanned the hide of every last boy and girl in Pin Hook."

We believed him. He had already whipped a girl seventeen years old and studying to be a teacher.

One afternoon, almost at the end of school, Mr. Jessee kept me in alone. He did not tell me why, but I knew it was for a whipping, and I knew why. The others had decided that he had put me last because he was not going to whip me at all. A girl had then told him she had heard me say a dirty word at recess. She told him and then she told the others.

When we were alone in the room, Mr. Jessee sat at his desk and made me stand before him. He seemed in no hurry to get to the whipping. He looked at me a long time and there was no anger in his face.

"You used to be a good boy," he said gently. "I used to brag about you when you first came to Spring Hill. You were a good boy and you studied hard. You were smart in your lessons. I used to tell people you would go a long way in spite of your mother being a widow woman. Then you moved to Pin Hook and got in with the crowd. It didn't take you long to be as bad as the rest of them. You know you've been wrong, don't you?"

"Yes, sir."

"I've got to whip you."

"Yes, sir."

"You know what for?"

"No, sir."

"You said a word at recess for the girls to hear—"

"They said I said it. I didn't."

He looked me straight in the eyes.

"You didn't say it?"

"No, sir."

He looked at me a long time.

"I believe you." He leaned closer to me. "I have to ask you. Have you done anything to deserve a whipping for?"

I thought of words written in books, and the words I had helped pass up and down the row of desks—enough for ten whippings, I knew. I felt my face get hot. I could lie, but he would know I was lying. Better to take a whipping. Then maybe he would quit looking at me that way.

"I reckon."

He stood up.

"Might as well get it over with, and make it one you'll remember. I hate to do it, but it's for your own good."

He looked down at my legs, and I thought he was going to tell me to roll up my duckings so he could whip me on my bare legs.

"Come here," was all he said.

"Yes, sir."

He took me by the hand and led me to the open part of the room in front of the blackboard. With his right hand he took a long switch from the corner and measured his distance from me. Then he swung with all his strength. The switch hit my legs and broke in pieces that hit the wall and rattled on the floor. I felt only a dull blow and no sting.

"They notched my switches," he said angrily. "Dirty little—" I missed some of the words and then I heard "Pin Hookers."

He took a switch and held it to the light. I could see fine rings cut with a sharp knife.

"I started with ten good ones," he said, "and I don't mind wearing out the last one o' them."

One by one he broke nine switches over my legs, and there was not enough pain for me to feel like crying. I could have laughed at the sound of sticks hitting the walls, but did not. The look on his face stopped me from laughing or saying anything.

When the last switch was gone, he kicked the pieces against the wall, away from his desk. Then he took my hand and shook it, man to man. His eyes were hard and his thin lips were pulled tight against his teeth.

"I don't hold anything against you," he said. "You didn't know what you were doing when you got in with this bad bunch. I can tell you. You stay with them, you're bound for trouble. This ought to a been a lesson to you. If you take it to heart, it'll do you some good. If you don't—" He let go of my hand. He did not need to tell me more. I felt scared enough as it was of what would happen. "You may go now."

I knew I had to say something.

"Thank you, sir."

He smiled, and I ran out of the schoolhouse. Outside, I looked around to see if any of the others had waited to listen. I knew what they would say if they heard me thank him for giving me a whipping. No one was around.

Alone on the road home, I thought of ways to tell my mother. I knew I would get it from her, with my duckings pulled up and a switch that had not been notched. But I had to tell her. It would be worse if she found out some other way. Better to tell her, and tell her I had been accused of something I did not do.

She was waiting for me at the gate, but she did not look angry and she did not have a switch.

"I heard he kept you in," she said. "Did you get a whipping?"

"Yes'm."

She opened the gate and looked at my legs as I walked in.

"I always said a child o' mine that got a whipping in school would get another one at home. Now I don't know. How come he whipped you?"

"They said I said a dirty word."

"Did you?"

"Not what they said I said."

"He whipped you, though."

"He whipped everybody."

From the look that came over her face I knew she was not going to whip me, or come close to it.

"That's what I've been saying," she said. "If it'd just a been you getting a licking, I'd warm you good and plenty. I cain't see the sense when it's everybody. It's got to be something wrong with the teacher if he has to whip everybody. I reckon he's just taking out his spite on Pin Hook."

She was wrong, but I did not tell her. I could not tell her the things the boys and girls had done to spite him. I could have told her that he was right and we were wrong, but I did not.

"Did he make you cry?" she asked.

"No'm."

She looked at me and I knew she was proud of me.

"I'm glad. I'd a hated it if he'd a made you cry."

She went inside the house and I went to the woods to get stovewood, without saying to her what I said to myself, "Mr. Jessee sure is a good teacher."

At school the next day I was more a part of the crowd than ever. Boys and girls met me at the road.

"He whipped you all right," they said. "We seen the switches broke all to pieces. Ain't you glad they was notched? Couldn't a hurt much, notched like they was. You ain't got no cause to stand up for him now."

I did not try to.

"He's lost the school for next year," they told me. "Trustees told him last night he ain't coming back."

No need to stand up for him. He was not coming back. I could feel bad at losing him for a teacher, but I did not have to tell it to the others. We stood in a group on the school ground, waiting for him to ride up on his pony, waiting to show him how far he would get, whipping everybody in school. I was part of the crowd, and as loud as any of the others talking against him.

He came and rang the bell. To show him that we did not have to mind, we waited till he rang it again to line up. At our desks, we sat staring straight ahead, not talking, answering his questions only when the look on his face told us we had better. It was a game, and we knew we had already won. The only fun left in it was in making him miserable. We studied on that more than we had ever studied our books.

I was part of all the mischief against him, but there were times when I wished I had not got in with the crowd. Mr. Jessee was right. I had changed. Pin Hook had changed me, and not for the better. I had books in my hands and wanted to read them, but I could not. The others would be against me if I read or studied. But if I did not study, I would never be a teacher. To be a part of them, I had turned against Mr. Jessee. In turning against him, I had turned against being a teacher. To be with them, I had to say I hated books and everything to do with books.

No one knew I wanted to be a teacher—no one at school or at home. At school they would have laughed at me. At home my brothers would have said I was trying to get out of work—that I was trying to find a job lazier than following old Beck down a cotton row. My mother had talked about getting an education, but she had never said she expected me to be a teacher. I thought they would say it was ruination of a good farmhand to let me think about being a teacher. I knew what the boys and girls at school would say. They had already had more books and teachers than they wanted. Talk of being a teacher would only set them against me.

I wanted to talk to Mr. Jessee, but there was no way without being caught. I tried waiting after school. Once he came out, got on his horse, and rode away, passing me, looking at me, but never giving me a chance to say a word to him. I knew why. I was a Pin Hooker, and not worth wasting time on. His eyes, when I called to him, were cold, unfriendly. It was his way of showing firmness. Another day I went to Pine Creek, to the bridge he had to cross to go home, and waited till I heard horse hooves thumping on the wooden floor. I came out on the road and met him. He nodded at me and rode on.

The battle between teacher and school, teacher and Pin Hook wore on through the last days. Pin Hook against Mr. Jessee. The trustees would not hire him again. The people knew that, and wanted him to have a hard time finding another school. They listened to the tales of their children and passed them on as gospel truth. Men stood around the store and blacksmith shop mornings and afternoons when he had to pass and laughed loud enough for him to hear them.

"How many you whupping today?" they asked him.

Every day he went to the woods before school and cut more switches. He dared boys and girls to cross him. Boys came to school with pocketknives borrowed from their fathers.

"I'll cut him before I'll let him tech me with a switch," they said.

One boy tried it. Mr. Jessee grabbed the knife and took it away from him. Then he whipped him so hard that the others kept their knives in their pockets. We knew then that he would not be run out of Pin Hook—that he meant to stay till the last day.

The last day was a big day in Pin Hook. The children went to get their report cards. Some men and women went to see that there would be no whippings. They did not speak to him, and he walked past them without a word. They moved close to the steps. He tied his pony near the front door and, without loosening the saddle girth, went inside. Then he rang the bell and marched the boys and girls in to the desks.

One by one he called them by name and they went up to get their report cards. Some he spoke to. Others he looked at with tight lips and steady eyes. They had won, but he was not giving in.

When he called my name I went up with the feeling that he might take a switch from the corner and wrap it around my legs. That would have been easier than the look he gave me when he handed me the card. I took it and waited, hoping that his look of friendliness would come, but it did not.

"You did not do well," he said. "I could not promote you on the work you did. I had to retain you in the sixth grade. It's a disappointment to me that I have to."

Unable to say what I felt, or to stand the look in his eyes any longer, I took my report card and went back to my seat. The others were whispering and laughing. I sat staring at the word "Retained," written in red ink in the handwriting I had tried to copy.

When the report cards had all been given out, we turned in our free books and, one by one, went outside to stand with the men and women. I was not the only one retained. Nearly all the boys and girls he had whipped had been kept back. For the others the grades were low.

Word spread fast along the four roads from the store: Fathers and mothers had better come and do what they could for their children. Men left their plows in the field and came. Women came in their dust caps and aprons. They passed report cards around and talked in low voices of what should be done to Mr. Jessee. No one talked of what should be done to the children. It was clear to them that some of the boys and girls had to be good scholars. If they all failed, the fault had to be the teacher's. They talked about what to say to him, but nobody was willing to march into the schoolhouse and say it.

By late morning the report cards had all been given out and all the children were standing around with the men and women. One by one Mr. Jessee locked the windows and pulled down the long tan shades. Then he came out and shut the door behind him. With a look at the men and women that dared them to say anything, he walked slowly to the tree and untied his pony. Still watching them, he climbed to the saddle and turned the pony toward the road. Without a word he crossed the school ground and rode toward the store. The people were silent till his back was turned to them. Then they said in loud voices all the things they had to say against him.

He was gone, but the report cards had been left behind. Something had to be done about the report cards before a new teacher came in the fall. The solution they arrived at was simple: The report cards would be torn up. The children could promote themselves if they felt like it. The trustees said any teacher they hired would take the word of the boys and girls.

School was out and we could all go home again. Mr. Jessee was gone and good riddance. He was too strict. Pin Hookers did not need his kind of education.

I watched the people going off in groups toward the store, talking, laughing. No one from my family had come. I had to go home alone, and all I could think of was how I had treated Mr. Jessee.

School out, I was changed from schoolboy to farmhand and told that I had to do my part of the work. My part was cutting sprouts and thinning corn, from daylight till dark, most of the time alone in the field, and lonesome for school. At one end of the rows I could look across a pasture to the schoolhouse, shut up and silent. I missed the other boys and girls. They were also working in the fields, and the only chance I had to see any of them was on Saturday after dinner. Then I had to shell half a bushel of corn, put it in a sack, and sling it across the back of a horse so that half went on one side, half on the other. Riding bareback, I took the corn to mill and waited my turn, sitting on the store porch with the other boys who had come to mill, or hanging around with them outside the blacksmith shop.

I missed the books. The free ones were locked up at school, and I had read the ones we had at home over and over. I was ready to go back to school, but a long summer lay between, with more work than all of us could do.

On a Saturday Monroe loaded some crossties he and Dewey had hewed out and took them to Detroit to sell. He went before daylight, on a back road that took him through miles of uncut woods before he came out on the main road. He came back after dark. He had sold the crossties for fifty cents a piece and there was money left over after he bought the things he had to buy.

He ate corn bread and milk at the kitchen table and told us about a tiehacker he had seen on the road. He lived in a little house back in the woods. He did not tell where he had come from. He did say that he was laying off to move on when the best tie timber had been cut. Standing on the road, he told Monroe that he liked to read and that he owned some books. Monroe named some of them, and they were books I had never heard of before.

"You reckon we could borrow some?" I asked Monroe.

"I never asked him. He didn't seem like the kind that would mind."

After dinner the next day I went to ask him, barefooted, wearing clean duckings and hickory-stripe shirt. It had been raining and water stood in brown pools in the post-oak flats and ran in leaf-stained streams to the bigger branches. I walked in water where I could, with the feel of mud and sodden leaves soft under my feet. Out of the flats, I crossed knolls where red oaks grew tall, and leafy branches hung close to the ground. On the low-growing leaves I found ink balls hard and green and round as marbles—each the nest of a pink-white grub. When I broke them open, purplish water ran out and stained my hands.

After more than an hour of walking I came to the house in the woods—a two-room house made of boxing planks and covered with hand-split boards. All was quiet around it. There were no chickens to run or dogs to bark. The front door was open but I could see no one inside. I went almost to the front door and called, "Hello." There was a sound of someone moving in the house but no answer. "Hello," I called again. Still no answer.

When I was about to turn away, a young woman came to the door with a baby in her arms. Her face was dead white and heavy about the lips and chin. A birthmark like smeared-on ink-ball juice covered one cheek and spread down to the neck of her dress. I could not keep from staring at it.

"Come in," she said. "We wasn't looking for company."

Her voice was friendly and when she turned her back she looked like any other woman.

"If I wouldn't be hindering I'd be much obliged."

"You're welcome. I'll get the mister."

She set a hickory-bark chair inside the door for me and I sidled to it. Then she went through a doorless opening to the other room.

Before I had time to look around, a man came through the opening, rubbing his eyes to wake up. He was not what I thought a tiehacker would be. He was tall and strong and young, with fair skin, a straight nose, pinkish lips, and heavy yellow hair which he pushed back from his forehead with long white fingers. He was too good-looking to be a tiehacker—too good-looking for the woman in the opening behind him.

"Howdy," he said.

He went past me and sat in the door with his back against the facing, close enough for me to get the green sap smell of his clothes.

"You getting many ties cut?" I asked.

He nodded but did not open his lips. I waited and then tried again.

"They say prices is good."

"Fair, you might say."

I had never seen a tiehacker with so little so say about crossties. People working in the woods nearly always talked about the woods, but not him. The woman stood in the opening, listening, saying nothing. I stared at her and then at him. They were not like other people, maybe from living back in the woods so long.

When I had nothing more to say about crossties, and the man and woman kept their lips tight shut, I sat staring out the door, past the man, to woods that stood like a gray-green wall, and sat till I could feel a cramp in my leg.

I knew there was no use putting off longer telling him why I had come.

"You like to read?" I asked.

It was like setting a match to the man's face. The color changed and there was light in his eyes. The woman spoke first.

"He'd druther read'n eat."

He looked at me and seemed not to hear the sourness in her voice.

"I read everything I can get my hands on," he said. "It don't make no difference what. Novels—history—anything comes my way."

He leaned toward me and he had the look, the sound of a teacher, only better than any teacher I had ever seen. He should have been in school, not in the woods, I knew, and I in the schoolroom with him.

"They ain't nothing like reading," he said.

He said it and meant it.

"You got many books?" I asked.

"I own twenty-five."

It was not the way a man would say, "I own ten pigs." Or cows. It was like owning horses, only prouder. With horses you have to show them off. He did not offer to show off his books, even when he could tell from my face how much I wanted to see them. He looked at me and then sat staring at the woods, his mind I was sure on what was inside the books. His wife stood in the opening, watching us, saying nothing. The books were there, in the house, and I began to feel that I would have to go without seeing them.

"What you got?" I asked.

He turned his eyes back to me, a boy sitting in his hickory-bark chair. He searched my face and eyes.

"You like books, don't you?" he said.

"Better'n I like to eat."

His wife had said it of him.

He laughed and stood up.

"No harm'n showing you."

The woman stood aside for us to pass. Then she sat in the straight-back chair I had left and began rocking the baby. The room we were in had a wood stove, a kitchen table, and two wooden benches. We went through the opening to the fireplace room. It had a bed with a quilt cover, apple boxes for trunks, and blocks for stools. In one corner, between the fireplace and window, he had built shelves of rough lumber against the rough bare wall. The shelves held books, more books than I had ever seen in a house before, or at school if the free readers and arithmetics were left out. The man went to the shelves and I followed close after him, looking at the books, reading the names: *Treasure Island, Light in the Clearing, Tom Brown's School Days*—enough reading for a month of Sundays.

The man took a book and put it in my hands.

"Have you read this'n?" he asked.

I felt the clean cool cover in my hand and read the title. *Penrod.* I had never heard of it before, or of Booth Tarkington.

"I ain't," I said.

"Would you like to borry it and read it? It tells about a boy."

"I sure would, if you don't care for me taking it."

He took it from my hands again and made a cover for it from a brown paper sack.

"I learnt a long time ago to take care o' books," he said. "I don't handle a book till I've washed my hands, and then I put on a cover while I'm reading."

I looked at the ink-ball stains on my hands and tried to rub them off on my duckings. He wanted me to take care of his book, but he wanted me to read it.

He looked at my hands.

"You can take it," he said. "When you get it read, you can

bring it back and get another one. You won't hurt it none, reading it."

I wanted to take it and go, but he wanted to talk about his books. I sat on a wood block and he squatted by the shelves.

"I can tell you about every book I've got," he said. "I've read them over till I've just about got them by heart."

One by one he took them down from the shelves and held them in his hands while he talked. He told the story of *Treasure Island* from beginning to end.

He held another book up and I read the name: *Martin Eden*.

"You read it?"

I shook my head no.

"This is about my best, in my way o' thinking. It's about a boy named Martin Eden that wanted to be a writer but didn't have any more to go on'n you or me—no education, no nothing. He did have something to say, and guts enough to stick with it till he got it said. He had a tough time of it, but he got to be a writer all right. Jack London sure knows how it feels to want to write. I read it and read it and get to feeling like Martin Eden. You know what I mean?"

I had never heard of Martin Eden or Jack London, but I knew what he meant. I had felt the same way, reading, and tried to tell him so, talking as I had never been able to talk to Mr. Jessee.

When the room was dark from the shade of trees I got up to go home. My work had to be done before night came on. Quietly he stood up and put *Martin Eden* in my hands. For a moment he laid a hand on my shoulder.

"You got a touch of the stardust," he said. "Don't ever lose it."

I did not understand the exact meaning of his words. I did not have to. He was talking about books and my feeling for books.

"I won't."

"That's good."

We went through the opening and past the woman, who was sitting in the door with the baby in her lap. She looked up but said nothing. She was there, but not enough to stop the lonesomeness I felt going away.

He walked to the edge of the woods with me.

"You coming agin soon?" he asked.

"Soon's I read what I've got."

He was still standing there when the trees and bushes shut him off from sight. When I was deep in the woods I stopped and looked at the books I held in my hands: *Penrod* and *Martin Eden*.

My work had to be done first. Then I could sit by the coal oil lamp, reading *Martin Eden* first, learning what he had to go through to be a writer.

Through spring and early summer I went to the tiehacker's house every time I got an hour or more off from work. Sundays he was always at home, reading from one of his books or sitting in the door staring out at the woods. Week days, after rain, when the ground was too wet to work in the fields, he kept on working in the woods. I listened for the faraway ring of a broadax and followed it till I found him hewing crossties. No matter where I found him, he took time out to talk to me about Martin Eden and Penrod and the other people I had met in his books.

When he was at the house, he picked out the books he wanted me to read. On the days when I could not find him his wife let me stand in front of the shelves and pick for myself. She may have read them but she did not talk about them, or hold them as he did. She never talked more than enough to pass the time of day. When I took back books she went through the pages one by one looking for marks or torn pages. Before I left the house, she made me write down the names of the books and promise not to keep them past Sunday.

In summer, when it was almost time for crops to be laid by, I finished reading *Treasure Island* and on a Sunday took it back, looking for a chance to talk about it to the man. I had questions to ask about it, and I wanted to tell him how I felt about Long John Silver. The book was another new world to me and I wanted him to tell me more about it.

The front door was shut and no one answered when I called "Hello." I waited as long as I could. Then I raised a window and laid the *Treasure Island* on the floor. I had read most of his books, but not all of them. I was sorry not to see him. I was sorrier not to have a book to take home with me.

As I walked through the woods I watched for him and listened for the sound of his axe. At the edge of the woods, at the beginning of first dark, I knew I was not going to find him that day.

The next Sunday I went to his house again. This time the doors and windows were wide open and the house was empty. They had moved and taken all their things with them. I went in and stood before the bookshelves. The books were all gone. There was nothing on the shelves but magazine pages pasted on for papering. I read words, lines of words that ended with cut edges. Stories had been chopped up till I could not find beginning or end. I looked at the pictures but they were no good without the stories. When there was nothing left to do in the house, I went out and walked slowly home through the woods.

I asked about him at the mill and store, but no one knew where he had gone, or where he had come from. They remembered that he had come to the house in the woods without a word to anyone. Now he had left the same way, leaving some good crosstie timber uncut.

"It could a been he was running from something," they said. "He might a been running from something when he come here."

There was never any more answer than that, and it was enough to make me wonder: How come a tiehacker's got twenty-five books? How come he never talked about the woods the way tiehackers did?

I went to his house again. It was empty and still. I could not help feeling bad about him and about the books I never got a chance to read.

I might have known that Monroe's Saturday nights and Sundays at Dock Farmer's were not all spent in talk about crops. I should have thought something was going on when Mae Farmer, wearing a dotted Swiss dress, came to our house to hear Monroe sing and pick the guitar. She sat at one side of the room with my mother, saying almost nothing, but blushing and laughing when he played and sang "Green Corn":

> Come along come along come along Jimmy John,
> Bring along bring along bring along your green corn.

Had an old cow and she had the hollow horn—
Took her to the house and fed her on green corn.

"Mae's about grown," my mother said, when she had gone home.

"Not grown enough not to be feisty." To my grandmother, any smiling or giggling at the boys made a girl feisty. Feisty to her was not the same as fast. "You never know when one's going to get to be the other."

In revival meeting time, when the crops were laid by, Monroe and Dock Farmer went to Paris in the buggy. It was an all-day trip that lasted till long after dark and meeting was over, and they had nothing to show for it.

The next day was not the same at our house. My mother and grandmother talked in low voices in the kitchen. Monroe shaved with my father's straight razor and then stayed in the fireplace room a long time with the door shut. When he came out he was wearing gray pants, yellow shoes, and a light-blue striped shirt, looking ready to go to meeting. He had on a necktie that showed burnished purple and green in the sunlight. He had set his felt hat on the back of his head to show off his sandy, roached hair.

"I reckon it's time for me to go off in the buggy," he said.

"Where you going?" I asked.

He laughed.

"Oh, knocking around."

He went, sitting in the middle of the buggy seat, out the lane and up the Blossom road, with us watching him till he was out of sight behind the willows on the branch. My mother looked sad, my grandmother frowned.

"I reckon it's for the best," my mother said.

"I reckon." My grandmother went back to the kitchen. "Once they get set on it, they ain't no stopping them."

I did not know what they were talking about. When I asked, they shook their heads and went on getting ready for meeting.

When I saw him again, we were under the brush arbor. Singing was over and it was time for the sermon to begin. He and Mae came walking into the light of the coal oil flares, walking close together, smiling, their faces reddened by the red light. She had on a white voile dress and had put her hair up in a knot on her head. She was fifteen, but she looked older.

They found a bench at the back of the arbor and sat down. My mother got up and went to sit with them. All at once I knew they were married, and I wanted to laugh and cry, mostly cry.

Monroe was married and it would never be the same with us again. I liked Mae. We had been in the same room at school, and she nearly always walked home with the rest of us. But I did not want Monroe married.

I sat through the sermon and the call to the mourner's bench. Then, after we had been dismissed by prayer, I went with all the others to stand around them and hear them tell about the ceremony.

They had gone to Post Oak looking for a preacher, and had found one there, at the brush arbor getting ready a sermon for the night. While they sat in the buggy, he said the words that made them man and wife.

"Didn't you feel funny, getting married in a buggy?" someone asked.

They laughed.

"No funnier'n getting married any other way."

In Pin Hook, people did not shake hands for a wedding. A few people wished them luck. Some said it looked like time for a shivaree. Someone asked my mother how she felt.

"The devil owes me a debt in daughter-in-laws," she said. "It's time he started paying me off."

She laughed and made others laugh while we were at the arbor. When they had gone off in the buggy, to hide out from shivareeing, and we were walking home, she did not laugh. She walked fast and I knew she was shaking her right forefinger against her skirt.

"You mind it?" I asked her.

"It's not that I'm minding them marrying. I do wish they'd got down out'n the buggy. It's bad luck getting married on wheels. Start out rolling, keep on rolling, they say. I don't think much of a preacher that wouldn't know better'n that, giving them a bad start."

58

On a clear warm night Cleaver took me outside and pointed to the evening star. He was leaving home that night. Before we heard from him again he would be under that star. Then he was gone, with no more word than that, though we thought he had gone out west to pick cotton.

Soon Monroe and Mae had gone. They had moved to the Womack farm at Blakeney on Red River, to pick cotton in the fall, to work a crop on the shares the next year.

In the time before school started, I had time to roam the fields and woods alone, to come again to the old family graveyard in a back field, to wonder about the Witherspoons, Halls, and Duvalls— my father's family—buried there. There were only a few markers, and the whole was grown over with black locust trees.

My mother told me the story. When the Witherspoons first settled there they had slaves to clear the land and build the houses. A child of one of their house slaves died and there was no Negro graveyard for her to be buried in. Wiley Witherspoon let them bury the child in the family plot, and the mother set out a locust to mark the grave. The grave could no longer be found, but in spring the graveyard was white and sweet with locust in bloom.

I walked the fields where the houses had stood. Only one was left: a square room and shed built of square hand-hewn oak logs. The logs showed marks of double-bit and broadax, and the careful work of slaves' hands.

When I asked my mother about the people who first settled there, she told me what she could, and let me look at one of the family keepsakes: a copy of *The English Reader* by Lindley Murray. She told me that Catharine Witherspoon had brought it to Texas in an oxcart. I had no way of knowing. On a blank page at the back I found: "Lewis Duvall one day after date promest to pay to." Those words and no more. He was Catharine Witherspoon's kinfolks, and somehow kin to me.

I read poems and parts of poems selected from Shakespeare, Pope, Dryden, names that meant nothing to me, and many others. I studied the prose pieces and tried to write descriptions like the ones I read from Addison and Goldsmith.

Then I was back in school. Edgar Latimer, a Pin Hook boy who had gone off to school at Commerce, had been hired to teach the big room. The boys and girls who had won out over Mr. Jessee soon knew how to torment Edgar, whom they never respected enough to call "Mister." They talked and laughed and passed notes during books. When he turned to write on the blackboard, paper wads flew. At recess they ran through the schoolhouse, playing leap-frog over the desks. Short of temper, Edgar yelled at us, words that got taken home at night. Soon the parents were saying that he had to be fired.

He never gave them the chance. He left about Christmas time, and they had to find another teacher to finish out the year. They hired DeRhon Stuart, a young girl from Woodland. She was young and blonde and as well dressed as any girl in town. She came with bobbed hair, at a time when many people in Pin Hook were argu-ing over whether a girl with bobbed hair could be decent. The girls all bobbed their hair and dressed up for school like going to church.

Every day was like a play day, with basketball at recess and forty-two games during books for the ones who had done their work. Books mattered less and less. Boys and girls were going steady, and she knew all their secrets. Pin Hook had not been so happy with a teacher in a long time.

Again I began trying to write. When I handed one of my pieces in to the teacher she read it aloud to the whole room. Then she came down the aisle to my desk.

"Where'd you copy it from?" she demanded.

"I didn't. I wrote it."

"You couldn't have. You're smart." She looked at the others. "But not that smart."

"I know I did—"

"I know you didn't. I won't take it—"

She went to the stove and dropped the paper in on the fire. The other boys and girls looked at me and laughed.

"I'll write more, and better ones," I said. "I'll show you."

She stood before the room, her face grim, her voice harsh.

"You can't show me a thing I don't know already."

She went ahead with lessons. At recess I went first to the woods to hide, and then across the fields and pastures home, too angry and hurt to cry, and ready to quit school because of the teacher.

At home I found Dewey clearing a new piece of ground, getting ready to plant it in corn.

"Good thing you got home early," he said. "Plenty of work for you, burning brush."

They had decided without telling me that it was time for me to quit school. Cleaver had come home again, but they still needed the work I could do. I never told them about the piece I had written, or what the teacher had said about it. School was over for me for the year, or for good. I did not care. I was not going to learn anything at Pin Hook.

While they sawed logs and split firewood I piled brush high and set a line of fires in the cleared part between the woods and rail fences. It was something to be doing, and I went at a trot dragging limbs and punching fires beginning to die down. The flames, pale yellow in the bright sunlight, turned purplish red at first dark, and bright red when night came on.

"You cain't come in till they all die down," Dewey told me. "We cain't risk letting fire get out."

For a time the flames rose high enough to make red patches against the black sky. Then they died down to beds of red coals, the sky grew lighter, and stars showed above the treetops. With the fires dying down, and the woods a black wall around, I kept close to the warmth and light, my mind on what was around me, on trying to say what was around me. At a time and a place people would believe I could make things up and write them down.

Tired of waiting but afraid to leave the fire, I took a burning stick and threw it high in the air. It became a fountain of sparks against a dark sky, beautiful to look at, frightening because of what it could do. It hit the ground and the night was blacker. I took another stick and ran with it, letting the sparks fall behind me like a shower of shooting stars. Up and down the new ground I went, running with burning sticks, throwing them, watching sparks glow bright and then fade, a boy out of school.

59

Days I worked in the field; nights I read from *The English Reader* and learned lines of poetry by heart. It was different from reading novels and stories—so many of the pieces labeled moral and didactic—but there was nothing else to read and I had to read something. Two lines of verse stuck with me:

> 'Tis education forms the common mind;
> Just as the twig is bent, the tree's inclin'd.

I memorized them and, in the field, went over them again and again, studying how they might be a part of me. They would not, I knew, if I worked in the field and never went to school. All I could see ahead of me was day after day working in the field.

What I had to say about education, the need for education, began to take shape in my mind. During the day I thought about it. At night I wrote down what I had thought, using as well as I could the words I had learned in *The English Reader*. Then it was finished and I had no one to show it to. School was out. I would have been afraid to show it to the teacher anyway.

There was a letter column for young people in the Dallas *Semi-Weekly Farm News*. One day it came to me that I should put my thoughts on education into a letter and send it in. That night I sat up late working on the letter. The next day, without telling anyone, I left it in the mailbox for Mr. Ragsdale.

The time of waiting seemed long. Then one day it was there in the paper, my letter printed every word as I had written it. I read it over and over and knew nothing like this had ever happened to me before.

I showed it to my mother.

"I knowed you could do it" was all she said.

On Saturday I took corn to the mill and stopped at the store. An old lady was on the porch.

"I seen your letter in the paper," she said. "Did you write it?"

"Yes'm."

"Well, I wouldn't a knowed you in it."

I was glad. It did not sound like Pin Hook. It might have been written by somebody outside Pin Hook.

Letters began to come from boys and girls in Texas and Oklahoma, four and five at a time, some answering what I had said about education, some asking only that we write each other. I began meeting the mail carrier every day.

"Looks like you got lots o' friends," he told me, with a laugh.

Then he was serious.

"I read your letter," he said. "You c'n go a long way if you have a mind to."

60

In the summer, when the corn was thinned, the cotton chopped, my grandmother washed and ironed her clothes and packed her old black valise.

"I'm going to Dallas for a spell," she said. "They say Vick's mind is getting worse. She'll know me now. They say she might not later on."

The letter was sent off to Maggie, telling her to meet my grandmother on the Santa Fe on Saturday. My grandmother called it *santafee*.

"I'd be afraid to go without being met," she said. "You go in at the Union Station, and it'd be easy to get lost, it's so big and so many people running through it."

Dewey was told to get the buggy and pony ready to take her to Paris Saturday morning. He would have to leave before sunup and get back after sundown. I wanted to go with him, but one more would be too much weight on the pony.

On the night before she left my grandmother sat on the kitchen steps not doing anything but watching the sunset. I sat with her and talked about the trip.

"You glad to be going?" I asked.

"In a way I am, in a way I ain't. It's a long way, and I ain't used to town ways. One day on the streets'll wear me out. If it wasn't for Vick, I'd as leave stay home. It might do her some good, seeing me again."

She talked about Aunt Vick and the hard trip but she did not talk about Dallas. She had been there and seen the tall buildings, the streetcars—all the things I wanted to know about—but she did not talk about them.

"I cain't set my mind on it," she said, "for thinking o' Vic's trouble."

I wanted to beg to go with her, but I knew there would be nothing to go on till cotton was sold, and not much then.

My grandmother went to bed soon after dark. Dewey played chords on the piano. There was nothing for me to do but sit in the dark and wonder what it would be like to go to Dallas.

We were up before daylight and by sunup the pony was hitched to the buggy and my grandmother was on the seat ready to go, in her black dress and starched white bonnet. Suddenly she called for me.

"I forgot the Jerusalem oak," she said. "Last time I was there Vick asked me to be sure and bring some more. She said it done more to clean out the mites in the hen house than anything else she had ever tried."

My mother was not so sure about it.

"They've moved to town now," she said. "They might not be raising chickens in town."

"If I know Vick, she'll have some chickens. Go get me some Jerusalem oak quick."

"How much you want?"

"It takes a right smart for a hen's nest."

I took some paper and string and went behind the barn where

Jerusalem oak grew thick and high like weeds. As I broke the stems the sharp, spicy smell rose around me. When the bundle was wrapped and tied, the smell stayed on my hands and came through the paper.

"Reckon that's enough?" I asked when I got back to the buggy.

"It looks like a plenty."

My grandmother took the bundle and put it on the seat beside her. Soon the air around the buggy smelled of Jerusalem oak.

"You reckon it's all right on the train?" my mother asked.

"Why not? It's a good clean smell."

Then they were on their way up the lane, my grandmother's bonnet whiter in the sunlight, and we were left behind. I took my hoe and went to the field to chop crabgrass and think what it would be like, going on the *santafee* to Dallas.

61

On a Thursday in August I was in the cotton patch, cutting weeds out of the middles, when I saw Mae stop at our mailbox, come down the lane to our house, and then cut across the cotton rows to where I was working. Cotton had been laid by on the river and she and Monroe were visiting us and the Farmers.

"You got a letter," she called when she was close enough. "From Dallas."

I went to meet her. She had walked a mile in the hot sun and her face was red and there were sweat marks under her arms. She did not slow down. She wanted to know what was in the letter.

I took it and saw that it was in Maggie's handwriting. When I tore the envelope open at the end a five-dollar bill slid halfway out.

"Just look," Mae said.

I looked at it and then she reached for it.

"It's not counterfeit," she said. "I can see the veins."

While she held it I unfolded the letter and read it. Maggie was asking me to come to Dallas on Saturday.

"That's the day after tomorrow," Mae said.

Maggie and my grandmother were sure it would be good for Aunt Vick if I would come. She was steadily growing sadder in mind. Seeing me would help her remember the good days at Pin Hook. Maggie did not want to take me away from home if it would cause any hard feelings. She was asking my mother to let me come, but only if my mother could make up her mind to it. All she could say was that she was sending five dollars for a ticket and she and my grandmother would be waiting at the station when the train got in Saturday night.

Mae took the letter and read it through.

"You going?" she asked.

I put my hoe over my shoulder and looked at the thin land and scanty crops. I had seen them before, year after year of the same thing, of working on land that would never make a living, of doing without, of being tied down by a rake and a plow and a grubbing hoe. My mind was already made up.

"I'm going if it's the last thing I ever do," I said. "I've got to go to the house and tell them."

We walked fast across the field and down the turnrow, and I talked about what I was going to do—the things I had dreamed about all at once close enough for me to touch, of getting away from Pin Hook, of making my way in a place where I would not have to tell people I was from Pin Hook. I talked as I had never talked to anyone before, trying to make her see the brightness that was burning my eyes. She saw and knew and we passed between us the five-dollar bill that had made the difference.

"You've got to go," she said. "You've just got to. If your mother don't want you to, I'll beg her. She's got to see. A boy like you has got to have a chance somewhere, and it's not to be had in Pin Hook."

Together we used worn-out words—getting an education, getting ahead—without any idea of how they were to be done. They sounded good, and we said them again slowly. Neither could tell the other about the world outside.

My mother was picking peas in the garden when we found her. She had on a limp bonnet and a floursack dress that hung loosely from her round shoulders. When I told her what was in the letter and showed her the money she took off her bonnet and wiped the sweat from her face with it. She took the letter and shaded it against the sun to read it. I watched her lips moving over the words and a look of sadness come around her eyes. I thought she was going to cry.

"I want to go," I said.

She took the bill and rubbed it between her fingers.

"I'll get a job and work hard. I won't get in trouble—"

She put her hand down at her side and I could see she was shaking it.

"It's a long way from home," she said.

"Not too far. The train makes it in less'n a day."

"You're nothing but a young'un."

"I'm nearly sixteen, and I won't get much bigger. I'll be staying with Maggie and Aunt Vick. They'll keep me outa trouble. I'm not afraid, staying with them. You've got to let me go. I couldn't stand it if I didn't go."

She read the letter again.

"When'll you have to leave here to get there?"

"Saturday morning, before daylight. I'll get Dewey to carry me in the buggy."

"He might not want to—"

"If he won't, I'll walk. I don't care how I get to the train, but I'll get there. I've got to."

She wiped her eyes with her bonnet.

"You got your heart set," she said, a trembling in her voice. "No use in me saying no. You c'n go, but the Lord only knows what you gonna wear. I reckon we c'n scare up something."

Mae went to my mother and put an arm around her shoulders.

"I'm glad you said he could go," she said. "I know he'll stay outa trouble and make good." She laughed a high, strained laugh. "He's got to make good. I want my children to have a rich uncle."

She took the sack of peas from my mother and we went toward the house. A fire had to be put under the washpot. The smoothing irons had to be set on the stove to heat. Clothes had to be brought out of dresser drawers and gone over.

Of my own things, I had a blue wool cap I had ordered the year before and a striped silk shirt Monroe had given me—those and a set of pink knit underwear Maggie had sent me for a present. Nothing else I had was good enough to wear on the train—not my duckings or blue chambray shirt—not the hobnailed boots I had worn all winter to school and to work. Anything else I had to borrow.

The suit was from Dewey—a light tan crash with pale green stripes. He had to try it on again before he would let me have it. On him, it was tight across the shoulders and short in the sleeves and legs. When he saw it was too small, he let me have it. As he was five inches taller, the sleeves came down to my fingers and the legs touched the floor over my feet. My mother wanted to shorten them but he would not let her. He thought he might want the suit back again. In the end my mother rolled up heavy cuffs on the sleeves and legs and ironed them in with a smoothing iron.

Cleaver had a pair of black shoes that he saved for Sundays. He let me have them after I promised to send them back parcel post after I had made enough money to buy a pair. Now I had shoes but no socks. My mother wanted me to wear heavy work socks but I would not.

"I'll go without," I said. "It won't be the first time I've gone anywhere without socks."

By Friday evening the clothes were ready for me to put on. My mother had washed my duckings and shirt and tied them up in a newspaper. I would need work clothes when I got to Dallas.

There was time, and at sundown I went out by myself and walked around the place, taking a last look at the barn and lot and a last pat at the ponies. Then I cut across fields and woods, following paths my feet had helped to wear. From the woods, where I had breathed the strong smell of hickory and sweet gum, I went across other fields to the watermelon patch. The good melons were gone, but there were small ones ripe enough to bust on the ground and eat. The red heart of a melon held in the fingers—something I would not have again ever in this life. It was something to put down on paper but I did not have time to try it.

After supper, Monroe played the piano and sang, as he had before he left home. I liked the sound of his voice and followed the words, but I did not feel like singing. When the others came to join him, I went to sit on the front steps in the darkness and think about what it meant, leaving this all behind me, going to something that might be not better but worse.

I was still there when they blew out the lamps and went to bed.

When the sky had turned to midnight white and I thought they were all asleep I heard my mother at the door.

"You get to bed," she said. "It'll be a hard trip for you, going all the way to Dallas."

In the dark I found my pallet and stretched out. The room was still dark when she called me in the morning. She had been up long enough to build a fire and cook breakfast. Dewey had gone to feed the pony. We would eat a little, he would hitch up the buggy, and we would go. *Forever*, I felt, now that the time had come. I mixed butter in molasses and sopped my plate with a biscuit, but it was hard for me to eat. In a few minutes I quit trying and brought my clothes to the kitchen to put them on.

Dewey went to hitch up. Feeling like someone else in the clothes, I said good-bye to the others, rousing them from sleep, and went out to the buggy. Dewey was already on the seat and I put my bundle of clothes down beside him. At that moment my mother came along the outside of the yard fence, her face gray in the gray light, her right hand shaking nervously along the side of her skirt. In her left hand she held a chicken, its feet tied together with a rag string.

"I cain't see a boy o' mine going off without socks," she said. She laid the chicken under the buggy seat. "You sell the chicken in Paris and buy a pair o' socks."

I wanted to kiss her good-bye, but couldn't remember ever having kissed her, and didn't know how to go about it. I hoped she would kiss me, but she did not. She stood back from the buggy wheels with her arms pulled close against her sides. Without touching her, I got up to the buggy seat and looked down at her.

"You be a good boy now and write me," she said.

"All right. I will."

Dewey clucked to the pony and we moved slowly down the lane and out to the big road. At the turn I looked back. My mother was watching from the door.

We left Pin Hook behind, sleeping. The sun was up when we passed the Novice Church. Dewey kept his eyes on the road ahead and talked.

"You've got to watch out for the women," he said.

He did not look at me and did not sound like himself.

"What women?" I asked.

"Bad women. Whores. Town's full o' them."

"I heard—"

"Where'd you hear?"

"At the store. They say—"

"I seen them but I ain't been clost to them. Scared o' what they carry. Bad diseases. It'd cost you three or four hundred dollars to get shet of. They say some never get shet o' them."

Questions came to my mind: Where would I see these women? How would I know when I met one? How would I get away from her if I did? I did not get a single question asked.

"I'm telling you so you'll know enough to stay away from them," he said.

For him there was nothing more to say about that kind of trouble. He did have advice on how to behave on trains and in railroad stations.

"If you have to go to the privy," he said, "you'll see a door with MEN on it. It holds only one at a time, so you got to watch your chances and wait till there's nobody in there. It ain't nothing like anything you've seen at home inside. It's all done by water. They got a little box on the wall with paper in it—two sheets folded together. You cain't get mor'n two sheets at a time, but nobody's stopping you from taking two more. Nobody'll be watching you in there."

He left me with the feeling that I would be watched everywhere else. When he was not talking I was wondering what it would be like to have people around me all the time. I couldn't scratch without being seen by somebody.

For the second time in my life I was on Lamar Avenue. I was no longer the little boy riding on a load of peanuts. I was almost a man and I was going off to Dallas. They said it was a heap bigger'n Paris. I was more than afraid. It was easy to get lost in Paris. It'd be a heap easier in Dallas.

Dewey sold the chicken at a store close to the wagonyard for a quarter. Then he stopped at a store on Bonham Street and traded it for a pair of black Sunday socks. There was no place in the store for me to sit down and put them on. I was afraid to put them on in the buggy. Somebody would see me and laugh at me.

It was close to train time and we went out Bonham Street with the pony at a trot. We tied up at a post across from the Santa Fe station and went inside. Dewey, who was carrying my five-dollar bill to keep me from losing it, went up to the ticket window.

"One way to Dallas."

It was easy for him to say it, but not easy for me to hear him say it. The agent did not look at either of us. He handed Dewey the ticket and change and Dewey handed them to me.

"Train's about due," the agent said. "You better wait outside."

No time now to put on socks. I stuffed them sack and all into my pants pocket and we went out to a platform, where station men pulled iron-wheeled baggage carts and passengers stood by their valises.

Before I could get used to the things going on around me a long lonesome whistle sounded down the track and the train came in with clanging bell and a roar and rush of steam that made my ears hurt. Suddenly a chill was about my heart and a tightness in my throat. The train was there to take me away and I would never come back. Much better not to go, I knew. Much better for me to be digging crabgrass out of the cotton. Nobody ever got lost in a cotton patch.

Dewey saw my face and must have known something of what was going on in my mind. He took me by the arm and put me in line for the conductor.

"Give him your ticket," he said.

With my bundle in one hand and my ticket in the other I let the conductor take my arm and help me up the steps. I looked down at Dewey standing by the conductor and tried to say good-bye. He held up his hand and I knew he was glad to see me go. A man pushed past me and went inside the coach. Not knowing anything else to do, I followed him.

The coach was no more than half-full—all men—farmers in duckings and straw hats—town men in suits and high top shoes. I found a seat by an open window and sat with my bundle on my lap. The air was close and hot, but I would not take off my coat. I was afraid they would laugh at my riding shirt sleeves. I was also afraid to take off my shoes and put on my socks. The smell of cigar smoke began to make me feel sick but I stayed on in the smoker, knowing somebody would laugh at me for being country if I went to another coach.

With a rush of steam and the far-off sound of the bell the train began moving out slowly past warehouses and an oil mill. I leaned my head as far out the window as I could. Better the smell of coal smoke than the cigars inside.

The trip was long and the train stopped at every station. I never moved from my seat for the water cooler or the privy. Either way I went, I would have to face all the people staring at me. I kept my head out the window watching the towns and farms we passed. It was Saturday and many people, in town for their day off, came to the station to watch the train go by. In the blackland, where cotton rows came up to the railroad track, people were picking cotton. It was good cotton, I could see, with thigh-high stalks white from the ground up. The people stood up and waved at the train passing by. When no one was looking at me I waved back. I knew them better than I knew the men around me in the coach.

It was near sundown when, across the flat hot prairie, I saw the tall buildings and acres of houses of Dallas. No one had to tell me it was Dallas. Nothing else could be that big. I saw the tall buildings against the sky. Then, when we left the farms behind, I saw shacks where people lived and all the dirt and junk along the tracks. What I saw made me know that in some ways Dallas was poorer than Pin Hook.

In the beginning of dusk the train stopped on a siding, waiting to back in to the Union Station.

"Next stop Dallas," the conductor called down the coach. "All passengers change at Dallas."

Then I could see the Union Station, white and clean against a blue-gold sky. Then I saw more, enough to make me know Dallas was what I wanted: automobiles on the Viaduct, streetcars coming and going to Oak Cliff, and, high above the city, an airplane circling. I had to be a long way from Pin Hook to see so many things all at once.

The train backed into the station and, with my bundle tight under my arm, I got off and followed the crowd up the long stairs to the waiting room. Each step brought something new—red-capped porters, sliding doors, so many people they had to go up one stair, down another. The waiting room, bigger than anything I had ever seen, had high ceilings, bright lights, and rows of benches filled with people. A Negro went through the waiting room calling trains in a hog-calling voice that rose to the ceiling and echoed from the ticket offices and newsstand. It sounded better than hog calling, the way he called the stops on the Katy: "Dennison . . . McAlester . . . Springfield . . . Sa-a-aint Louis . . . and all trains to New Yawk . . . Chicago . . . Washington. . . ."

Slowly I went down the rows of benches looking for Maggie and my grandmother. They were not there and I was afraid they would not meet me. I had the address on the letter but how was I to find one little house in all the houses I had seen from the train? I also had the telephone number to call if we should miss at the station.

I went up to a woman in a wire cage.

"Could you use the telephone for me?" I asked.

She stared at me and then smiled.

"What's the number?"

I read from the letter.

"Haskell five thousand one hundred and eighty-three."

"Haskell five one eight three," she said quickly and picked up the receiver.

Before she got the call through I saw my grandmother come up the steps to the waiting room and go toward the benches. She had on a long black dress she had worn from Pin Hook and a black straw hat with a purple ribbon. I had never seen her in a hat before and as dressed up. She saw me and put her arms around me in front of all the people. Then Maggie, who had been to see if my train was in, came up and kissed me on the cheek. Her black dress was as pretty as anything in the station, and her wide white lace hat showed she was used to living in town. They made me feel country, but I was glad they felt like looking their best.

We started toward the stairs to the street, with me between them, the bundle under my arm.

"What's that bulging your pocket?" Maggie asked.

"My new socks."

I stopped and pulled out the sack. My grandmother looked at it and then at my ankles.

"You mean to say you come all the way from home bare shanked?"

"Yes'm."

Maggie sat down on a bench and laughed till tears ran down her cheeks. My grandmother laughed with her—two women laughing while I stood on one foot and then the other and the Negro man filled the station with "Sa-a-aint Louis . . . Chicago . . . New Yawk. . . ." When Maggie could laugh no more she stood up.

"Let's go home," she said. "If you've come this far with your socks in your pocket you might as well go the rest of the way."

We went, with me walking stiff-legged so my ankles would not show, out of the station, across a street where cars whizzed by every minute, and on to a Junius Heights streetcar, in a glare of lights, in noise that made us put our heads together to make ourselves heard.

Riding a streetcar was not like riding a train. People took all the seats and crowded against each other in the aisle. A conductor took the money. A motorman rang his bell and we went right down the middle of the street, with cars passing on either side and people jumping to get out of the way.

"Watch 'em jump," my grandmother said with a laugh.

Maggie had advice for me.

"You got to learn not to be poky in front of a streetcar."

We were standing behind the motorman when the car turned on to Elm Street and the lights of stores and moving picture shows stretched in two long lines ahead of us, moving lights in red and blue and green that made wheels and waterfalls over and under lines of light running up and down and across, with names in lights standing still: GEM, JEFFERSON, PALACE, MELBA.

"Look at the lights," Maggie said. "You could go a long ways and not see anything as pretty as Elm Street at night."

I shook my head, too taken by what I was seeing to talk about it.

Far ahead I saw the word MAJESTIC and above it a strange and beautiful bird in red and green and yellow with crane's legs that stepped up and down, up and down, not going anywhere but, staying where it was, its red and green topknot high against the sky, making me forget everything but the knowing that I was in Dallas and this was a part of Dallas. Without a word I went to the back of the car and watched till we passed the curve that separated the light and dark parts of Elm Street.

"Deep Ellum," Maggie said when I went back to her, and I knew why. There were Negroes on the street and the sound of their laughter and the smell of fish frying. "You couldn't pay me to get off the streetcar on Deep Ellum."

We left the streetcar at Fitzhugh Avenue and walked south.

"You could a seen our house from the train if you'd a knowed which one it was," Maggie said.

After two blocks we came to the railroad track and walked a path at the end of the ties another half a block. We stopped at a bungalow dark in front but with light showing through a back window. It was as small as any of the houses I had seen, but new enough to smell of fresh pine lumber. Maggie unlocked the door and turned on the light.

"You all come on in," she said.

It was a small room with pine walls still unpainted, with the door to the kitchen open, the next door locked with an iron lock. Maggie turned a key in the lock and opened the door.

"We got him," she said. "Come see if you know him."

Aunt Vick shuffled through the door, barefooted, her gray hair falling down on the gray chambray of her dress. Her face was gentle as it had been when she left Pin Hook, but her eyes were different. They had a faraway, unseeing look.

"Hello, Aunt Vick," I said.

She came to me and ran her fingers over my face. I thought she was blind and then knew she was not. Her mind, not her eyes, had failed her.

"She don't know you tonight," Maggie said. "Maybe in the morning. Some days are worse'n others. You'll be a heap o' company to her. She always thought Jessie ought to give you to her."

She took Aunt Vick back to her room and locked her up again, out of sight but there on the other side of the door. I could not shut her out of my mind. She was worse than I thought. Her son was dead in the Navy and this was what his death had done to her. None of her days would ever be better.

Maggie and my grandmother put supper on the table but I could not eat. I sat with them and they told me the things we would do on Sunday—a hunt through the paper for a job for me, a list of places to apply on Monday, and then a walk to the Fair Grounds.

After supper they made a pallet on the floor for me and turned out the light. I lay awake a long time, listening to them talk, and then listening to Aunt Vick talking to herself on the other side of the wall.

The job I got was at the Sears, Roebuck mail-order house out on South Lamar, a red brick building with white trim set between the streetcar line and railroad tracks. Maggie took me there after a week of trying to get me a job as laborer, after a week of having bosses look at me and tell her I was too young or too lightweight for the jobs they had. I was glad to go with her on the streetcar out to Sears, Roebuck's. All my life I had wished on their catalogues. The orders we made out went to them. Dewey had ordered the suit I had on from Sears, Roebuck. My cap had also come from there.

I knew the building before the streetcar stopped. It looked just like the picture on the catalogue, only bigger, the bricks redder, the stone around the windows whiter. In the picture the wide concrete space in front was empty. Now there were people coming and going or standing in bunches waiting for streetcars. We got down and, without stopping to talk to anybody, went straight to the front door and through it, and to the right to the employment office, where Maggie had been before.

People waited in the rows of chairs around the room, mostly boys and girls close to my age. From them we soon found out that Sears, Roebuck was hiring. It was time for fall orders to start coming in from the farms. Town boys and girls laughed at getting jobs from cotton-picking money.

A girl gave me an application blank and a pencil and told me to sit at a table to make it out: name, address, age. I looked at Maggie and she nodded. In the blank I wrote sixteen. It was only a little lie—I would be sixteen in November—and it was lie or no hope to get a job at Sears, Roebuck. For education I could say seventh grade; for experience, farm work. For reference I gave two names; Maggie Tippitt, 4914 Santa Fe Avenue, Dallas, and U. S. Swindle, Route 3, Blossom. I handed it back to the girl and we sat down to wait while a man took the others inside one by one.

Some got jobs, some didn't. We could tell by the looks on their faces when they came out of his office.

My name was called and I went inside. The man looked me over and told me to sit down. He read my application over, glanced up at me, and read it over again.

"Sixteen, eh?" he said.

"Yes, sir."

"No experience working in town?"

"No, sir."

"Can you roller skate?"

I shook my head. I had never seen roller skates.

"I could learn."

I said it with such fear of missing a job that he laughed.

"You won't have to. I have a job for you that you don't have to be on roller skates."

The words brought me half out of my chair.

"I'm much obliged—"

He wrote something on my application.

"You report to me eight o'clock Monday morning. I'll turn you over to somebody else to break you in. You will be paid ten dollars a week, and a dollar for supper money the nights we work late. All right with you?"

"Yes, sir."

I said it fast before he could change his mind. A dollar a day was all I had hoped for. He stood up and I had to make room for the next one. I wanted to thank him but he was already calling another name.

"I got a job," I told Maggie in the waiting room.

"I know. See, I told you you would."

She put down the catalogue she had been reading and we went out of the room, past the rows of waiting people. Outside, I looked up the front of the building.

"I got me a job at Sears, Roebuck," I said. "Now I can tell the people at Pin Hook I'm making good."

She laughed, but she was not laughing at me. She knew what it was to come from Pin Hook and get a job in Dallas. She had done it all by herself, with nobody helping her the way she was helping me. She was no longer a country girl playing "No Not One" on the organ for a man twice her age. She lived in town in a house she had bought with her own money, and she had another house to rent out. She still worked at the shirtwaist factory but only when she wanted to. The scrimping she had to do at times was better living than nearly anybody had at Pin Hook.

On the streetcar she talked about how we could scrimp together and get ahead faster. I would pay her five dollars a week for room and board and she would build on a little room for me. From the rest I would save for clothes. We would go together to all the free things in Dallas till nobody would know I was from the country.

When we got off the streetcar she took me down a shady street and stopped in front of a house tall as the trees and painted white. It was the kind of house anybody would be glad to live in.

"That man come from the country when he was a boy," she said. "He got a job in a store on Main Street and worked himself up to the top. Now he's got a fine house and plenty o' money. He didn't have any more'n you've got to start with."

With a job, I knew getting ahead would be easy. I had no trouble seeing myself in a house like that.

63

With tokens for going and coming in my pocket, with lunch—not dinner—in a paper sack, I took the streetcar to Sears, Roebuck on Monday morning. It was a long ride—the length of Elm Street and then nearly as far again out South Lamar, the last part of it crowded with people going to work or to ask for a job. I got off with them and went to the employment office, eavesdropping on their talk, the talk of the ones who had worked there before, the ones who said they had been order pickers, checkers, stock boys, cleaning women, dolly pushers in the freight rooms. It sounded easy for them, going back, but not for me. I would have to catch on fast to keep up.

Eight o'clock by the clock over the door and the girl at the desk started calling out names, ten to twelve at a time.

"You worked on five before," she said to a boy in the first group. "Take them up to five."

Names were called, groups led away. I waited, afraid for my name to be called, and then afraid it wouldn't be—that the man had made a mistake in telling me. New people came in asking for application blanks. The girl moved the rest of us against the wall by her desk.

When there were only a few of us left, a man in blue serge pants and a tan pongee shirt came in with a paper in his hand.

"Ready, Mr. Morrison?" the girl asked.

He nodded and began reading names. I heard my name and went to stand with the others around him, close enough to see the dark shadows under his eyes and the even cut of a black sideburn. I liked his face and was glad to be going with him.

He led a dozen of us, all new, across the hall and into an

elevator. I guessed what it was and braced my shoulders against the wall, afraid to let them know I had never been in an elevator before, and that I would rather walk than ride. When we started up, my stomach seemed to stay behind and I swallowed hard to keep down the sick feeling. I gripped a wooden railing put there for holding on to and gritted my teeth to keep from asking them to stop.

The elevator stopped with a jerk at the sixth floor and we followed Mr. Morrison out.

"You wait here for me," he said to me.

He left me by a row of open windows where I could look out on South Lamar and get a breath of fresh air. A sleeve across my face and I felt better.

"Come with me now."

Mr. Morrison took me through heavy steel doors out into a wide open floor where rows of men and women worked at long tables and shouted above the grinding roar of machinery. The roar seemed to come from a sheet iron chute in the middle of the floor. Men checkers checked goods on orders. Women tied the goods in bundles and dropped them down the chute, and they made a rattling, rasping, bumping sound all the way down through the middle of the building.

Out from the tables rows of bins from ceiling to floor made aisles that stretched to the windows on the other side of the building. In the dim light of the aisles boys and girls on roller skates with orders in their hands went from bin to bin, picking out pieces of goods. Orders filled, they skated up to the tables, fast like racing, and the skates rumbled on the wooden floor. New orders in their hands, they swerved and darted back to the aisles, dodging each other, at times steadying themselves with a hand on a shoulder or the edge of a bin.

Mr. Morrison showed me a wire paper holder on the end of a table.

"Pick up your orders here," he said. "Bring them back here when they're filled."

He led me down a dark aisle at one side of the building to a long table halfway between the east and west windows. It smelled of oilcloth and rubber and creosoted floors. Rolls of oilcloth hung in racks behind the table; a strip of pink rubber sheeting was on the table.

"Denny?" Mr. Morrison called.

A tall thin young man came from behind a row of bins with a roll of oilcloth on his shoulder.

"Denny, here's your new helper. It's up to you to break him in."

Not my name, not anything about me.

"Yes, sir." Denny smiled. "I'll do my best."

Mr. Morrison went back down the dark aisle leaving Denny and me facing each other across the table. He smiled again and I liked his looks. He would be easy to work under.

"What part of the country did you come from?" he asked.

I thought he might be making fun of me, but he was not. It was only friendly talk.

"Pin Hook."

"Never heard of it. What's it close to?"

"Paris."

"Oh, I know where that is."

From then on I would be from Paris. It was only a twenty-five-mile lie.

"You been here long?"

"A whole week now."

"Well, stick around. We'll try to pick the hayseed out of your hair."

He was laughing at me, in a way that made me laugh with him. I liked him when he was laughing at me.

He took some orders from a wire paper holder and handed them to me to read. They were from people in country places, written in pencil, the words and numbers crowded into little places —all asking for oilcloth. I looked up at the rolls in the racks. Enough oilcloth for all the eating tables in the country.

He showed me how to match an order number with a roll on the racks; how to measure the cloth by the tape on the table; how to rip a straight line with scissors. The piece cut, it had to be rolled on a stick, wrapped in brown paper, and tied with brown twine. When there were enough orders for a load, I carried them in my arms like stovewood to the table up front, where a checker checked them and sent them down the chute. It was easier than any kind of work on the farm, and I liked watching the bright-flowered patterns opening up on the table.

Denny went to the warehouse. Denny went to the buyer's office. I stayed behind the table, matching order numbers with rolls of oilcloth and cutting piece after piece. Before I rolled a piece up again, I tried to think how it would look on a table, or on the table back home. Oilcloth was more fun than rubber sheeting. It could be red or pink or yellow roses, or patterns of checks or squares or running lines. Rubber sheeting was white or pink and nothing else. I soon saw that people ordered more oilcloth than rubber sheeting.

Without letting on to Denny, I watched the way he moved and listened to the way he talked. He had never lived in the country a day of his life, and looked it. I could never be as tall as he was, or as good-looking, but I could pick up city ways.

A bell rang and the noise of roller skates and machines stopped.

"Lunch time," Denny said. "You get forty-five minutes."

I wanted to eat with him but he was off to the elevator before I could get washed up. With my lunch sack in my hand, I went down the elevator alone, and going down was easier than going up.

Outside, in a parkway lined with benches, I found a seat by myself and ate by myself. I could see the tall buildings straight ahead and the Viaduct to Oak Cliff to my left, and I was glad to be there. I was in Dallas and I had a job. I would get ahead as fast as the next one.

While waiting for the work bell, I walked up and down the street in front of the building. Through a restaurant window I saw Denny at a table with some of the order pickers, talking, laughing, his thin face flushed, his eyes bright. I wanted to go sit with them, but the streetcar token in my pocket would not buy anything in a restaurant.

Back on the sixth floor, I opened a catalogue on the table and began going through it, page by page, starting with oilcloth. All the patterns in the catalogue were on the racks. It was the same with everything else. If it was in the catalogue it was in the building, waiting to be ordered. All I needed to order it myself was to work and get the money.

Denny came back and we finished the orders for the day. Order pickers, with nothing more to do, skated slowly up and down the aisles or came to lean on our table and talk to Denny.

"See you got a new helper," they said.

I kept on straightening rolls of oilcloth.

"Yep."

"Any good?"

"Green as grass but steady."

I felt their eyes on me and burned at what they were thinking: country, farmer, hick. They did not have to say the words, or ask where I was from. They could tell by looking at my blue duckings and shirt. They came and went and to them I was not a name: I was Denny's helper.

In the washroom, after the quitting bell, I changed back to my suit for the streetcar ride home. A boy with Denny passed me and looked at my suit and rolled-up cuffs.

"Where'd you get those clothes?" he asked.

I knew he was making fun of me.

"Ordered them from Sears, Roebuck."

He slapped Denny on the shoulder and bent over laughing.

"He orders his clothes from Sears, Roebuck."

Everybody in the washroom began laughing. For the first time I wished I was back in Pin Hook. Nobody laughed at Sears, Roebuck clothes in Pin Hook.

The boy came close to me and put out his leg.

"I wouldn't buy work pants at Sears, Roebuck," he said. "I wouldn't buy anything made to sell to country folks."

He held up the cloth of his pants leg.

"I paid fifteen dollars for these in town."

Denny stopped the laughing.

"Let's go," he said. "I'll show you how to punch out."

He went with me to the time clock and took my card from the in rack. After he showed me how, I punched it and put it in the out rack.

Then we were separated in the rush for the streetcar and I was packed in with people I had never seen before. It was not going to be easy, I knew now, living in town, being laughed at for looking country.

64

Learning how to cut and wrap oilcloth took little more than a day. Learning how to get along in a place as big as Sears, Roebuck took longer. I could read and write, add and subtract well enough

for the orders that came in. I did not have enough words or anything else to stave off the jokes made on me in the aisles and
washroom. It was easier, I soon found out, to get to the washroom
early and late, and to eat my lunch on the cutting table. Then I was
never alone without Denny, and he saved me as much as he could
from their joking. Some things he could not save me from.

One afternoon when there was a lag in work, bells began ringing all over the building. Far down a dim aisle I heard someone yell
"Fire!" and the aisles were full of the sound of skates and running
feet. Alone at the cutting table, I thought of all I had ever heard of
fires, pictures of buildings burning in flame and smoke. I went
down the aisle to look. Men and women had dropped their work
where they were and run. I had to run, too.

The first aisle to the stairs had been shut off by an iron door. I
got to the second just as two men were pulling the door to. They
tried to stop me but I got through and to the stairs ahead of everyone else. Down the stairs I went and the bells were ringing again,
and a siren blowing. The elevators had stopped and crowds of
people were on the first floor. I worked my way among them and got
to the outside, safe in the bright sunlight.

The fire engines were not there, and they did not come. I
waited and watched, but there was no sign of fire. I could see people
getting on and off the elevators.

"They must've put it out in a hurry," I said to myself. "Nobody'd be going up if they hadn't."

I went up and nobody was talking about the fire. On the sixth
floor the order pickers and checkers were at work. The iron doors to
the stairs stood open. Mr. Morrison walked slowly down the aisle
toward his office.

I went back to the cutting table and found Denny wrapping an
order.

"Where'd you go?" he said.

"Outside."

"Outside? What for?"

"To get away from the fire."

"What fire?"

A look of laughing began to glow in his face.

"The fire up here. The one the siren was blowing about."

He fell on the cutting table and laughed till his eyes were
squenched shut. He stood up and then had to sit down on a stool.

"I never heard anything to beat it," he said.

I began to feel green and country and small.

"It wasn't a fire," he said. "It was a fire drill."

"A what?"

He laughed till he had to get hold of himself.

"You never heard of a fire drill?"

"Never."

He stopped laughing and leaned on the table across from me.

"It comes once a week, but we don't know when. All we know is to run like hell and get a clip and do what it says. You know the red wooden clips across from the chute?"

I had seen what looked like a row of red wood boards hanging from nails.

"Yes."

"On the back they tell you what to do."

He was friendly and not laughing.

"I got Captain today."

I could see he was proud of it.

"Is that the best?" I asked.

"The pure D best."

He sounded like back home saying *pure* D. He was the Captain and he was friendly. I hoped he would not tell the others what I had done.

It was too much to hope. After he had made a trip up to the chute with orders the order pickers began skating by.

"How'd you like the fire?" they asked.

I knew enough to keep my mouth shut, but that did not stop them from laughing. They crowded around the cutting table and looked at me in a way that made me want to run.

"He's a Captain all right."

They were talking about me—not about Denny—and making fun of me for being too country to know about fire drills.

While they were still standing around, Mr. Morrison came back to talk to me. He sounded kind, but he could not quite keep the laughter out of his eyes.

"Didn't anyone tell you about the fire drill?" he asked.

"No, sir."

"We slipped up. Come on and I'll show you."

He took me to the front of the building and to the rack where red clips hung from nails. Order pickers, order checkers stopped to watch and listen and get another laugh out of me. I could see their eyes and the jerk of their heads, but I had to listen to Mr. Morrison.

"We've got to have fire drill, so if we do have a fire we won't panic and lose a lot of lives. When the bell rings, everybody's got to take a clip till they're all gone. Them with jobs have to take over."

He took down a clip and turned it over. I read NORTH FIRE DOOR.

"The one who gets it has to run to the north fire door and shut it. Understand?"

"Yes, sir."

He called the others to come listen. Then he took down several boards and pointed out all the fire stations on the floor. He showed us the axes, helmets, and red buckets hanging on the wall but did not take them down. They were to be used only for fires. So was the hose folded in a rack.

"You know what to do when the fire bell rings?" he asked me.

"Yes, sir."

"Well, go on back to work."

There were winks from the others, but not from Denny. In the washroom I heard them calling me "Captain" behind my back. I could feel my face hot with anger, but there was nothing I could do against so many. They could laugh at me now, but next time I would show them.

I was on my way from the warehouse with my arms full of oilcloth when I next heard the bell ring. I dropped the rolls on the floor and ran as hard as I could, ahead of the stock boys but behind the order pickers on roller skates. Men with clips were heading for the fire doors. Order checkers were running from behind the tables and past the chute.

As I came around a bin I saw there was still one clip on the rack. I pushed my way through and grabbed it. I turned it over and saw the word "Captain." When I turned around there was a burst of laughter. Stock boys, order pickers, order checkers—all of them bending over and slapping their thighs, slapping each other on the back, yelling "Captain."

Not knowing what to do—knowing only that it was a put-up job—I stood holding the clip while the others went through the motions of a fire drill. Then Mr. Morrison came from his office and named me "Captain" for the week. He hung the clip back on the rack.

"Fire drill's over," he yelled.

Back at the cutting table Denny told me what he could have told me before.

"You can lag behind and let the others run."

From then on I did more than lag behind. I hid under the cutting table and stayed there till the fire drill was over. No one knew but Denny, and he never told.

In October, cotton selling time, when farmers had some cash, orders piled up on my hook and on the tables. More order pickers and checkers came to work. The chute sometimes clogged and overflowed and boys had to climb down through it to clear it. When there was more work than we could get done in a day, we worked at night. Day after day I left the house at seven in the morning. At night I came home after eleven so often that I was always tired and sleepy.

After a while I knew I was as much alone in Dallas as I had ever been at Pin Hook. My grandmother had gone back home. Aunt Vick never really knew me. Maggie and I could never go anywhere together because one of us had to stay with her. I tried walking the Santa Fe tracks with a red-headed girl down the street but we had nothing to talk about except our jobs at Sears, Roebuck. After that I walked the tracks and streets alone, talking to myself.

I was not getting ahead at all. The money I made barely kept me going. If I had not been living at Maggie's I would have run behind every week. I could not save anything to go to school on, and I had to work too many nights to try to go to night school. If I stayed at Sears, Roebuck the rest of my life I would end up without an education.

The first week in November I walked my feet weary on the streets of East Dallas. It was my birthday week and I was sixteen. I knew I had reached the point where I had to go one way or the other. I had to choose between going back to school or being a day worker the rest of my life. I was afraid to tell anyone what was on my mind.

On Sunday night, toward midnight, I knew what I had to do. I sat up in bed in the darkness.

"I'm going back to school."

My voice was loud enough to rouse Maggie and she came to my bed, crying. She had put so much faith and hope in me, and she needed me, alone as she was with Aunt Vick. As for me, she said, going back to Pin Hook was going back to where I had started from.

"I'll be going back to school," I said.

"Pin Hook's not much of a school."

"It'll be better with Jesse and Lemmie Swindle teaching it."

They had been off to school at Commerce. I could learn

enough from them to go to Commerce in a year or two. Then I
could take the examinations and be a teacher.

"If you have to go you have to go," she said, "but you'll live to
regret it."

I stopped Mr. Morrison near the chute the next day and told
him I was quitting Saturday.

"What for?" he asked.

"To go back to school."

"Where?"

"Pin Hook."

"You're giving up a good job."

"Yes, sir."

"You sure you want to?"

"Yes, sir."

"Your pay will be ready Saturday."

He brought a boy in from the stock room to take my place and
told me to break him in, a job that took the rest of the week, and
work every night to keep up with the orders.

On Saturday I went through all the oilcloth patterns and cut a
piece to take home with me. At the end of the day I took my pay
envelope and went by the time clock. My card was not in the rack. I
no longer worked for Sears, Roebuck.

It was late at night when I walked the last miles to Pin Hook
and down the lane to our house. My mother, awake at my first call,
made supper for me on the fire in the fireplace and sat with me
while I ate and talked.

"I come home to go to school," I told her.

"I'm glad you did. It's been mighty lonesome, just me and Roy by ourselves."

Dewey and Cleaver were off at work, Dewey on a farm, Cleaver at a sawmill. My grandmother was living for a while at Aunt Niece's.

"I've got to have more education," I told her.

"It won't hurt you none."

She put the oilcloth on the kitchen table and I told her what it was like working at Sears, Roebuck. I did not try to tell her how I felt, being at home again.

"You better go to bed," she said. "Morning comes early on school days."

The next morning I was back at school with Jesse Swindle as a teacher, in the seventh grade, studying reading, arithmetic, and spelling.

New people had moved into Pin Hook. Every house and shack in walking distance of Pin Hook had a family living in it, and every desk in school was taken, some by boys and girls seventeen and older. During books they sat around the stove and courted. At recess they courted on the benches under the brush arbor. School nights they courted at holy-roller meetings in the schoolhouse. Saturday nights they courted at parties, snap parties given for young people but anybody who wanted to come was welcome, or at least told to come in. Sunday nights the courting groups met for secret suppers—something never heard of before in Pin Hook.

These Sunday night suppers did not last long. Boys not asked put a stop to them. News went around that there would be a picked party on a Sunday night. Sunday night the boys caught a goose, picked it clean, and turned it loose at the party with a board tied around its neck. On the board they had printed:

One picked party, one picked goose.
Next time you pick, we'll pick the whole bunch.

The holy rollers—calling themselves Pentecostals—held their meetings Sunday, Wednesday, and sometimes Friday nights, in a schoolroom dimly lit with coal oil lanterns. Mostly women, they came at first dark or soon after, walking from the store or from up the Blossom road, and a few of them across the fields, holding their long skirts up out of the mud, praying as they went, at times stopping to kneel and shout and sing a holiness song. They took the seats in the front of the room and boys and girls took the ones at the back, where they could whisper and hold hands and make fun when the sisters got the spirit enough to go into unknown tongues. It was almost the same at every meeting: songs, prayers, testimony from the faithful, a sermon, more songs, and the call to sanctification or the second blessing.

Night after night women who had achieved the first but not the second threw themselves on the floor, rolling and praying, while the others prayed over them and begged them to throw the devil out of their lives. In the lulls I sat with my head down, trying to remember my reading, or any other lesson of the day. Then I put thoughts of school out of my mind when someone broke through to the Holy Spirit, when there was shouting and dancing and the strange *shibboleth* sounds of unknown tongues.

They might work over one sister till midnight and not help her through. Then she would rise to her knees and raise her hands above her head.

"God help me, I cain't get it tonight," she would cry.

It was a sign for praying and begging to fade away, for the meeting to break up, for the people to start the long walk home, the women quieted down, the boys and girls in couples walking slowly, courting all the way home.

66

The Interscholastic League was a part of the Pin Hook school for the first time that year. A part of extension teaching at the University of Texas, it was set up to sponsor athletic and academic contests among schools in every part of the state. In years past, Pin Hook had gone to Woodland or Woodland had come to Pin Hook for basketball games and spelling matches, but the contests ended there. Now a school could work its way up to a county meet or even to the state. Pin Hook had a chance to put itself on the map.

By the rules Pin Hook had only two possible entries: girls' basketball and spelling, the one in the winter, the other in the spring.

School very nearly gave way to basketball, not because of the teachers but because of the community. A new court had to be marked out in the sand, poles cut and brought in from the woods, backboards built and set. The blacksmith made new hoops and the girls made black bloomers and middies for themselves. We had basketball games before school, at recess, and after school. People who usually sat their time away at the store hunkered on the ground at school and watched basketball. Friday afternoons most of the people in Pin Hook were on the sidelines. For the games away from home, a line of buggies and wagons left the school ground at the dinner recess. For the home games, older boys and girls, no longer in school, came to visit the whole day and before game time the school ground was full of wagons and buggies.

Girls who made the team could go out to practice during books on good days. So could the boys who were line watchers, referees, or good talkers. Not any of these, I stayed with my books and had my papers copied by boys and girls too busy with basketball to get their lessons.

Then, after all this, the Pin Hook girls lost an early game and the chance to go to the county meet. This did not stop them from playing basketball. Only the cold and rain of winter stopped them, when the court was deep in mud and the ball too wet and heavy to bounce.

The spelling meet was to be held at Paris in the spring, with each school in the county sending two contestants. Soon after Christmas Jesse and Lemmie put us through several spelling matches to choose the best from Pin Hook. As the tests ended, it was clear that I had first place, a girl in the eighth grade second, another girl in the eighth grade third.

"The way you spell, you ought to win something," Jesse said.

Then, at the time for sending the names in to Paris, I did not have the money for the student registration fee, and there was no way to get it in time. Jesse dropped me from first place and moved the two girls up. Then he assigned me to teach them spelling.

For weeks we went to the girls' cloakroom and I gave out the words for them to spell: *abattoir, synthetic, hyperbole, secede, recommend,* and all the others on the list of eight hundred or so sent out by the Interscholastic League. The door was shut. No one could tell how much we spelled, how much we talked, how much we laughed. All of us knew that the nearer we got to the meet, the less we worked on spelling.

One morning one of the girls kept missing words she had spelled the day before. On one word she gave up and put her face in her hands, and let the words burst out.

"Oh, God, if I have a baby I'll die."

The other girl turned red in the face and looked down at the floor.

"I cain't talk at home and I've got to tell somebody," the first girl said. "I'm so scared. I've kept it to myself three weeks and I've got to talk."

The other girl and I kept quiet and let her talk.

"We were playing snap and I let him. Somebody left us outside a long time and I let him."

We did not have to ask who it was.

"Oh, God, I just laid down on the ground and let him, and I wish I hadn't. I wish I could take it all back."

She began to cry and the other girl put an arm around her.

"Wait and see," she said. "Ain't nothing you can do but wait and see."

All of us waited, day after day, sometimes working on spelling, more often whispering about the chances.

Then one morning she came in and told us that everything was all right, and we were glad, for the spelling meet was the next Saturday.

The girls went to the meet and lost in the first round.

Pin Hook was not surprised. Pin Hook did not care. Pin Hook was so busy playing rolyholy that nothing else mattered. Rolyholy is a game of marbles with three holes in the ground in a line and one to the right to make an L. Players start at a taw line ten or fifteen feet from the first hole and shoot all the holes in the L and back. A player keeps going as long as he hits a hole or another player's marble.

The game started at school with little boys crawling on all fours on the ground. Big boys and girls took it up and soon every house in Pin Hook had a rolyholy game in the front yard. Men sitting around the store started their own games: in front of the store, in front of the gristmill, and between the blacksmith shop and the row of mailboxes. Grown men wore the knees out of their duckings and their thumbnails to the quick shooting marbles. Three games went on all day Saturdays and Sundays, with some betting on the side.

Marbles went from the clay of the little boys to glass for the big boys and men and agate for the men with money enough to buy them. Players began to brag how many marbles they had busted. Plowing was held up while men tried to bust each other's marbles.

The blacksmith watched the rolyholy games while he worked at bellows and forge and anvil. He watched marbles busted and said nothing. Then on a Saturday, when three big games were going, he let the fire die down and came out to play rolyholy, with a steel ball taken from a bearing. The others let him go first and watched as the ball went straight from the taw line and dropped into the first hole.

"He's been practicing up," they joked. "I'll bound he's on his knees behind his house night and morning."

The blacksmith said nothing, but waited till the other marbles were on the ground. Then he took good aim on a clear glassy. There was a sharp click and the glass split in half. The men laughed, but there was no fun in their laughter.

"You busted him," one of the players said. "He's out."

"Danged right."

He said it and took aim on another glassy. Another click and another glassy broke.

"Is steel balls fair?" one of the players asked.

"Nobody never said it wasn't."

The one man with an agate put his foot between it and the blacksmith. The others saw it.

"Aw, come on," they said. "Le's see c'n he bust a agate."

He never got a chance. He did sell a handful of steel balls at two bits apiece and men with glassies got out of the game.

Soon it was steel balls at school, steel balls at the store, and rolyholy stopped as fast as it started.

67

Out of school long before school was out, study of reading and arithmetic behind me, cotton and corn rows ahead of me, dead brown with stalks and stubble, I knew how wrong I had been to leave Dallas, how wrong to think I could get an education in Pin Hook. Farm work had to be done, and too much of it depended on me—all of it on Cleaver and me. Dewey was working his way through a business school in Fort Worth. My mother was too old for heavy farm work, my little brother too young for anything but light jobs. Cleaver was as stout as a mule and as steady. He took over the plowing. I kept up with the hoeing as well as I could.

We worked a few acres on the homeplace and rented a piece of black dirt two miles up on the Blossom road. This was better land, but we had to be on the road early and late to work it.

Through spring and into the heat of summer we worked six days a week in the field and on Sunday we tried to catch up with jobs around the place. Pin Hook might have been miles away for all we saw of it other than the Saturdays when we went to mill or the Sunday nights when we went to a singing.

In August we finished laying the crops by. In August we knew the cotton was good, but not good enough to see us through the winter. One of us would have to hire out for work for a while. Cleaver could keep things going at home. I would have to work out—out on the prairie or down on the river. Before the fall was over, I worked both places.

After supper one night I told them I was going and walked out the front door. My mother followed me to the gate crying, but she knew one of us had to go. At the time she could do without me better.

With stops for rest and a short sleep on the ground, it took me all night to get to Paris, my first stop on the way to the blackland. I was leaving Pin Hook again, but not for long. I had told my mother I would be back when cotton picking was over. At times I was not sure. It was enough to walk over the red hills once. I could save my money and keep traveling, and never see them again. Any job in Dallas would be better than what I was doing.

It was daylight when I walked along Lamar Avenue, past houses and churches and stores. At any of them I could have stopped and asked for something to eat but I did not because of something my mother always said: "Never steal—never beg. You'd better go hungry than steal or beg." It was up to me to find some-body who would hire me and feed me.

I walked once around the square and then north on Main Street to the wagonyard. In front of the courthouse a man got up from the steps and stopped me.

"You looking for a job picking cotton?" he asked.

He looked more town than country in his white shirt and blue pants. His straw hat could be town or country.

"On the blackland?"

He laughed and I saw how young he was.

"Way out on the blackland."

"How much you paying?"

"Seventy-five cents a hundred and board."

"You got you a cotton picker."

"My truck's on the square in front of the bank. I'll round up the other boys and meet you there."

I went back around the square to the truck. Two boys were already on the front seat. A third boy came with the man.

"My name's Thompson," the man said. "You all ready to travel?"

"Couldn't be no readier. Where we going?"

"Out clost to Enloe."

I climbed up to the back of the truck with the other boy and stood holding to the cab. From there I could look into stores and houses as we went around the square and out South Main Street.

Soon after we left town we were on the blackland. Cotton was opening and picking looked good. Whole families went up and down rows dragging heavy sacks. At seventy-five cents a hundred and board I could make good money.

Thompson lived on the road between Lake Creek and Enloe. He left the other boys at his father's place and took me on to his house, to eat early dinner with him and his wife, to help her set up a cot for me on the back porch, and to take a brand new sack to a field white with cotton.

"Get grabbing that cotton," he said.

No need telling me twice. The more picked, the more pay. What I did not pick, somebody else would, and there were plenty of pickers, coming on foot before daylight, or coming in trucks from town. Thompson had to go at a gallop to keep up with the weighing and ginning, with two wagons going at once—one in the field with the tongue up and scales hung from it, the other on the road. When he was not there to weigh, his wife stood by the scales and took down the weights in a book.

It was a good job while it lasted. I had time for a letter home, a letter back. From the second, I knew I was going back to Pin Hook. Dewey was home again and I could go to school in the fall. The first picking was good. The second would be better I could see from the bolls still green on the stalks. I would stay for the second picking and then go home.

Then I was home again before the second picking was half over, carrying my clothes in the cottonsack I had paid for, sick with the third day chills, sent home because Thompson and his wife did not have time to take care of somebody chilling. My mother, glad to see me, glad for the money I brought, put me to bed and got out the blue quinine bottle.

School started by the time I was over the chills and fever, but I was off to work out again, this time in the river bottoms. I stayed with Monroe and Mae and picked in cotton higher than my head.

When the cotton was too thin to pay picking I worked by the day gathering corn, following a wagon, breaking off the ears, throwing them to the wagon body. Scorpions nested in the dry shucks and at times I was near crying from the stings in my hands. Men on either side of the wagon, sometimes white, sometimes black, knew the hurt.

"Another'n get you?" they would ask.

"The way it hurts, it could a been two."

"Don't I know it. Ain't nothing worse'n a scorpion stinging you in the pam o' your hand."

Then corn gathering was over and there was no more work for me on the river.

I went home again and back to school, starting late, trying to catch up on the algebra I had missed, learning to say *amo, amas, amat* without laughing. Jesse Swindle, with all Pin Hook against him, had put in the study of algebra and Latin.

It was soon clear that I would do well in Latin, and just as clear that I would not do well in algebra. Neither mattered very much. By Christmas I knew that I would have to quit school and get a job.

I made up my mind one night at a holy roller meeting in the schoolhouse. A woman preacher had prayed and preached. Then she opened up the door to heaven.

"God help them that come too late," she cried.

She danced across the front of the room with her arms upraised.

"It's a time for the second blessing," she shouted. "It's a time to be sanctified. Anybody want to be sanctified?"

Women and a few men fell on their knees and prayed in loud voices. A large woman went up and fell to the floor.

"God help me," she cried. "Help me get the Holy Spirit."

Women crowded around her, kneeling, praying, begging her to

try harder. Girls who studied algebra and Latin with me put their heads down and cried. Older men and women went down on their knees and talked in unknown tongues. A man not right in his head lay on the floor on his back shouting over and over "Shibbola, shibbola, shibbola."

When they were wet with sweat and their voices harsh whispers the woman stood up with a groan.

"I cain't get it tonight," she cried. "I've been turned back again tonight."

If she had come through, there would have been shouting and dancing, but not now. She had given up. The praying and talking in tongues stopped. People went back to their seats and wiped their faces. They needed only the benediction to send them back on the dark roads home.

Pat Swindle was waiting for me on the steps.

"You want a job?" he asked.

"I might."

"Papa said tell you he needs a hand. He says come to see him if you're looking for a job."

68

Within a week I went to see Mr. Swindle, knowing that a job as a farmhand was not what I wanted, knowing at the same time that my only chance was to hire out and get enough money to go to school somewhere else. My mother was ready for me to drop out of school. I was seventeen and past the time when I could expect to learn anything at Pin Hook. She was not ready for me to work out: She needed me at home, helping work our own land. She knew at the same time that I had to start somewhere away from home if I wanted to get ahead.

"Being a hired hand's not like being at home," she told me.

"I've hired out before."

On a warm sunny day I went through fields and woods, crossed Pine Creek on a footlog, and came out on the Novice road in sight of the Swindle house. It had not changed, and in a way it looked like home. Many a time I had sat on the front porch resting before starting back up the road with my buckets of water. It would be easy to go the rest of the way, except that I was still a little afraid of Mr. Swindle.

I waited and looked and then went on up the road. I might as well face him and get it over with. I turned off the road and went past the well. It had the same oak curb but a new bucket hung from the chain. I stopped with my hand on the gate latch.

"Hello."

Mr. Swindle opened the door of the west room and came out on the porch.

"Come on in, Bill," he said when he saw me. He was the only one who had ever called me Bill and he made it sound friendly.

I went up the sandy path and stopped at the steps.

"I reckon you've come for a job," he said.

He might have been smiling. I could not tell because a heavy moustache hid his mouth.

"Yes, sir."

He sat on a cane chair and I dropped down to the steps. His back was against the white painted wall, close to the facing where he kept his record of weather. I could see enough to read words but not figures. NOVEMBER . . . NORTHER. . . . : DECEMBER . . . KILLING FROST. . . . ; JUNE . . . CYCLONE. . . . ; FEBRUARY . . . THUNDER. . . .

Thunder in February, frost in April, I thought, but did not say it. He might laugh at the saying.

"I'll pay you fifteen dollars a month and board."

I knew this was customary.

"It's all right with me."

He wrote a date on the wall.

"Beginning next Monday."

"Yes, sir."

He was now my boss and I had to listen while he told me about the work to be done: wood to cut, land to be bedded, fences strung —all this before the work of spring—all to be worked at six days a week from daylight till dark—and Saturday e'enings off when the work was caught up.

"Fifteen dollars a month's a lot o' money for a boy your age."

"Yes, sir."

"What you going to do with it?"

"Save it. Go to school when I can."

"Where?"

"Commerce."

It was the only place I had ever heard of. Four of his children had gone there; the other three would go when they were ready.

"You want to go to school?"

"More'n anything."

He looked across the field, ready for plowing, and back at me.

"You work hard and save your money," he said. "I reckon I can help you some when you get ready to go to Commerce."

"How?"

"I reckon I could loan you a dollar for every dollar you save."

I counted quickly in my head. Winter to fall I could save a hundred dollars. With another hundred from him I could go to Commerce and work the rest of the way through.

"I'd sure be much obliged," I told him.

He nodded.

"I'll count on you to come Sunday. Bring your duds. The madam's not at the house now, but she'll fix for you to sleep in the shed room with Pat."

"Yes, sir."

I went out the gate and down the road—the long way home by the bridge over Pine Creek—glad that I had gone to Mr. Swindle. It would be months of hard work and then I would go to school.

On Saturday my mother washed and ironed my clothes and packed them in a floursack for me. On Sunday I put the sack over my shoulder and went up our lane. At the schoolhouse I stopped long enough to sit at the desk that had been mine and carve my initials in the oak top. Then, Pin Hook school behind me, I took my floursack and went the shortcut to Pine Creek.

69

It was not easy to be a hired hand. Morning after morning we ate breakfast by lamplight, after we had fed the stock and washed up at a pan on the back porch. Breakfast was good, with hot biscuits every morning, with Mrs. Swindle working over the stove, shadowy in the lamplight. By good daylight we were through breakfast and out to work.

Thurman Swindle lived up the road and worked on shares with his brother. It was my job to work double with him. He was a man in his thirties, stout as a mule, and always in a hurry. It was backbreaking for me to try to keep up with him.

On dry days we plowed or harrowed fields that ran to deep sand or post-oak clay, keeping our teams side by side, the same number of times at the turnrow for each of us. Long after sunup I could see Pat and his sisters on their way to school. By the time Mrs. Swindle hung a rag on a bush to call us to dinner I could see myself dragging a row behind. At night, when the mules were unharnessed and fed, I went slowly to the back porch to wash my face and soak my feet before supper.

So much walking, following a plow, galled me and there was never enough time for the swelling to go down or the rawness to heal. Afraid to tell anyone I was galled, I walked straddle-legged and tried to keep up. Thurman could have known by watching me, but he never slowed down or gave me any extra rest.

On Friday night one of the older girls came home from teaching school. When I came in from the lot, she was waiting for me on the back porch, a shape in the darkness.

"I know you are hurting," she said. "I could tell it the way you walked."

I was glad she could not see my face.

"It's hurting me some."

"Sit for a while in a tub of cold water," she said. "I brought you some meal to put on it."

I stripped in the darkness and sat in a tub, feeling the water burn, and the rough boards of the outside wall against my back. Then I dried myself and dusted my crotch with cornmeal. I was still raw but the pain was less, and I knew what to do next time.

On wet days Thurman and I cut wood, each on a side of a log, a crosscut saw between. Hour after hour we pulled the saw back and forth till my arms hurt and my back ached. Then I would forget and ride the saw.

"Pick up your feet if you're going to ride," he would say.

When the sawing was done the wood had to be split with sledge and wedges and hauled to the woodpile in front of the house. It was heavier work than plowing and it left me every night with sore muscles and a dread of wet weather.

Week nights we sat around the fireplace reading or talking. At times I played songs on the pump organ in the front room and Mrs. Swindle sang. These nights I felt a part of the family.

Saturday nights Pat and I walked down the road across Pine Creek to Pin Hook to have what fun we could at candy breakings or parties. On the way, we were boys together. At the parties, I was the hired hand.

One night in late spring, after the others were in bed, Pat and I slipped out of the house and went down the road toward Pin Hook. When we were away from the house he took a pistol from his pocket and carried it in his hand.

"Where'd you get it?" I asked.

"Out of the dresser drawer."

"You'll catch it if they find out."

"Let 'em find out. They c'n kill me but they cain't eat me."

I was scared. If he got in trouble, I would be in trouble.

"You better be careful," I said.

"I'm not scared. I'll show 'em I'm not."

When we were in the Pine Creek bottom, close to the bridge, an owl laughed a wild laugh from the top of a tall sweet gum. Pat took aim at the top of the tree and fired once. The owl stopped laughing and with a rush of wings flew away from the road.

"They can hear at the house," I said.

"That don't scare me none."

We walked on to Pin Hook and found every house dark. Nothing to do but walk back, and we were in no hurry. We stopped on the store porch and at places along the road. Pat talked about running away from home. I talked about leaving Pin Hook.

Late at night, when we had walked and talked ourselves out, we slipped back to the house and, careful not to make a noise, went to bed, with the door latched inside.

While it was still black outside there was a hammering at the door and Mr. Swindle began yelling.

"Where's my pistol? Open the door and give me my pistol."

I slid out of bed and grabbed my clothes. Pat opened the door.

"Here."

I could not see him but I knew Mr. Swindle was in the room.

"Get your clothes on and get going," he said. "Get to the cotton patch and don't come in till I tell you."

It was still black when we took our hoes and went to the field. We waited at the end of the rows for it to get light enough for us to see the cotton.

"I'm leaving," Pat said. "First time I catch them not looking I'm leaving."

Mr. Swindle watched us all morning and let us come to the house for dinner. He stopped me in the yard.

"I've give up trying to help you," he said. "I wouldn't loan you a dollar for anything."

There was only one thing for me to say.

"I'm quitting."

"Not till crops're laid by. You give me your word to stay and you're going to stay. Then you can go where you want to. I thought you wanted me to help you."

Feeling at the end of everything, I agreed to stay. All day I worked in the field. At night I wrote Maggie a letter asking her if I could come back. Then I met the mail carrier down the road and gave it to him.

When I came back to the house, Mrs. Swindle was waiting for me on the porch.

"I know what you want to do," she said. "You want to go to Dallas. You'll be waiting for a letter from your cousin in Dallas. Am I right?"

"Yes'm."

"We'll hate to see you go. You've been good company."

She had been good to me, but I could not find the words to say so.

Saturday morning Mr. Swindle sent Pat and me to chop cotton in a field in sight of the house. Then he and Mrs. Swindle went to Paris in the wagon.

When they were out of sight, Pat put his hoe over his shoulder and started toward the house.

"I'm leaving," he said.

"Where you going?"

"I don't know, but it'll be so far nobody'll know how to find me."

I went with him to the house, to the shed room, and watched him tie his clothes in a bundle.

"You could pack up and go with me," he said.

I wanted to, but I was afraid. I had half a month of pay coming to me. I would never get it if I left.

"I cain't," I said. "I've got to stick it out till crops is laid by."

Back in the field, I stood leaning on my hoe handle and watched Pat go with his bundle under his arm up the Paris road. All day long I leaned and looked, with only a little hoeing in between. Mr. Swindle would be mad, but let him.

He was.

"Where's Pat?" he yelled when he drove up to the gate.

"Gone."

"Gone where?"

"He didn't say. He left home."

Mrs. Swindle got down from the wagon, crying, and went to the house.

"Unhitch and unload," Mr. Swindle said to me.

He went across to the field and came back.

"You didn't hurt yourselves hoeing," he said.

"Pat left early."

"That's no excuse for you."

From then on the work was something to live through day after day. It was laying by work. The only good thing about it was that every time I came to the turnrow, hoeing or plowing, laying by was nearer over.

Then Mrs. Swindle came to the field, bringing a letter from Maggie. She waited but not for long. There was only one page to read. Maggie had married a policeman and turned her house into a boarding house. She would make room for me if I was willing to sleep on a pallet on the back porch.

"You going?" Mrs. Swindle asked.

"Yes'm. As soon as we get laid by."

After that, my work was slower, with more trips to the well for a drink of water and more rest in the shade at the end of the row. It was late July. Time for anybody to get some rest, crops or no crops.

In the middle of a morning Mr. Swindle called me in from the field.

"You're fired," he said. "You know why?"

"Yes, sir."

"You know what it means to be fired?"

"Yes, sir."

"Then you better pack your duds and go."

"Yes, sir."

"You're not the boy I thought you were."

He stayed in his rocking chair on the porch and I went to the shed room. Mrs. Swindle came to help me pack, and cried because I was going and Pat had never come back. I felt bad over the firing, but I was glad to be going. I knew that I was through being a hired hand on the farm.

Six months and more a hired hand, and only a little money at the paying off—enough for a ticket to Dallas, enough after that to keep me a few days and no more. This time I had clothes of my own to wear: blue serge pants, white shirt, and tan shoes, all ordered from Sears, Roebuck. And clothes to work in. My mother helped me get them ready, crying because I was going but urging me to go.

"Hiring out didn't help you none," she said. "Nothing like a job in Dallas will. I hate to see you go but I wouldn't stand in the way for the world."

It was September when I took the train to Dallas. I knew what to do on the train but I did not know what I was going to do with myself. Get a job. But after that? Go to night school if I could. Save money and go to Commerce.

The house on Santa Fe Avenue was not the same. Cain, Maggie's policeman husband, was red-headed and big. He worked nights and the house had to be kept quiet for him to sleep days. Maggie had added on a room for the two girls boarding with her. They worked in a laundry in the daytime. At night they washed their own clothes in the tin washtub we used for baths.

Aunt Vick did not know me at all, and her mind was of little use to her. She had a little room at the back to herself and they kept the door locked to keep her from going out on the streets. My pallet was on the porch next to her room and I could hear her talking to herself and walking back and forth.

"Turn on the gas," she would say early in the morning. "Vick's cold."

When no one else was in the house I would go in and light the gas in the open stove. She would stand over it and hold up her skirts to warm her legs.

I got to Dallas on Saturday. On Monday morning I went to Sears, Roebuck and was put to work at once, this time as a stock boy in ladies' underwear. My pay was fifteen dollars a week and I had to keep bins filled with kinds of clothes I had never seen before. Each piece was sealed in a brown envelope with the catalogue number and price printed on in purple ink. It was not heavy work but I had to keep running or let the order pickers report me for empty bins.

Night school started and I talked of going but did not. I knew I would have troubles making the change from Pin Hook to Bryan Street High School in Dallas. Also, I was unwilling to spend the money for tuition and extra streetcar fare. I wanted to go to Commerce. I wanted to save every nickel and go to school at Commerce.

Maggie took me to the Dallas Public Library at the corner of Commerce and Harwood Streets and signed a borrower's card for me. There were books to be read, hundreds of books, and I knew I had to read as many as I could. Once or twice a week I walked from Sears, Roebuck to the library after work, taking back books by Zane Grey, Harold Bell Wright, Gene Stratton Porter, borrowing more books by the same writers, till I had read all that were on the shelves.

One night I found *In Memoriam* on a shelf and, looking through it, came on the part beginning "Ring Out, Wild Bells," the poem I had learned by heart at Spring Hill and said before the room at Pin Hook. I saw that it was from a longer poem, and only a part of a long story. Now I had all of it in a book that I could carry with me and read on the streetcar. I made up my mind to learn all of it by heart, taking it a section at a time. I could say it to myself if not to anybody else, and nobody would call me "Wild Bells" for saying it.

Near the end of a day in November I was called to the office of the floor manager.

"You're to go home at once," a girl told me.

"How come?"

"It's your aunt. She's bad hurt and they want you to come home."

"How?"

"They didn't tell me how. They just said for you to come home. You better punch out and go."

Without taking time to wash up I changed clothes and punched out. Then I ran for the streetcar.

When I got to the house a woman from down the street opened the door.

"Where's Maggie?" I asked.

"At the hospital. She went in the ambulance with your aunt—"

"How's Aunt Vick?"

"Bad burnt they say."

"Burnt? How'd it happen?"

I knew but I had to hear from her.

"She was locked in the room with the gas stove and her clothes caught afire. You could hear her screaming clear down the street. Maggie and Cain run as fast as they could. They got the door unlocked and put the fire out, but she was bad burnt."

She opened the door to Aunt Vick's room.

"Here. Let me show you something," she said.

Inside the door, in a corner near the door, there were burnt places on the wall high as my shoulders.

"She got this far and couldn't get any farther, till they got to her and put out the fire. Then they took her in the ambulance."

"How bad off is she?"

"They say she ain't got much chance. They sent for your grandmother."

"Anything I can do?"

"Nothing for any of us to do but wait."

She took a pan of water and a rag and began washing burn marks from the pine wall.

"I wouldn't want Maggie to see these," she said. "She's going to feel blame enough as it is, locking her mother up with a gas heater. It ain't easy, taking care of somebody like that, but it wasn't right, locking her up that way. They could a got to her faster."

The woman did not know as much as I knew, living in the house with them, the trouble it was to wash and dress and feed her, the worry that she would go off in the streets by herself. Life for her was already death. And I might be as much to blame as Maggie. Not on this day but on others I had lit the gas for her.

While we waited we washed the walls and floor of the room and opened windows to get shet of the smell of burning.

Toward midnight Maggie came in and crossed the room to me.

"She's dead," she cried, her arms around me. "Your Aunt Vick's dead."

She dropped down to a sofa and sounded like praying.

"Thank God she's out of her suffering."

The night passed, and in the morning I went back to work—to keep filling bins, my mind not on my work but on Aunt Vick.

That night after work I went to the Union Station to meet my mother and grandmother. When the train from Paris was called I saw them coming up the steps. My grandmother in her long black cloak, my mother in a new hat and coat from Sears, Roebuck. They saw me and began crying.

"Vick's dead. It don't seem right, Vick's dead. Does she look natural?"

I knew what they were asking: Did the fire burn her face?

"I don't know. They hadn't brought her when I left. I had to work all day."

I took them down to the streetcar and by the time we turned on Elm Street I was pointing out to my mother the things she should see in Dallas. She looked and listened till we passed the big bird on the Majestic Theater. Then she looked at me in a way that made me stop talking.

"I'm going to marry Lank," she said. Her face was red in the streetcar light and sweat showed at the edge of her hair. "I told you about Lank before you left home."

I remembered letters in the mailbox addressed to my mother. In one corner they said: "If not delivered in five days return to Lank Smith, Gem, Texas." Gem was in the Panhandle, a way out in West Texas. Lank Smith had lived at Pin Hook before I was born. He had homesteaded out west. Now he was a widower and writing to my mother to find out about his friends at Pin Hook.

"Yes, you told me about Lank. You didn't tell me you were aiming to marry him."

"I didn't know till lately—after all you big boys left me."

I knew that Dewey was working away from home and Cleaver was roaming. She had been left with my little brother.

"It got so lonesome I couldn't stand it, so when he asked me to marry him I said yes. I ordered a new hat for the wedding."

"When'll it be?"

"Before Christmas, when he gets things in shape to come."

I felt bad then about leaving her.

"You want me to come back to Pin Hook?"

She shook her head.

"You wouldn't stay. I couldn't count on it, and I'd hate to hold you back any. You're already here and got a job. It's better for me to marry Lank and move to West Texas."

It was settled, I knew, and better for her, better for me.

We walked through the dark to the house and found it full of people. They had brought Aunt Vick home and she lay in the front room in a gray casket. They had combed back her white hair and put too much powder on her face. I stared at her a long time, glad the fire had not touched her face.

My grandmother stood by the casket crying.

"Poor Vick," she said, "it's a hard way to die."

My grandmother sat up through the night and my mother stayed with her. At times Maggie came in and the three of them stood over the casket. Hedley came, a dark, sad-faced man, no longer in trouble, a married man settled down out in West Texas. I could not remember him, but I could remember Aunt Vick worrying over him.

"I recollect when we were children on the Ouachita," my grandmother said.

They had come a long way from the Ouachita, a long way from Pin Hook.

The next day we went to a little Methodist Church for songs, prayers, a sermon, and a last look before the coffin was closed.

"You want to go to the cemetery?" they asked my grandmother when it was over.

"I'm going with her just as fur as I can," she said.

We went to the grave and stood beside it while the coffin was lowered and till the last spadeful of dirt had been mounded over it.

Then I went with my mother and grandmother to the Union Station in time for them to get the train to Paris.

72

To me, ladies' underwear was boxes and bales and bins of brown envelopes of many different sizes. I had to read the labels but I was told never to open envelopes. Things would get dirty opened. Day after day I unpacked, carted, and stacked envelopes without ever seeing what was inside. I had to put the right envelope in the

right bin, so order pickers could memorize bins and fill orders without coming to a stop. There were corsets and breast confiners,
bloomers and princess slips, chemises of crêpe de Chine, petticoats of
black taffeta. I learned the names but not what they looked like.

Thanksgiving passed and we began working late most nights in
the week. Still we could not keep up with the orders. With every
mail they came like leaves. New pickers and checkers came to work.
Other stock boys unpacked boxes for me. I went at a trot pushing a
cart that was like a box on wheels.

Stocks ran low; in some sizes and styles they ran out. The man
in charge of stocks went up and down the aisles. On some bins he
put a sign: "Back Order." Order pickers had to stop at these long
enough to write "B/O" on the orders. On other bins he put "Substitute" and added the number to be substituted. The order picker
lost time reading the new number but he could fill the order.

Two weeks before Christmas the man in charge of stocks quit
and they gave me his job. The floor manager took me off the four-
wheeler and sent me to the bins, with a clipboard of papers in my
hand.

"It'll be easy once you catch on to it," he said. "Look up the
number here. If it says 'On order' put 'Back order' on the bin. If it
says 'Not on order' put 'Out' on the bin. Substitute every time you
can. If you're out of forties give them forty-twos. A size bigger is all
right in most of the things. If you run out of something in one
price, substitute something in the same size in a lower price if you
can. Make sure you put the substitute number and price on the bin.
Use your head and substitute. Most people are ordering for Christmas. They'd rather have a substitute than their money back."

It did seem easy at first. I went up and down the aisles checking
empty bins and yelling for the stock boys to fill them. When they
were out in the stock room, I wrote changes on the bins in purple
ink. The first day I kept up, and the second by working straight
through lunch and coming back early after supper. The third day I
was behind and the order pickers began yelling at me.

Orders came faster. The stock boys got farther and farther behind. At times they could not tell if a number was in stock or not.
To keep the order pickers quiet, I made substitutions on my own,
first to a size smaller and then to prices higher or lower. Then I
began substituting one name for another. By the end of the week I
was substituting any dollar ninety-eight number for any other dollar ninety-eight number.

On Monday before Christmas the orders began coming back with letters: "Too large." "Too small." "Send size ordered by return mail." At first the order checkers and order pickers could handle the returns and order the refunds. Then there were too many and the floor manager had to be told.

I was in a back aisle making a substitution when I saw him coming toward me waving a letter and carrying a brown envelope under his arm. I knew he was mad from the way he came at me.

"God damn it," he yelled, "don't you know a corset from a princess slip?"

I had to say I did not.

"You never looked to see what you were substituting?"

"No, sir."

"Why not?"

"I had to keep ahead of the order pickers."

"Well, this woman ordered a corset and you sent her a princess slip and she's as mad as a wet hen. You done a lot of these?"

"I reckon."

He went down the aisle checking substitutions and I heard him say, "Oh, God" at one bin after the other. Then he turned on me.

"Don't you make another substitution till I check it."

"Yes, sir."

A little later he called me to a table up by the chute. The table was piled with brown envelopes, each with a letter clipped to it. A line of order checkers stood behind the table.

"Look at this," he said, and I could feel the anger in his voice. "More returns than orders. More hot letters than this department ever had before. It'll take weeks to straighten out."

Order checkers were mad at me. Order pickers skated up close.

"Listen to some of the letters," the floor manager said.

He began reading and everybody began laughing as each mistake I had made seemed worse than the one before it. It was not only corset for princess slip, I had substituted nightgowns for bloomers, long drawers for vests, and cotton knit for tub silk.

"No telling how many more we've got coming back." He looked at me and his smile was not friendly. "How much you know about ladies' underwear?"

"Not much." I thought of the catalogue pictures and the sealed brown envelopes. "I never got enough time to look."

I knew it was the wrong thing to say but I could not stop

myself. People all around me heard me and began laughing. They did not stop till he sent me back to pushing a four-wheeler in the stock room.

On the last work day before Christmas I got my pay envelope and there was a pink slip inside. I had been laid off because the Christmas rush was over—laid off, not fired. I could not see much difference. I was out of a job at a time when jobs were hard to get.

I walked to the library and then walked all the way home. It saved me a streetcar token.

Looking for a job in January was worse than I thought it could be, going from building to building, walking in cold or rain, hearing again and again that no more applications would be taken till spring, or that I did not have enough education and experience to apply. The money in my pocket ran out and I had to draw on the savings I had put away for Commerce. Some mornings I would have stayed at home but Maggie would not let me. Anybody staying at her house had to be out working, or out looking for work.

"You're eighteen," she said. "You've got to make out like you're a man."

Other mornings I went straight to the library, after telling myself that a job would not turn up that day.

In the middle of January there was a letter from Pat Swindle, mailed from Texarkana, the first word I had heard from him since the day he walked off from the cotton patch. He had a job with a lumber company in Texarkana, working on a timber crew in the woods of Arkansas. He wanted me to come and work with him.

"I'll meet you at the post office in Texarkana January 22. You've got to be there. You cain't let me down."

I looked at the calendar and studied his letter. If I left the next day, I would have four days to meet him in Texarkana. It was warm outside, the sun bright. It would be a good thing to hit the road and meet him, to get a job on my own and not have to tell anybody how much money I was making or what I was going to do with it. Pat was a good friend to me. I would be as good a friend to him.

I kept the letter from them and did not tell them what I meant to do. I knew Maggie would try to stop me, and I did not want to be stopped.

The next morning I went to look for a job but came back to the house in the middle of the day, when I knew they would all be out at work. I put on clean overalls and shirt, work shoes and socks, my black coat and cap. I could send for the rest after I got a job. I wanted to go without leaving a word, but could not. I wrote a note telling them I had gone to meet Pat. I did not say when or where. Then, with the two dollars I had left, I walked out the Santa Fe tracks away from Dallas.

It was a bright winter afternoon, just cool enough to make me feel good walking. For some miles I stayed on the Santa Fe track, stepping on crossties, singing old songs I had learned at Pin Hook. "Send me a letter, Send it by mail." All at once I was happier than I had been for months. What I was doing was right. I would go where I pleased, work when I pleased, and move on when I got tired of working. Pat was the right one to go with. He was younger, but he had been hoboing for months and knew how to get along.

When I came to where the highway crossed the tracks at Rinehart, I took the pavement. Better to try catching rides on the highway than riding the rods, when I had never been on the rods. I took the road and walked along, flagging rides, and glad for the ones I got. I knew that Paris was not on the direct road to Texarkana, but at the first turning off place I went toward Paris.

At sundown I walked into the town of Wylie, knowing I could not get another ride that night. I ate a bowl of chili in a café and went to the railroad station. When the stationmaster left, I stretched out on a bench by a warm coal stove and slept through the night.

The next day I made it to Paris and then to Blossom. It was late in the day when I walked past the Blossom school and the line of stores. I saw people I knew but they did not know me. It was hard not to ask them for something to eat and a place to stay all night. "Don't steal, don't beg." My mother's words came to mind. It was harder to pass the road to Pin Hook and not turn down it. Somebody else lived in our house at Pin Hook. Somebody else would have to give me grub and bed if I went there.

The next morning I was on the road again, after sleeping at the house of people who had been our neighbors when we lived at Blossom, with eighty miles ahead of me to Texarkana and a day and a half to make it in. The skies were gray with clouds and I was beginning to get a cold. There were a few cars on the road between Blossom and Clarksville, but not many. By the middle of the day I was catching rides on wagons when I could, walking when I could not, and beginning to feel dragged down by the cold.

Out of Clarksville I missed the road and in the late afternoon came to English, a place with store and school and houses at the edge of the pine woods. At the store, men told me the road was too boggy for a wagon all the way to Avery. At the school I stopped to rest and watch the end of a basketball game. The school was like Pin Hook but bigger. When the game was over I walked along the road with children ahead of me, children behind me till the last ones stopped at a house out in a field. There was nothing left for me but to keep on walking.

It was late at night when I got to Avery. The last mile or so was on gravel. It rattled under my shoes but was easier to walk in than the bogging clay. The town was asleep and dark, and dogs barked at me from house to house as I went along. I looked for a place to buy supper but everything was closed. Almost to the other side of town I saw a light burning on a porch and a sign: "Rooms, Fifty Cents." Hungry, worried about my cold, I stood at the edge of the porch and yelled "Hello" till an old man came with a coal oil lamp.

"You want a room?" he asked.

"Yes, sir."

"Four bits, cash."

I gave him half a dollar and he took me to a room in another house. He set the lamp on a washstand and went to the door.

"Privy's out back," he said.

"Any grub anywhere?"

"No grub tonight."

After he had gone I went to bed with my clothes on and wrapped the thin quilts around me, with a layer over my head. I needed to breathe warm air to stop coughing. I slept some, but was awakened in between by the sound of wind and rain on the tin roof over me.

I left Avery in gray daylight, before anything had opened. There was a heavy cloud to the north and a strong wind was blowing from the northeast. In January that meant bad weather and I was still forty miles from Texarkana. In a few hours Pat would be waiting for me at the post office.

At the edge of town a touring car with the curtains up stopped beside me. A young man unbuttoned a curtain on the driver's side and looked out.

"You want a ride?" he asked.

"I sure do."

He opened the door on the other side and I got in. He was about my age. An older man and woman sat together on the back seat with a black lap rope pulled up to their waists. The car started moving and gravel ground under the wheels.

"Where are you going, boy?" the woman asked.

"Texarkana, ma'am."

"What are you going there for?"

"To get me a job. Work. Make me some money."

She looked at me, at the man beside her, and back at me, and I could see a change in her face.

"You're running away, aren't you?"

"No, ma'am. Nothing for me to run away from."

"There must be something. You've got to tell us so we'll know. We don't want to be helping boys run away from home."

Out of the wind and weather, with a ride all the way to Texarkana, I talked and answered their questions. Better to talk than walk. I told them about Pin Hook—mostly about school in Pin Hook—my job at Sears, Roebuck and why I lost it—the job I hoped to get in Texarkana cutting timber.

"You're a peart boy," the woman said. She looked at the man. "Don't you think he ought to go to school some more?"

"It never hurt anybody."

They were right but I had to say something.

"I quit school to work. All I need is a job."

They let me out in Texarkana, not far from the post office, and I had not told them how hungry I was or how little money I had. They might have given me something and that would have been begging.

Hungry as I was, I went straight to the post office and up the front steps. A cold wind shipped around the brick building. Pat would be inside where it was warm. I went the length of the building but did not see him. I went through again slowly, looking in every possible place. Pat was not there. For the first time I was scared. I asked at the general delivery window but there was no letter for me—nothing. That meant he would be there later in the day.

At an alley cafe I bought a bowl of chili. A girl set a bowl before me and shoved a tray of crackers and a bottle of catsup down the counter. The smell of chili made my mouth water and my stomach growl. With shaking fingers I crumbled in crackers and covered them with catsup. I could fill myself up with chili and crackers and catsup. But the waitress was watching me. She let me have crackers and catsup once and moved them out of reach. What I got was enough to hold me but not to fill me.

Back at the post office I sat in a corner waiting for Pat. There were men close to me, bums in to keep out of the cold, rod riders on the way south from places like Chicago to places like New Orleans. From them I learned that Texarkana was a tough town on hoboes. Police arrested hoboes and made them work out their fines.

"You better warm up and move on," they told each other. "The law'll get you if you don't keep moving."

Pat did not come. I walked up and down, keeping away from the bums, but he did not come.

A policeman came in one door and I went out another, into the cold and gathering darkness. There was no other place for me to go and I did not have enough money for a bed. Cold and afraid, I started walking out the street I had come in on that morning, with nothing in mind now but to get away from the police. I walked past the edge of town and out on the highway, and felt safe in the dark on the highway.

When I knew that I could not walk another mile the road passed through heavy woods. Build a fire, I thought. Build a fire and get warm. I would feel better warm and not cough so much. Back from the road, I piled up leaves and sticks and struck a match to them. Soon I had a good fire going and bright flames whipped in the sharp wind.

The fire could warm my body, but it could not take the chill from me. I was sick, hungry, and with no place to go. It was not my fault; it was that I had been born poor, and at Pin Hook. Then I was warm through and I sat up looking into the fire. I was sick and hungry now, but, by God, the time had to come when I would not be. I had been soft—too soft. I had to be hard—hard enough to make what I needed to fill my belly and warm my back. I had to do it by myself, without Pat or anybody.

Before daylight a fine drizzle fell on my face and woke me. I put more wood on the fire but the rain turned heavy enough to wet me and put out the fire. I went back to the road and walked west till I came to a country store. The owner was building a fire in the stove. I bought a piece of candy and waited by the stove for the rain to stop.

"You mind if I stay awhile?" I asked.

"You ain't bothering me none."

I sat on a keg of nails with my head against a counter and slept through the morning. When I woke up the rain had stopped, and I went on the road again, walking west, thinking only of getting back to Dallas. There had to be a job of some kind for me in Dallas.

Water stood in ruts deep enough to bog a car. I got a ride on a wagon that took me half the way to Avery. At Avery I bought a loaf of bread and warmed myself in the railroad station. Then I walked on the tracks. I would not get lost in the dark if I kept on the tracks.

When daylight came I was still walking; it was not a night for the open. The sky was clear and a cold wind blew from the north. Rainwater froze where it stood on the road and in the fields. There would be no rides that day, maybe for three or four days. I could be in Dallas in that time, if I could hold up to walk forty miles a day.

I went from the Texas Pacific to the Santa Fe tracks at Paris, stopping only to buy a piece of cheese to go with the bread I had left. It took the last of my money, so I put half of each in my pockets for the next day. To keep down hunger and thirst, and to ease my burning throat, I broke pieces of ice from the ditches to suck on as I walked. They helped my throat but not my cough. I had nothing for it or for the rawness in my armpits and crotch.

At Ben Franklin I warmed myself in the station and watched a train pull out for Dallas. I knew that hoboes rode the blinds and the rods. I found the blinds but was afraid to swing on when the train started moving. I watched it out of sight and then followed it down the tracks.

Somewhere in the darkness I saw the shape of a barn close to the tracks. Knowing I had to stop and rest, I went inside the barn and climbed up to the hayloft. There was no loose hay, and I was afraid to break the bales that stood in straight stacks. I could get in trouble breaking bales. I crawled between stacks of bales and shut myself in with others to keep out the wind and cold. It was not warm enough but I could rest and sleep a little.

By daylight I was on the track again, eating the last of my bread and cheese, knowing that I should keep some of it for the time when I would be hungrier. I felt weak and my legs wobbled when I stepped from tie to tie. I thought of trying to find a highway but the fields were sheets of ice and I could not see where to go. I took to the ditch when freight trains passed. Nobody riding the rods, I could see. Anybody would freeze to death riding the rods on a day like that.

At times I saw houses across icy fields and thought of going to them for help. "Don't steal. Don't beg." I had never lowered myself that much, and I was not ready to begin.

Sundown came and darkness, but I went on, finding it harder and harder to make my feet move. They were sore and swollen—too swollen for me to take off my shoes.

"A little piece more," I kept telling myself. Then I could rest in a barn or haystack. The next night I would be in Dallas.

It was bare prairie and there were no barns or haystacks, or a patch of woods where I could build a fire. I had to keep walking or freeze.

Then I stopped and rubbed my eyes. Ahead of me and off the tracks a light shone at the level of the barbed-wire fence. Without thinking, I started toward it. I crossed the ice-covered ditch, climbed a frozen bank, and rolled under the fence. After crossing a narrow stretch of prairie I came to a small house. The light was shining through a window. Inside I could see people sitting in front of a fireplace.

"Hello," I called.

I could see them leave their chairs and look out the window.

"Hello."

A man came to the door and opened it.

"What you want this time of night?" he asked.

"I want to warm myself."

He might not let me. I had not thought before that he might not let me.

"Who are you?" he asked. "What's your name?"

I gave it, and then gave it again.

"Never heard tell of you. Where do you live?"

"Nowheres right now. I was walking down the tracks and saw your light. I've got to get warm."

He closed the door and I could see him with the others around the fireplace. Then he opened the door again.

"Come on in."

He held the door open for me to pass. I went past him and straight to the fire.

"You cold?"

A woman in a rocking chair asked the question.

"Yes'm."

"Don't stand too close. It'll hurt if you stand too close."

I stood back a little, on the other side from her chair. She was older than my mother, thin, and wrapped in quilts—sickly looking but friendly. The man sat beside her. On her other side there was a young man in a blue suit and a boy my age in a blue shirt and overalls. She handed each an apple from a bowl in her lap.

"Want an apple?" she asked me.

"Yes'm."

I took it and ate it down to the core without stopping, with all of them watching.

"You ain't et for a spell," the woman said.

"No'm."

"We've got bread and milk."

The young man brought a glass of milk and a piece of corn bread from the kitchen. The man pulled a chair up to the fire for me.

"Eat and warm yourself," he said. "Then tell us how you got to Celeste."

Celeste. Closer to Dallas than I thought.

While I ate they told me about themselves. The woman was a cripple and had to do most of her work from her chair. When she was by herself the man had to come in from the field to move her from one job to another. The young man was a teacher in a country school. The boy went to high school in Celeste.

"We could make a bed for you if you want to stay all night," the man said.

The way he said it, I was not begging. It was not like being a tramp coming in begging for a place to stay.

"I'd be thankful."

They gave me warm water for washing and cough syrup for my cold. Then they let me sit by the fire and talk. It was easy to tell them about Pin Hook and the jobs in Dallas. It was easy to talk to a teacher about how I wanted to go to school. I could not tell them about my days on the road. They could see that I was hungry and cold.

"What will you do tomorrow?" the man asked.

"Go on to Dallas."

"Walking?"

"It's not so far now."

But they would not let me walk. The man would let me have money for a ticket and pay him back when I could. The teacher would take me to the station and put me on the train.

When I could keep awake no longer they put a mustard plaster on my chest and put me to bed in a featherbed.

When I woke up again it was late morning and the man was in the kitchen helping the woman cook dinner. We ate and talked again of what I would do.

"You c'n work your way through school," the woman said. "Anybody can if he wants to bad enough."

After school the teacher came in his Ford and took me to Celeste. On the way he told me what it was like to go to school at Commerce, and what he said made me want to go there more than ever.

He bought my ticket and when the train came in he gave it to me and shook my hand.

"I'm glad you saw our light," he said.

I knew he meant it—they all meant it.

"Me, too."

Then I was on the train looking out at the ice-covered fields.

It was warm in the Union Station, cold and dark outside. I thought of sitting on a bench all night and going from there in the morning to look for a job, but I went out and walked down Commerce Street. They were going to fuss at me anyway. Better to get it over with.

When I got to the house, Maggie, Cain, and the two girls were sitting in front of an open gas stove in the front room. I could see them through the window and went in without knocking.

"Where've you been?" Maggie asked.

"Rambling."

I had made up my mind to tell them that and no more—nothing of the places I had been, the hard times on the road.

"Did you find Pat Swindle?"

"No'm."

"I don't see why you thought you would. You know how long he's been hoboing it. It's a good thing you didn't. Next thing you hear, he'll be behind bars. You could a been with him."

I thought of the bums in the Texarkana post office, and the policeman walking through. I knew better than to tell them how close I had come to being arrested because of Pat. It was bad enough to have to think of it myself.

As I got warm again my coughing got worse.

"You sure caught a cold all right," they said.

They gave me warm milk, soup, and salve to open my head and ease my throat.

"You want us to take you in again?" Cain asked.

"Yes, sir. For a little while—till I get a job."

"Or go off bumming agin?"

"I won't. Not any more. I'll get me a job and pay you every cent I owe you."

"What do you think, Cain?" Maggie asked.

"It's all right with me if he gets a job. I won't have him hanging around the house in the daytime."

"You c'n make your pallet tonight," Maggie said. "In the morning you've got to look for a job and you cain't be choosy."

The girls had got their laundry jobs from an employment agency on Lamar Avenue.

"I'll show you in the morning," one of them said. "They're bound to have something."

They helped me make my pallet. Then they went to bed.

"Get a good night's sleep," they said. "You've got to look peart in the morning."

74

The employment office opened at eight. I got off the streetcar at Commerce Street a little after seven and walked back to it. A dozen or more men waited on the sidewalk, in front of two blackboards nailed to the wall by the door. I worked in among them close enough to read notices in chalk of jobs open for farm hands, dishwashers, ditchdiggers. I read them and read them again.

"Yistiddy's jobs," a man told me. "Mostly tuck up. They'll chalk on some more today maybe, if they's any left after the calling out."

At eight a man opened the door from the inside and we followed him up wooden stairs to a big room. Men who knew him leaned on a counter reading jobs on a pad. The rest of us waited on benches around the wall. I was the only boy. The others were middle-aged and older, all in work clothes, some of them needing shaves, all of them looking down and out.

The men at the counter got slips of paper and went out. Then came the calling out time.

"Dishwasher," the man behind the counter called. "Anybody want a job pearl diving?"

Five men went up. He looked them over and gave one of them a slip.

"If it don't suit, come back," he said. "Plenty besides you'd like a crack at it."

The man with the slip went out without looking back. The man behind the counter called out more jobs and sent more men out with slips. Then he looked at me.

"Hey, boy," he said.

I went toward the counter.

"Yes, sir."

"How old are you?"

"Eighteen."

He opened a door in the counter for me and gave me a chair by his desk.

"Old enough." He wrote my age and name on a piece of paper. "Education?"

"Two years in high school."

I did not tell him it was part a year in the eighth grade at Pin Hook. He wrote it down and looked at me.

"Catholic?"

The question had never been asked me before.

"No, sir."

He put the paper against his lips and whistled past it.

"They didn't say it had to be a Catholic."

He looked at the men on the benches, and then back at me.

"I'll have to try it. No more boys around this morning. It's a Catholic school over in Oak Lawn. They called in for a boy to be a priests' waiter."

I heard the word school and liked it. I was not so sure about

Catholic or priest, but it was a school. Any school would be better than no school at all.

"What's the job like?"

"Priests' waiter. I don't know what it's like. It's at a Catholic school and it pays thirty dollars a month and board. You want it?"

Thirty dollars a month and board. I did not think it over.

"Yes, sir."

"You got two dollars for me?"

"No, sir."

The job was not mine if I had to have two dollars. He looked me over again and asked for a number on the telephone.

"Father O'Keefe?" he said to the receiver. "I've got a boy for you. Trouble is, he don't have the two-dollar fee. If you would stand for him I could send him right out. He looks all right to me. O.K.? Coming right out."

He gave my name and hung up. Then he wrote the address on a piece of paper.

"It's the University of Dallas. Take the Oak Lawn car to the end of the line. Then walk straight ahead four blocks and you'll see a big red brick building all out by itself. That'll be it. Ask for Father O'Keefe."

"*Father* O'Keefe?"

"That's what they call him."

He gave me a slip of paper and I went out. Down the stairs, down Elm Street to St. Paul, and out it, following the Oak Lawn tracks. I would be later getting there, but I would save a fare.

It was a long walk and I had plenty of time to think about the job, and to worry that it was in a Catholic school. Any other kind and I would be all right. I could work and get along. As far as I knew, I had never talked with a Catholic, but I had heard what people said in Pin Hook.

I also had plenty of time to look at the fine houses I passed on Turtle Creek Boulevard and up through Oak Lawn. It would not be like living on Santa Fe Avenue.

I passed the end of the streetcar line and saw the University of Dallas ahead of me—a three-story red brick building with white crosses on top and another cross on a little church by it. It was above Turtle Creek Boulevard and high enough for a view of Dallas from the grounds. I went under a wrought iron arch and up a long walk, thinking that it was good for a school to look like this.

It was just past lunchtime and there were boys in the entrance and in the halls, boys my age and younger with books and tablets and pencils, pushing and scuffling in halls that smelled of cedar oil, crowding through doors into classrooms that were gray with wear and chalk dust. I felt like a homecoming scholar.

In the hall I stopped a younger boy.

"Where can I find Father O'Keefe?" I asked.

He looked at my black coat and overalls and took me to an office where a pink-faced, white-haired man sat behind an iron partition.

"Father O'Keefe," he said. "Someone to see you."

Father O'Keefe stood up and brushed a black skirt back with a stroke of his hand. A man in skirts? In the next room there were more of them. Men in skirts. Father O'Keefe came close to the partition. His face was smooth and smiling under a black cap with a black ball on top.

"What do you want?" he asked.

"They sent me from the employment office."

"Oh, yes. I expected you earlier."

He went around to an open counter and we stood face to face while he asked questions and wrote my answers on a printed form. His questions were the same the man at the employment agency had asked.

"Are you a Catholic?"

There was a difference in the way he asked it.

"No, sir."

I could feel the job slipping away from me. He read again what he had written down and looked me over again.

"That won't matter," he said. "You work hard and we'll get along. You want to work, don't you?"

"Yes, sir."

"Then it's settled. I'll show you where to sleep and then turn you over to the chef."

He opened a door and came from behind the counter.

"We'll call you Billy," he said. "We don't have a Billy."

I followed him down a hall, hearing the drone of voices from classrooms. It was time to talk to him about school.

"I went to high school two years—"

"Yes, you told me."

He kept on walking. I had to try again.

"This is a school. I wish I could go to it some when I'm not working."

He glanced at me and kept walking.

"Maybe you can if you're a good boy and work hard."

"I'll work hard. I'll work like anything to go to school."

He said no more, but in my mind we had come to a bargain: I would work hard and he would help me go to school.

We came to a large basement room with seven bunks and some wardrobes against the walls.

"This bunk is yours," he said.

It was not much, but it was a place to sleep.

Then he took me to a huge kitchen, where a man in white apron and tall white cap was eating at a scrubbed oak table.

"The chef," he said to me. To the chef he said, "New priests' waiter, starting tomorrow morning. You'd better show him around."

He went out and I could see him going down the hall with a student on either side of him.

"You waited tables before?" the chef asked.

"No, sir."

"Done any scullery work?"

"Any what?"

"Scullery work. Washing dishes. Cleaning up. You ever washed dishes before?"

"At home, sir."

"This is different, but you'll learn fast enough. Where are your belongings?"

"In East Dallas."

"Go get them this afternoon. Tonight you can watch somebody else on the job. Tomorrow you'll be on your own."

He showed me the priests' refectory with its long oak table and oak chairs. Then he took me to the scullery and showed me the deep vats for washing dishes.

"You eat yet?" he asked.

"Not yet."

He took me back to the kitchen and sliced two pieces of roast beef for me. Then he pointed to a cart with bread and butter, pickles and jams.

"Priests' cart," he said. "Help yourself to anything on it."

I made sandwiches for myself and ate at the serving table, watching the chef getting food ready for supper. There were more things to eat than I had ever seen before, and more of everything. I could see myself working there and going to school till I had an education.

There was a letter from Pat Swindle for me in Maggie's mailbox. He had not met me in Texarkana because he had lost his job and gone on roaming. He had been riding the rods up and down the country and was writing from Terre Haute, Indiana. He was broke and hungry. "I could eat horse manure," he wrote, "if I had some horse manure."

I brought my things from Santa Fe Avenue in a box and slid it under my bunk. Then I was ready to go to work, glad to have a job, glad not to be roaming.

Father O'Keefe called me the priests' waiter; everybody else called me the scullery boy. The first to call me that was Bouquet, the second cook, whose name was Flowers, and who had the best bunk by the best window in our room. At four-thirty the next morning I heard bare feet on concrete floors and soft whispering— the Catholic boys saying their prayers. At five o'clock Bouquet shook me.

"Get up, scullery boy," he said. "Times a-wasting."

He went out and down the hall to the kitchen. I washed and put on a white shirt—the priests' waiter had to wear a white shirt— and a white apron that came down to my ankles. Then I went to the kitchen.

Bouquet was alone in the kitchen, his cap and jacket bright in the white overhead lights, his dark pants reddish in the lights from the stoves. On one stove he had bacon frying, on the other batter-cakes, and he danced from one to the other, flipping with a turner, and singing "Yes, We Have No Bananas."

He saw me and stopped singing.

"Priests start at six," he said, "when the first ones come in from mass. Table's set up, all but the butter and jam and cream for the coffee. Here, use this cart."

He pushed the cart to me and showed me where to find things in a big icebox.

"When they come in, you be there to take their orders. We tell the boys what to eat. The priests tell us. They get what they want. You run the orders to and from the kitchen. I'll go show you."

He went down a long hall that was lighted only by the lights in the boys' dining room at one end. I pushed the cart behind him, to a serving room across from the scullery. From it I could watch the priests come in, and go out to take their orders. From it I could see the crucifix on the wall and the silver on the sideboard.

Two priests came in and took chairs across the table from me, one tall and light, the other short and dark, both of them in robes and bareheaded. They stood behind their chairs for a prayer and the sign of the cross.

When they sat down I went out of the serving room and went toward them. They saw me and shook their heads.

"Another one?" the tall priest said. "Every week we get another one."

"Every one worse than the last."

The short priest laughed out loud.

"This one can't be as bad as the last. They don't make them that stupid."

My face burned but I had to do my job. I went around the table and stood by them for their orders.

"What's your name?" the tall priest asked.

"Father O'Keefe said I'd be called Billy."

"Well, Billy, I want sausage, eggs, and toast, and I want them hot. Tell the chef I want my breakfast hot."

"Yes, sir."

"Bring me the same," the other priest said.

I ran to the kitchen and told Bouquet what they said.

"I cook it, you serve it," he said. "If it's cold it's off your nose, not mine. Stand right where you are and you'll get it hot."

I did—hot sausage and eggs and toast on platters so hot they burned my hands. I slipped napkins under them and ran.

When I got to the refectory some other priests had come in, Father O'Keefe among them. I put the platters down and the tall priest put his fingers on the toast. Then he looked at Father O'Keefe.

"This is more like it. You got us a better waiter this time."

The orders came fast: bacon and eggs, sausage and eggs, wheat cakes and sausage, poached eggs on dry toast. Enough to fill the cart. I pushed it at a trot to the kitchen.

"How you making out?" the chef asked after I had turned the orders in to Bouquet.

"All right, I reckon."

Again I pushed the cart at a trot, back to the serving room. Then I knew I was in trouble. The priests, in black cassocks, looked alike. I knew Father O'Keefe but not any of the others, or which platter went before which priest. It could be the end of my job.

I set Father O'Keefe's platter in front of him, and one in front of another priest. He looked at me and smiled.

"It's not mine but I'll pass it down."

All the other platters got passed down and I went back to the serving room. I did not know their names but I could learn their faces.

Breakfast over, I loaded the dishes on the cart and hauled them to the scullery. When I was running hot water over them Father O'Keefe came by.

"We keep a clean scullery," he said. "No meal is through till the scullery is clean and everything put away."

This was the part of the job to hate: stacking dishes in deep vats, the hot water and strong soap, up to my elbows in water three times a day, all in a place called the scullery, and because of it to be called the scullery boy. For thirty dollars a month I was a scullery boy. Getting ahead would be slow without some help.

Father Carney always came late to breakfast, after the last mass. He was a dark, thin, serious priest, and he taught English to the boys in school. He always brought a book to read at breakfast. Sometimes he spoke to me only to give his order and spent the rest of the time reading. Other times, he talked to me about the boys in school and the books he was reading.

"What mass do you attend?" he asked after I had been there several mornings.

"None, sir."

"Why not?"

"I was raised a Baptist."

"I see."

Another morning he started talking before he gave his order.

"You want to be a Catholic?"

"I don't know, sir."

"You want to think about it?"

"I might, sir."

"I'll say a prayer for you."

After that, we were good friends. I waited every morning for him to come in. He read a little, but most of the time he talked to me about books. Most of them I had never heard of, but I liked hearing him talk about them. It was like being in school, but in a way better. Some mornings he talked till the bell for his class rang and he had to rush out in the middle of something he was saying.

I had talked to Father O'Keefe once again about going to some classes. He listened and then told me how hard it would be to arrange. Most of the classes were in the morning; my free time came in the middle of the afternoon.

"We're paying you to do a job," he said. "We couldn't give you time off from your job."

He was firm and I began to lose hope. Then I thought of asking help from Father Carney.

"How much education have you had?" he asked one morning.

"Two years of high school at Pin Hook."

I almost believed it by now.

He laughed.

"That doesn't sound like much."

He pushed his book aside and I told him what it was like to go to school at Pin Hook, and why I had left. I told him the hope I had felt when I took the job as priests' waiter—the hope of going to classes. I was old enough to be finishing high school, and the chance was passing me by.

"Could you help me?" I asked.

He waited a long time and then he spoke.

"You are a bright boy," he said. "I can see how much you want to go to school. I am sure you would do well if you had the chance. We do have some boys going free here, but they are Catholic. I could help you at once if you were Catholic—"

"I'm not."

He looked at me for a long time.

"We have instruction," he said. "If you want instruction—"

"I couldn't be a Catholic. My mother—"

I did not tell him what my mother always said: "I'd rather see one of my boys in his coffin than in the Catholic Church."

"You might write your mother about it."

"She wouldn't change her mind."

He looked sad when he left the table.

"Think it over," he said. "Any time you want to talk about it, I'll be glad to help you."

Alone in the refectory, I stacked dishes on the cart and rolled it to the scullery. I ran hot water over them and washed till my fingertips shriveled. All the time I was thinking of what he said. I could be a Catholic and get to go to school free. I could be a Catholic and get out of the stinking scullery at once. I would have, had it not been for the things I had heard all my life against Catholics.

I also thought of a trick. I would join the Catholic Church long enough to go to school and get an education. All the time I would be a Baptist underneath. All day I thought of how I would tell Father Carney. Then when I saw him I could not.

One day Father O'Keefe stopped me in the hall and I knew Father Carney must have spoken to him.

"Come with me," he said.

He took me to an upstairs classroom that was full of tables and typewriters.

"You can study here in your time off," he said. "Nobody uses it in the afternoon."

He gave me a typewriter book and showed me how to work a typewriter.

"You can teach yourself to type. You don't need a teacher to learn how to type."

He went out and I worked with the book and typewriter the rest of my free time.

One day when I came down from the typewriting room I found Pat Swindle waiting for me on a stool in the scullery. He had come in on the rods and found Cleaver, who had come to Dallas and got a job at the Union Station. He had cleaned up some, but he still showed signs of riding the rods.

"Cleaver said you were pearl diving out here," he said. "He said you could get me some grub."

It was Saturday and I had the table ready for supper. It was easy to spread bread with butter and jam for him. He wolfed a piece and looked at me.

"You got any meat? I could sure use some meat. I'm so hungry my guts think my throat's cut."

I knew there was sliced meat in the icebox. I also knew what the chef would say if he saw me giving anything away. But Pat was hungry. His face showed how hungry he was. Better to take some meat than see him go hungry. When the chef was not looking I slipped slices of meat under bread on a tray and took it to the scullery.

"I didn't make it to Texarkana," Pat said. "Did you?"

"I made it there and back."

"You got my letter from Terre Haute?"

"Yes."

"I would a met you but I got fired and had to move on."

I did not ask him how. It was easy enough to guess.

"You like pearl diving?"

"It'll do till I get something better."

"Not me, bud. I got a job at a café one time washing dishes. They just about worked my—"

"Be quiet," I whispered. "They're coming to supper. You better stay out of sight."

Half a dozen priests came slowly down the hall and entered the refectory from the other side. Pat watched them and then grabbed my arm.

"What're they dressed up like women for?" he whispered.

"They're priests. That's what they wear. Stay here. I've got to wait on them."

When I got back from the kitchen with the cart they were through their prayers and sitting down. Tonight there was no reading in Latin. They talked and laughed and hurried through supper, and went out the way they had come. I was glad to see them go. There would have been trouble if they had found Pat in the scullery.

When they had gone, I filled two plates from the table and took them to the scullery. Pat took one and looked at the roast beef and mashed potatoes.

"Them old women eat good," he said.

"They sure do."

"I bet they drink good, too."

There were bottles in the storeroom—boxes and boxes of bottles—altar wine kept there when it was against the law, locked up and nobody but the chef had a key, and another bottle in a chest in the refectory, kept handy if a priest needed it. I knew they were there but I did not tell Pat.

"God, I'd like a drink," he said. "You got any handy?"

"No."

"You know where a man could get a drink, if he had some money? A bootlegger or something?"

"No."

He looked at my long white apron.

"You ain't learnt much since you left Pin Hook, have you?"

"I reckon not."

All the time I was thinking that I had learned a lot and that I had to show him.

"I'm off tomorrow night," I told him. "We could go to town. Cleaver could meet us and we could go to town."

"And get something to drink?"

I knew a way to show him how much I had learned.

"We might."

"How?"

"If I told you, we'd both know. Meet me tomorrow night and I'll show you."

"Where?"

"Down by Turtle Creek."

He watched me wash dishes, sitting on a stool, looking tired and sleepy. Long before I was through he was ready to be on his way to meet Cleaver. I made a roast beef sandwich for him and wrapped it in waxed paper. He put it inside his shirt and went out through a basement door.

After supper dishes the next night I waited till the chef had gone. Then I went to the box where he kept the key to the store-room. It was not there. It was not in the clothes the chef had left in his closet. All day I had thought of the bottle I would take with me that night, of how I would show Pat I had changed since Pin Hook. Now the storeroom was locked and I was afraid of trying to break in.

When it was time for me to go I remembered the altar wine in the chest in the refectory. It was never taken out at night. I could put one in its place before mass in the morning.

In my Sunday clothes, I went along the dark hall to the dark refectory and to the chest under the crucifix. I could not see it but I knew it was there and Catholic. It had nothing to do with me. I opened the chest and lifted out the bottle of wine. With it under my coat I went out the basement door and along the line of trees down to Turtle Creek.

Pat and Cleaver were waiting for me under a streetlamp at the beginning of Oak Lawn Park. Pat saw I had something under my coat and touched the bottle.

"Godamighty," he said, "you got a bottle. Let's look at it."

We went down a dark path to the lake and I took the bottle from under my coat.

"It is not whiskey," I said.

Pat took it and struck a match.

"What is it? Home brew?"

"Better'n that. It's altar wine."

Pat was trying the cork with his fingers.

"That don't bother me none," he said. "It'll warm the belly."

He pulled at the cork with his teeth till it was loose. Then with a squeak and a light pop it came out. Then he raised the bottle and took a long swig.

"Good drinking," he said.

He handed the bottle to Cleaver and then to me. The wine was hot in my mouth and stinging in my throat. Tears came to my eyes but I took another swallow, to show them.

Pat took the bottle away.

Afraid of getting caught with it, we drank fast, swallow for swallow, and threw the bottle into the lake. I began to feel warm and light-headed.

"Let's go to town," I said. "Let's see the bright lights. I don't want to see a priest. I don't want to dive for another dish."

"You feel all right?" Cleaver asked.

"Never felt better."

I knew better, but we took the Oak Lawn car and got off on Elm Street, in the bright lights of the picture shows, the Palace on one side, the high-stepping bird of the Majestic ahead and high up. We walked to Akard and turned back to St. Paul.

"Prettiest street in the world," I said.

My feet were unsteady and they walked on either side to catch me if I stumbled. They were laughing at me and giving me time to walk it off.

"The prettiest town in the world. Some day—"

We were coming up to the Majestic and I could see the bird stepping higher, higher, in lights that went up. Somebody made that bird. Not just anybody. Somebody.

"Some day I'm gonna be somebody in Dallas," I said. "I'll make money and go up and down Elm any time I want to."

They began to laugh.

"How you gonna make money pearl diving?" Pat asked. "How you gonna get anywhere working for men that dress like women?"

"I'm going to school."

"How?" Cleaver asked.

"Work. I'm going to get me a job that'll give me time for school."

"Where?"

"Commerce."

It was the only place I had ever heard of where everybody could go to school.

"I've got thirty dollars and a payday coming. I'm going to take it and go to Commerce—"

"You won't go far on that."

I knew he was right and I began to cry. All that time working and only thirty dollars saved up.

They kept walking me, up past the Majestic, and I stopped crying. The bird was stepping high over me.

"I'm going to school," I said. "It may not take me far but I'm going as far as it'll take me. I've got to go to school."

People in front of the Majestic stared at us. Cleaver and Pat took me off Elm Street and walked me in the dim lights of Pacific as far as Akard and back. Then they put me on the Oak Lawn car to go back to work.

I went. The priests would be coming into breakfast at six in the morning. I would wait on them and then tell them I was leaving.

Nearly two weeks passed before I told Father O'Keefe that I was going to quit and go to school. He came in after the last mass one morning and was still there when the others had gone. I went and stood across the table from him.

"You want to say something?" he asked.

"Yes, sir."

"What is it?"

"I want to quit, sir."

"You want to quit? Why? We're not overworking you?"

"No, sir. It's not that. I'm going to Commerce."

"What are you going to do there?"

"Go to school."

"What school?"

"East Texas State Teachers College—the high school department."

I would have left then but he was not ready for me to go.

"We have a better school than that here," he said. "You could stay here and go to school."

I thought of my first day there.

"I talked to you about it before," I said. "I wanted to go to some classes, but there didn't seem to be a way for anything but the typing room."

"I remember now. You did talk to me about classes. I meant to work out something for you but it was late in the year and I never got around to it. Next fall, if you'll stay on with us, I am sure we can do something for you."

"I don't want to stay."

"Why not?"

"I don't trust what you say, sir."

"You don't trust me?" He laughed, but I did not like his laugh. "That is a new one for me."

He stared at me and I leaned on one foot and then on the other.

"This school has never turned anyone away," he said. "You work here through the summer and we'll make arrangements for you to go to some of our high school classes. Will that be all right?"

"No, sir. I've got to go."

"When?"

"Saturday night, sir. I've got to find a job in Commerce."

"You can't go Saturday. You've got to serve the banquet Sunday. We've got parents coming for commencement. You've got to help us with that."

"Can I leave then?"

"You can go, but I think you're making a mistake."

Then he started me getting ready for the banquet. The walls had to be cleaned, the silver polished. The furniture had to be waxed and rubbed. All this took the hours I should have had free.

Thursday morning Father O'Keefe decided that the floor had to be cleaned and revarnished. The chef mixed lye and water in the big bucket.

"That's strong enough to cut varnish," he told Father O'Keefe.

The chef gave me a long-handled floor brush and a hand brush. Father O'Keefe set me to work.

"You'll have to go fast," he said.

All morning long I pushed lye water over the floor with the heavy brush. Around radiators I had to get down on my hands and knees and use the hand brush. Soon my hands and feet were stinging. Before the old varnish was gone, seams came loose in my shoes and the soles flapped. I took my shoes off and my feet were raw and red.

"I cain't stand it any longer," I told Father O'Keefe when he came by.

"It won't be much longer," he said. "You can't stop now. The room has to be ready." He stooped down and looked at the gummy floor. "You've got most of it off. You can wash it with clear water and scrub the rest of it off."

Barefoot because I could not walk in shoes, I washed and scrubbed the floor till it was wet white. It was dark before Father O'Keefe would let me stop, and the priests had to eat with the boys.

I wanted to leave that night but I was afraid they would not give me my money. I had to have it for Commerce.

Friday morning I sanded down rough spots, still working barefoot. Friday afternoon I put on varnish, and went to bed while it dried. Saturday I waxed the floor on my hands and knees and polished it with rags. Saturday night I packed my clothes in a paper suitcase. My hands and feet were peeling and tender. The chef had my money. I saw Father O'Keefe give it to him.

Sunday I set the table in the refectory and put on the flowers brought in by the women. Then I got the serving room ready for the students who had been brought in to serve the tables.

Mass over late, priests and men and women in Sunday clothes came down the long hall to the refectory. There was laughter, a silence for prayers, and more laughter. I watched them through the sliding window of the serving room, waiting for the signal to start serving.

My job was to load the cart with plates of food in the kitchen and bring it to the serving room. From there the boys took the plates to the table. They also brought them out again and stacked them in the scullery. Back and forth, back and forth, I ran, pushing the cart. Then at last the plates I brought had squares of cake, squares of ice cream. One more trip, to bring silver pitchers of coffee, and my job was over.

Through the window of the serving room I took one long look at the table and the people. Then I went past the scullery. There were stacks of dirty dishes and somebody else would have to wash them. The chef gave me my money in the kitchen.

Not wanting anything to eat, I went back to the room where I slept. It was dark and empty. I slipped out of my dirty clothes and left them lying on the floor. Then I washed and put on my Sunday clothes. Still alone, I climbed out of a window with my suitcase and went into darkness, limping and crying as I went.

Late the next afternoon I got off the train in Commerce and started toward the red brick buildings of the college, walking slowly, looking at the strange streets and buildings, a stranger in the town wondering where to go for the night, where the cheapest room might be found.

On a wide street, when I was coming close to the square, a boy older than I came over and walked beside me.

"You a student?" he asked.

"Yes, sir."

I was glad to be thought one.

"New student?"

"Yes, sir."

"You got a place to stay?"

"Not yet. I just got off the train."

"We rent rooms for boys. Good clean room cheap. Close to the campus."

He was friendly and I wanted to go with him, but I had to tell him the truth.

"I don't know where I'll stay. I've got to work for my room and board."

"You don't have much money?"

"Not much."

"How much?"

"Thirty-five dollars."

He looked at me but did not stop walking.

"You'll need more'n that all right, but you can make it if you get a job waiting tables somewhere. You have any experience?"

I told him about my job as priests' waiter, the kind of work I had done but nothing else. Better not to tell anything else if I wanted a job.

"You won't have any trouble," he said. "You could stay at our house till you get a job. It'll cost you fifty cents a night—a whole lot cheaper than a hotel—and you can add it to the month if you decide to stay."

I went with him and was glad that I did. His mother was running a rooming house to help her three boys through school. They all worked in town and knew of jobs coming up, and they were all ready to help somebody else. By noon the next day they had found a job for me waiting tables. The money I had would pay for a room with them and fees. Anything else I would have to do without, but I would be in school.

Then they took me to the college, to the office of the registrar.

"How much education have you had?" he asked.

"Eighth grade."

"Where?"

"At Pin Hook."

I had to tell him that it was in Lamar County, close to Paris.

"Oh, yes," he said. "Is it affiliated?"

I did not know. He studied me a long time and then turned slowly through the pages of a catalogue. Then he shook his head.

"We do have a subcollege department, but we've dropped everything but the last year of high school. You're not ready for that. I don't see how we can take you."

This was not what I had expected.

"Some people from Pin Hook come here," I said. "People in school with me."

"Maybe before we changed. We used to take anybody that came."

He wanted to help me.

"If you had another year of school, I might let you in. Why don't you take another year at home and then come?"

He must have know at once how impossible that was. He interrupted me before I could say more than "I cain't—"

"Probably not. I'm not surprised. I was a country boy myself. I did not make the rules. I just have to follow them. You know what I mean, don't you?"

I did not, but told him I did. He nodded and walked with me to the door.

"Go to school somewhere and then come back. We'd be glad to help you then."

That night I began waiting tables at a boarding house a block from the campus, without telling them that I could not go to school. I was not ready to give up yet, not after I had spent money for train fare to Commerce.

I did tell the boy who had rented me a room.

"Did you see the dean?" he asked.

I had only seen the registrar.

"Go see the dean. He might know some way. He was a country boy and knows how hard it is for a country boy to go to school."

I was waiting for the dean the next morning when he opened his office. He listened to me and shook his head.

"You're a whole year short," he said. "Last year we could have helped you. You've got to have another year somewhere else."

That night I packed my clothes, but the people who had rented me the room did not want to see me go. They needed to rent their rooms. They wanted me to go to school.

"Why don't you see the president?" they asked. "Anybody that wants to go to school as bad as you do ought to have the chance."

The next day I was in the office of the president, after hours of waiting, after hours of feeling that it was useless for me to wait. It was a quiet, darkened office and he sat quietly letting me talk, a thin-faced man, with thin fingers never still.

"I know what you are up against," he said when I stopped talking. "I was a country boy myself. If I had the only say, I would let you in without a word. That's the way this school was before it was turned over to the state. It has been taken out of my hands. New rules have been set to make it better."

He stood up but I did not feel he wanted me to leave. He went to the window and stood looking out, his thin face lined in the glare from outside.

"We have to raise standards," he said, "and somebody's going to be hurt. The first ones hurt will be country boys like yourself. I don't see any other way. We've got to cut out third grade certificates if we ever hope to stop third-rate teachers from teaching country schools. As it is now, you can finish our high school work and get a certificate. We've got to stop somewhere."

"You don't see a chance for me?"

"Not a chance. If you had one more year, it might be different."

I was close to crying when I left his office. I waited tables at the boarding house and then walked all over town. I looked at the railroad track and thought of striking out on the crossties. I looked at roads and wondered which one to take out. Then I came back to the college, to the red brick buildings. That was where I wanted to be.

That night there were more students at the boarding house, some of them there early to take entrance examinations. They had finished the tenth grade in the country or in small towns. If they did well on the examination they would stay. If they did not, they would have to go home again.

That night I thought of the examination and was glad I had heard of it. It was something I could do—something I could do for myself.

The next morning I was outside the president's office when he came down the hall.

"What do you want this morning, son?" he asked.

"I want to take the examination. You've got to let me take the examination."

He took me inside his office and telephoned the dean. They talked about me and then about the examination. Then he hung up the receiver.

"You take the examination," he said. "If you do well on it, we might figure some way to let you in."

He shook hands and walked with me to the door.

"I'd like to study for it," I said. "What can I study?"

"Nothing. Any studying you could do now would not help at all."

I went out and again walked over the town. I had my chance. Now I had to make the most of it.

I was in the room more than half an hour early. From a seat in the back row I counted the others as they came in—a hundred and forty, some of them boys and girls, some men and women with graying hair, all from the country, all of them trying to get ahead by examination.

The time came and the dean had the papers handed out. Name, address, school. I wrote nervously. Then I turned the page and took a quick look down the questions. There in front of me was

Long John Silver. Who was Long John Silver? I told who he was and felt better. I found myself going back in my reading—to the fireplace when I read United States history to my grandmother, to the tiehacker's house, to the Pin Hook school. I wrote what I knew, and guessed when I did not know.

Then it was over and we were told to come back in two days. In two days we were to come back to the same room.

In two days I was in the room again, ahead of time, watching the others come in. When we were seated the dean came to the front of the room and sat at a table. In front of him he had a stack of white slips.

He took up a slip, cleared his throat, and called a name. A girl got up and went to the table. We could not hear what he said to her, but she took the slip and went out. Slowly he called other names and people left the room.

When my name was called I went to the table and held out my hand for the slip. Then I knew that the dean was shaking my hand.

"Congratulations," he said. "You were second highest. On the basis of this we can take you. They will tell you outside how to plan your program."

"Thank you, sir," I said and went out.

A student clerk met me at the door and took me down a hall to an adviser's room, close to the library, where I could see rows and rows of books. She was a middle-aged woman, thin faced, but friendly when she saw my score on the examination. Then she began filling in forms: name, address, age.

"You going to work for a degree?" she asked.

I looked at her, ready to write down the answer.

"Not yet, ma'am."

Nobody had ever told me anything about a degree, and I was afraid to commit myself.

"It wouldn't change your program now," she said. She filled out a card and gave it to me. "This is your class schedule."

I took the card and went downstairs, out into the hot June day. In light that edged the blackish with green I read "Geometry, English. . . ." I was in school, with an hour between now and waiting tables at the boarding house—long enough to walk back through town, to look at the railroad tracks and know that I was not going to leave. Across the square I walked at a steady pace. Close to the station I broke into a run.

AFTERWORD

In 1966 I ended the first edition of *This Stubborn Soil* as follows:

> In writing the book, I put down speech as I remembered it.
> When I could not remember, I wrote it as the person would
> have said it. In the twenty years the work has been in progress
> I have gone back to Pin Hook again and again, listening to
> catch the exact flavor and rhythm. Then I recorded them as
> faithfully as I could. In that sense, this might be called fiction-
> alized autobiography.

Now, in 1986, another twenty years later, I go back to Pin Hook
searching for faces long gone, listening for familiar voices long
stilled, hoping to find new resources in things wrought by change, or
in new thoughts and impressions from people walking the dusty
roads or kicking up dust in their pick-ups. Either way, their looks,
the sounds and rhythms in their voices curiously alien. There was
nothing left for me but to reprint the book, to recall Pin Hook from a
time that was.